Make History with this fantastic CGP book...

OK, so the new AQA GCSE History exams are pretty tricky... but with this brilliant CGP Revision Guide, you'll be ready to go into battle!

It's packed with everything you need to get your head around the subject, including crystal-clear notes, maps, diagrams and photos for each topic.

We've also included exam-style practice questions throughout the book, plus plenty of advice on how to pick up top marks. After all that, you'll be like an heir to the throne — destined to succeed.

CGP — still the best! ☺

Our sole aim here at CGP is to produce the highest quality books — carefully written, immaculately presented and dangerously close to being funny.

Then we work our socks off to get them out to you — at the cheapest possible prices.

Contents

How History Works

Exam Skills for the Period Study

America, 1840-1895: Expansion and Consolidation

Germany, 1890-1945: Democracy and Dictatorship

Exam Skills for the Depth Studies

Conflict and Tension, 1918-1939

The League of Nations and International Peace

The Origins and Outbreak of the Second World War

Elizabethan England, c.1568-1603

Elizabeth's Court and Parliament

Life in Elizabethan Times

Troubles at Home and Abroad

Exam Skills for the Historic Environment

Exam Skills for the Thematic Study

Health and the People: c.1000 to the Present Day

Medicine Stands Still

The Beginnings of Change

A Revolution in Medicine

Modern Medicine

Published by CGP

Editors:
Chloe Anderson, Emma Bonney, Izzy Bowen, Emma Cleasby, Alex Fairer,
Catherine Heygate, Andy Park, Jack Perry, Rebecca Tate and Louise Taylor.

Contributors:
Peter Callaghan, Rene Cochlin, Paddy Gannon and John Pritchard.

With thanks to John Broadbent, Dan Heaney, Catherine Heygate, Anthony Muller,
Jacqueline Richford, and Sabrina Robinson for the proofreading.

With thanks to Ana Pungartnik and Holly Poynton for the copyright research.

Acknowledgements:
With thanks to The Art Archive / Palazzo Barberini Rome / Collection Dagli Orti for permission to use the image on page 1.
First extract on page 4 from 'What we Knew: Terror, Mass Murder and Everyday Life in Nazi Germany' by Eric A Johnson and Karl-Heinz Reuband, copyright © 2006. Reprinted by permission of Basic Books, an imprint of Perseus Books, a division of PBG Publishing, LLC, a subsidiary of Hachette Book Group, Inc.
Second extract on page 4 from 'Rise and Fall Of The Third Reich: A History of Nazi Germany' by William L. Shirer.
With thanks to Photo Researchers / Mary Evans Picture Library for permission to use the images on pages 7, 27 and 109.
With thanks to Mary Evans/Classic Stock/C.P. Cushing for permission to use the image on page 10.
With thanks to Mary Evans/Interfoto for permission to use the image on page 11.
With thanks to The Art Archive / Granger Collection for permission to use the images on pages 14, 15, 25, 90 and 108.
With thanks to Illustrated London News Ltd/Mary Evans for permission to use the images on pages 19, 33 and 128.
With thanks to Mary Evans Picture Library for permission to use the images on pages 31, 35, 64, 67, 71, 77, 85, 92, 95, 112, 121, 125 and 129.
With thanks to Thaliastock / Mary Evans for permission to use the image on page 41.
With thanks to Mary Evans / Sueddeutsche Zeitung Photo for permission to use the images on pages 44, 46, 53 and 74.
With thanks to Mary Evans / Everett Collection for permission to use the images on pages 45, 60 and 117.
With thanks to Mary Evans / SZ Photo / Scherl for permission to use the image on page 49.
Extract on page 50 from 'School for Barbarians: Education Under the Nazis' (Dover Books on History, Political and Social Science). Dover Publications Inc.; Reprint edition (28 Mar. 2014).
With thanks to Mary Evans / Imagno for permission to use the image on page 55.
Quote on page 64 from John Maynard Keynes, (2012), "The Collected Writings of John Maynard Keynes", Elizabeth Johnson, Donald Moggridge (eds.,), "The Economic Consequences of the Peace", Series: The Collected Writings of John Maynard Keynes, Cambridge : Cambridge University Press.
Extract on page 77 from A. J. P. Taylor, 'The Origins of the Second World War' (London: Hamish Hamilton, 1961).
With thanks to Mary Evans / Iberfoto for permission to use the image on page 82.
With thanks to National Museums NI / MARY EVANS for permission to use the image on page 87.
Image on page 90 copyright Anthony Masi. This file is licensed under the Creative Commons Attribution 2.0 Generic license. https://creativecommons.org/licenses/by/2.0/deed.en
With thanks to Mary Evans Picture Library/DOUGLAS MCCARTHY for permission to use the image on page 91.
With thanks to Antiquarian Images/Mary Evans for permission to use the image on page 101.
With thanks to Historic England / Mary Evans for permission to use the image on page 114.
With thanks to INTERFOTO / Bildarchiv Hansmann / Mary E for permission to use the image on page 116.
Poll from public survey on page 134 from King Fund analysis of NatCen Social Research's British Social Attitudes survey data.
AQA material is reproduced by permission of AQA.

Every effort has been made to locate copyright holders and obtain permission to reproduce sources. For those sources where it has been difficult to trace the copyright holder of the work, we would be grateful for information. If any copyright holder would like us to make an amendment to the acknowledgements, please notify us and we will gladly update the book at the next reprint. Thank you.

ISBN: 978 1 78294 604 5
Printed by Elanders Ltd, Newcastle upon Tyne.
Clipart from Corel®

Based on the classic CGP style created by Richard Parsons.

Sources: the Building Blocks of History

Historians have such an easy life. They read old documents and rewrite them... right? Actually, they do a bit more than that. For GCSE History, you have to become a historian, so you'd best be sure what they really do.

Historians use Sources to Find Out about the Past

1) Sources are things that historians use to find out about and make sense of the past.
2) They can be written (e.g. newspapers, government reports) or visual (e.g. photographs, maps, films).
3) Sources can be categorised as either primary or secondary:

Primary sources — evidence from the period you're studying

For example, a newspaper report on the First World War from 4th September 1914, or a picture of Henry VIII that was painted during his reign.

Secondary sources — evidence about (but not from) the period you're studying

For example, a 1989 book called 'Origins of the First World War', or a website providing information about all the portraits ever painted of Henry VIII.

Historians have to Interrogate and Interpret every source

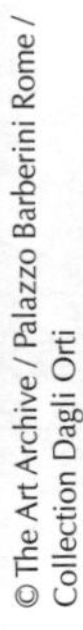

King Henry VIII, 1540

1) Historians have to be very careful with sources. To make sure they're using sources accurately, historians interrogate every source they use. This means they ask themselves a series of questions about the source's background.

- **What** is this source?
  E.g. It is a painting of King Henry VIII.
- **Who** made this source?
  E.g. It was produced by the King's official painter, Hans Holbein.
- **Why** did they make the source?
  E.g. He was asked to paint it by the King.
- **Where** and **when** was it made?
  E.g. It was made in the Palace of Whitehall in 1540.

2) Historians use their answers to work out how useful and how reliable a source is. For example:
   - This is a professional painting made during Henry's reign (meaning the painter could have met Henry). So this should be a useful source for finding out what Henry looked like.
   - BUT perhaps the painter would have been punished if he didn't show Henry looking good, so it may not be entirely reliable.

A source that presents a one-sided view is biased.

3) After they've interrogated a source, historians need to interpret it.

This means deciding what it tells them about the topic they're studying.

4) For example, Henry was probably quite a large man with fair hair and a beard. But the painter may have been told to make the picture to Henry's liking — so based on just this picture, you can't really say for sure how big he really was.

Henry was the king — people would have done what he told them to.

5) Historians look at lots of sources, and compare them against each other. If sources contradict one another, they'll try to work out why, and what this tells them about the past.

For example, another painting might show Henry as very unattractive. But a historian might interpret it differently, depending on whether Henry had seen and approved of the painting, or whether it had been made by one of Henry's enemies and was perhaps biased against him.

And if you're really good at history — they'll let you on the telly...

When you're studying GCSE History, you need to interrogate and interpret every source you see. Don't always assume what you see or read is an exact description of life way back when.

Building a Picture of the Past

Historians can use the information in various sources to get a better understanding of a particular period. This involves linking events together, and working out why things happened the way they did.

Historians study Change and Continuity

1) One way to get an idea of what happened in the past is to look at changes and continuities over time.
2) Change is when something happens to make things different.
   - Changes can be quick — e.g. a law making secondary education free.
   - Or they can be slow — e.g. a gradual change in a society's literacy levels.
3) Continuity is the opposite of change — it's when things stay the same — e.g. people believed for hundreds of years that disease was God's punishment for sin.
4) These ideas are opposites — think of continuity as a flat line going along until there is a sudden change and the line becomes a zigzag:

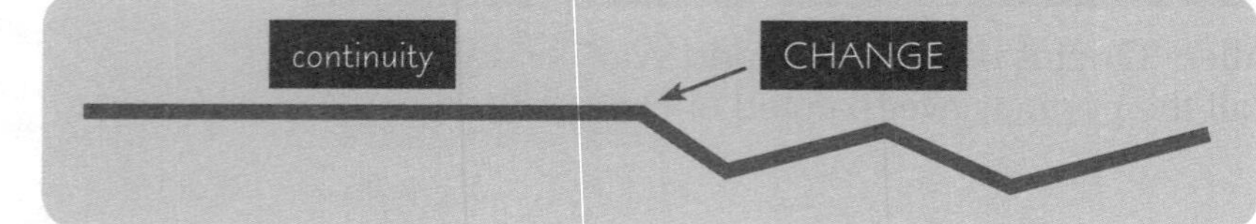

The most important changes in history are called turning points. After a turning point, life might never be the same again.

5) Change and continuity can happen at the same time in different parts of society.
   - For example, when the Normans conquered England in 1066, many of the richest people in English society lost their jobs and status (= change).
   - But life didn't actually change very much for peasant farmers (= continuity).
6) There are all sorts of things that a historian might look at for change or continuity. Some things might be obvious (e.g. a new king or queen would be an obvious change). But historians are also very interested in whether more everyday aspects of society are showing change or continuity — e.g. attitudes, lifestyles, beliefs, fashions, diets... the list is endless.

Historians think about Causes and Consequences

1) Cause means the reason something happened — e.g. the causes of the First World War.
2) Consequence means what happened because of an action — it's the result of an event, e.g. a consequence of the First World War was that a lot of young men were killed.
3) Causes and consequences can be either short-term or long-term.

Any time you have an event in history, think about what caused it and the effect it had — it's a really good way to show the examiner how different historical events are linked to each other.

Short-term cause: protest march on Washington

Long-term cause: growing resistance to discrimination against African Americans

EVENT: The introduction of new civil rights laws in America

Short-term consequence: an increase in the number of black voters

Long-term consequence: some people start to challenge discrimination against other groups (e.g. women).

4) Historians also think about how different causes and consequences interact. For example, there might be a chain of causes that lead to an event, or one consequence of an event might be more important than all the rest.

You can think of these as the Four Cs of history...

As you use this book, make sure you think about 'the Four Cs' on each page. When you identify causes, consequences, changes and continuities, add them to your revision notes and learn them.

Exam Skills for the Period Study

These two pages are all about how to do well in the period study section of your exam.

Period Studies are all about how Events Unfolded

1) The period study covers around 50 years of history in one country. It focuses on the relationships between different events, so you'll have to know all the crucial moments of the period you're studying.
2) You should also have a good knowledge of context, and know what led to significant events and what their consequences were. This includes their impact on people's lives.
3) You'll need to understand that an event or issue can have many different interpretations, all of which can be considered correct as long as they're based on evidence.

Before the exam, it's a good idea to practise analysing interpretations.

There are Six basic types of exam question

1) You'll be given two interpretations and asked three questions about them. The first one will ask you how the interpretations are different.

   How does Interpretation A differ from Interpretation B about what life was like in Nazi Germany in the 1930s? [4 marks]

2) The next question will ask you why you think the authors of the two interpretations might hold different opinions.

   Why might the authors of Interpretations A and B have a different interpretation about what life was like in Nazi Germany in the 1930s? [4 marks]

3) The third question will ask you which interpretation you think is most convincing. You'll have to use your own knowledge to help you decide.

   Which interpretation do you find more convincing about what life was like in Nazi Germany in the 1930s? [8 marks]

4) The next question will ask you to describe two features of the period you've studied.

   Describe two problems faced by Germany at the end of Word War I. [4 marks]

5) The fifth question will look at the impact an important event or development had on a particular group or situation.

   In what ways were the lives of young people affected by Nazi social policies? [8 marks]

6) The last question will focus on cause or consequence, or look at how something changed in the period you've studied. You'll be given two bullet points to discuss, and will have argue in favour of one of them.

   Which of the following was the more important reason why Hitler became Chancellor in 1933:
   - Hitler's popularity
   - economic problems?

   Refer to both reasons in your answer. [12 marks]

You'll need these Skills to answer the questions

1) When you're working with interpretations, you need to figure out what the author is trying to say — look at what information they give, what their tone is and if they emphasise anything in particular.
2) To decide which interpretation is more convincing, you need to consider the event or issue that the interpretations are discussing and decide which interpretation you think describes it most accurately. Make sure you explain your decision using your own knowledge and refer to both interpretations.
3) When you're answering the final question, you need to talk about both bullet points to get high marks. Analyse each reason and make a judgement about which was the most important. Make sure the information you include is relevant, too — the question will give you a specific area to focus on.

For more general advice on how to answer exam questions, see p.136.

Exam Skills for the Period Study

Here's a sample answer for one of the questions in the period study section of your exam.

Have a look at this Sample Answer

Interpretation A

...once Hitler came to power, it was wonderful. Everybody had a job and there weren't any more unemployed people. They were happy to have a job and the foodstuffs were cheaper and the wages were raised a bit. Somehow, things were going better in the first years.

Extract from an interview published in 2005 with a German woman who lived through the Nazi regime.

Interpretation B

It was at that time, in the late summer of 1934, that I came to live and work in the Third Reich. There was much that impressed, puzzled and troubled a foreign observer about the new Germany. The overwhelming majority of Germans did not seem to mind that their personal freedom had been taken away, that so much of their culture had been destroyed and replaced with a mindless barbarism, or that their life and work had become regimented to a degree never before experienced...

Extract from 'Rise and Fall Of The Third Reich: A History of Nazi Germany' by William L. Shirer, published 1960.

This sample answer will give you an idea of how to approach the question about why different authors might have different interpretations of events. Use the information you're given about the authors to help.

Why might the authors of Interpretations A and B have a different interpretation about what life was like in Nazi Germany in the 1930s?
Explain your answer using both interpretations A and B and your contextual knowledge. [4 marks]

Although both interpretations are recollections of Nazi Germany, the authors have two very different perspectives. Interpretation A is from a German woman, who claims that 'once Hitler came to power, it was wonderful'. She would have been able to compare life in Germany before and after Hitler became Chancellor in January 1933, and would have personally experienced the devastating impact that the American Wall Street Crash had on Germany in 1929. As a result, her positive view of life shortly after the Nazis gained power isn't surprising — life did initially improve for many Germans.

Interpretation B is the perspective of 'a foreign observer' who moved to Germany in 1934. They wouldn't have witnessed the economic hardships in Germany seen by the author of Interpretation A. This could be why the second author doesn't concentrate on the economic benefits the Nazis initially created, but instead is 'puzzled' that so many people 'did not seem to mind' the lack of 'personal freedom' in Germany. They are comparing life under the Nazis in the early 1930s to life in another country. The 'mindless barbarism' of the Nazis may have seemed more striking to somebody from a different cultural and political background, who hadn't experienced the changing political mood in Germany.

The first sentence directly addresses the question.

A very quick summary of the interpretation shows you've understood its message.

The answer talks about the authors' different experiences.

The answer uses the information given about the authors and looks at how their experiences may have affected their views.

History — just one thing after another...

The period studies are pretty short, so you're expected to know them well. You'll find events easier to remember if you build up connections between them — plus, it'll get you more marks in the exam.

North American Geography

Knowing a bit about the geography of America is really important to understanding this topic. European settlers initially lived only on the east coast, leaving many regions of America unsettled.

America has very different Geographical regions

1) In order to understand the events covered here, you need to examine how the environment has influenced the American people — so we'd better start with a look at the geography of North America.
2) North America can be divided into several geographical regions, all of which are quite different from each other.

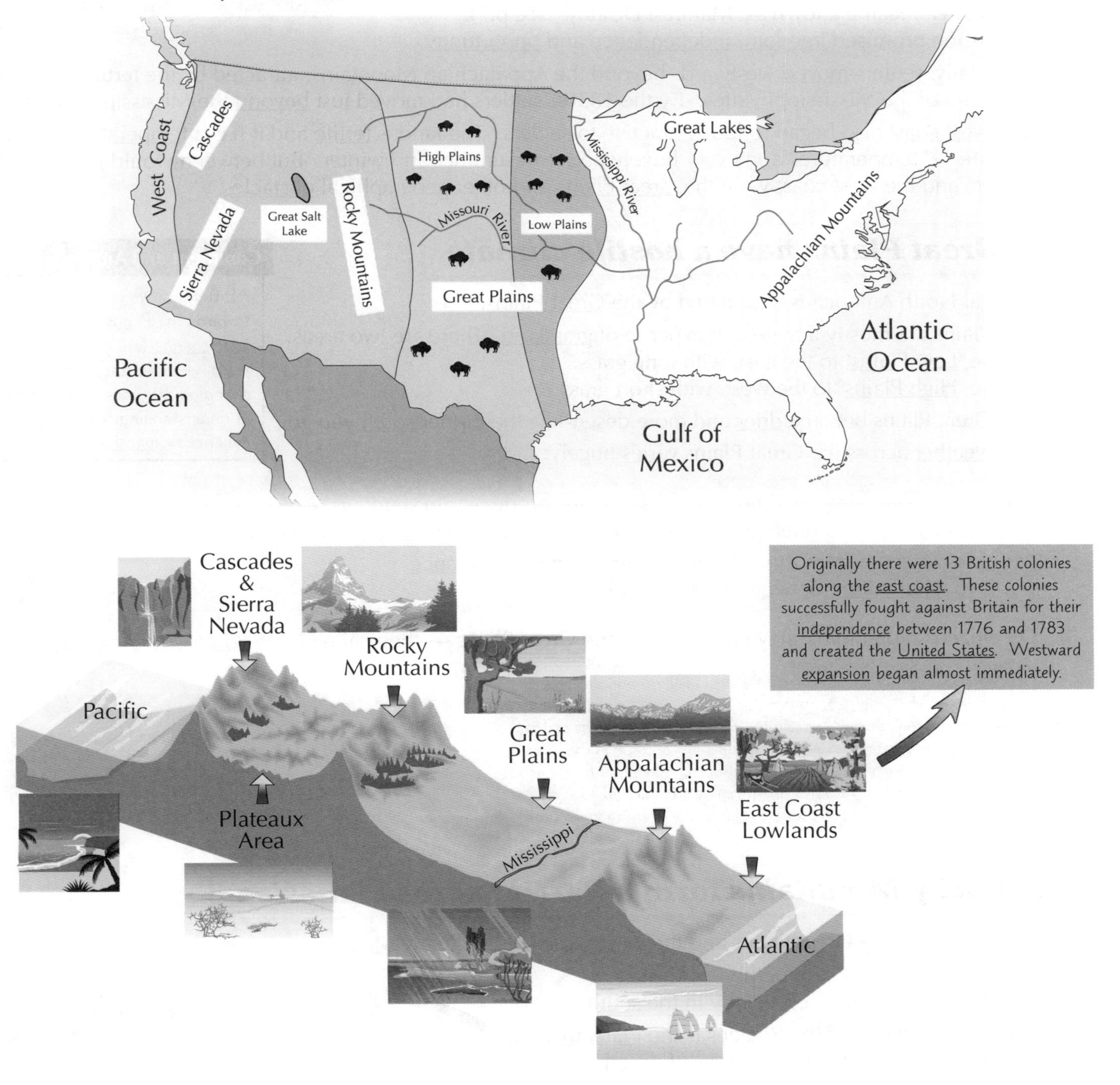

Originally there were 13 British colonies along the east coast. These colonies successfully fought against Britain for their independence between 1776 and 1783 and created the United States. Westward expansion began almost immediately.

You'd better learn the geography — or you're history...

Yep, you're still studying history, but geography was really important in the story of the expansion of the USA. So make sure you learn it to show you have a good grasp of the topic in the exam.

The Geography of the West

Over time, settlers began to move west. Some went all the way to Oregon and California on the west coast — but there were geographical barriers that people had to cross to get there.

Many US citizens wanted to settle land in the West

1) The US population didn't stay concentrated in the East for long. The population and the demand for land was increasing.
2) There was also a growing belief in government and among US citizens that it was the USA's 'duty' to expand westwards. This belief became known as 'Manifest Destiny' (see p.7). Expansion promised freedom, independence and opportunity.
3) Gradually, settlers moved westwards beyond the Appalachian Mountains, attracted by the fertile farmland of the Mississippi Valley. By the 1830s, settlers had moved just beyond the Mississippi River.
4) The west coast also began to look attractive to settlers. The land is fertile and it has a temperate climate — temperatures don't vary hugely between summer and winter. But between would-be settlers and the west coast were the Great Plains and other geographical obstacles.

Thomas Jefferson, president from 1801-1809, believed that land ownership and farming would create a healthy, moral population. Extra land could only be gained by expanding further west.

The Great Plains have a hostile climate

1) Central North America is dominated by the Great Plains.
2) The Plains are mostly a huge, flat expanse of grassland. There are two areas:
   - the 'Low Plains' to the east, with long grass.
   - the 'High Plains' to the west, with short grass.
3) The Great Plains become drier and more desert-like the further south you go.
4) The weather across the Great Plains varies hugely:
   - The mountains on either side of the Plains produce rain shadows (regions with little rain). You often get droughts in the summer and severe snow in the winter.
   - Being so far from the sea means there's a huge difference in temperature between summer and winter.
5) US citizens didn't think they could live on the Great Plains — they called it the 'Great American Desert':

Comment and Analysis

Attitudes of white settlers towards the Plains would later change (see p.12 and p.24) — understanding these changing attitudes is important in understanding the course of America's expansion.

Major Stephen H. Long explored the area in 1820 and said that it was 'almost wholly unfit for cultivation, and of course uninhabitable by a people depending upon agriculture for their subsistence... the scarcity of wood and water... will prove an insuperable obstacle in the way of settling the country... This region, however... may prove of infinite importance to the United States, inasmuch as it is calculated to serve as a barrier to prevent too great an extension of our population westward'.

This contributed to the widespread view among US citizens that the Great Plains were wild and harsh — many believed they were unsuitable for living and farming because of the extremes of weather, sparse rainfall and hard ground.

The Rocky Mountains form a Barrier across America

1) Lying between the Great Plains and the west coast are the Rocky Mountains — a major mountain range.
2) The slopes on either side of the Rockies are heavily wooded — especially in the south.
3) Towards the centre of the Rockies is the Plateaux region. It's relatively flat but contains areas of desert.

Water can run onto the Plateaux region and get trapped, only escaping by evaporation. This has created the Great Salt Lake — important later on (see p.9).

Can't study geography without drawing pretty pictures...

Try scribbling down a map of America without looking at the maps on the previous page. Label the main regions and write a little about each one, using the information from this page.

Wagons Roll

Settlers made the journey to the west coast for a variety of different reasons.

People went to the west coast in Large Numbers from the 1840s

1) The first people to explore the West were mountain men who hunted animals in the 1820s and 1830s to sell their skins. They didn't settle in the West, but established westward trails that settlers would later use.
2) Missionaries were among the earliest settlers on the west coast in the 1830s. The aim was to convert the Native Americans there to Christianity.
3) Later, larger groups of people who wanted to make new lives for themselves went to the west coast. The first of these was the Peoria Party in 1839. Others followed in the 1840s — their routes became known as the Oregon and California Trails.

They had many Different Reasons for heading west

The Great Migration of 1843 saw a sudden increase in settlers — a party of around 1000 people moved to the west coast. This was because life in the East was hard, and there was promise of better things in the West.

Problems in the East

- Economic problems — Recession in 1837 caused banks to collapse and businesses to fail. Wages and profits fell and unemployment rose.
- Overpopulation — High levels of European immigration, particularly from Ireland and Germany from 1846-1854, led to overcrowded cities, fewer jobs and a lack of land for people to farm.
- Disease — Overcrowding and poor sanitary systems led to epidemics of yellow fever and cholera.

Comment and Analysis

Reasons why people went west can be split into push and pull factors — things that pushed them out of the East and things that pulled them to the West.

Attraction of the West

- A new start — Land was fertile and cheap.
- Government encouragement — The government passed acts which allowed settlers to claim land in Oregon — they wanted people to settle in the West to strengthen the USA's claim to the land there.
- Gold — Gold was found at John Sutter's sawmill in California in January 1848 (see p.10). In December, President Polk confirmed that there was gold in the area. In 1849 there was a gold rush, as tens of thousands of people made the journey to California, hoping to make their fortune.

In 1841, Congress passed the Distributive Preemption Act, which allowed settlers to buy 160 acres of land at a very low cost if they'd lived there for 14 months.

Only about 8% of early migrants to California during the Gold Rush were women. More followed later as their husbands and families settled in California.

Settlers also moved west because of a belief in 'Manifest Destiny':

- Many US citizens believed that they were destined to occupy and govern all of North America. They saw it as their god-given right.
- They believed they were superior to Native Americans and that they should civilise the continent.

The term 'Manifest Destiny' was coined by John L. O'Sullivan in 1845.

Paintings which created a romantic, idealised image of moving west promoted expansion and 'Manifest Destiny'. For many, the journey wouldn't have been as pleasant as this image suggests (see p.8).

Migrants crossing the plains towards the Rocky Mountains.

More facts you're destined to learn...

EXAM TIP

You should be able to explain the reasons why people went west. For example, there wasn't enough land in the East, but there was the promise of fertile land in the West.

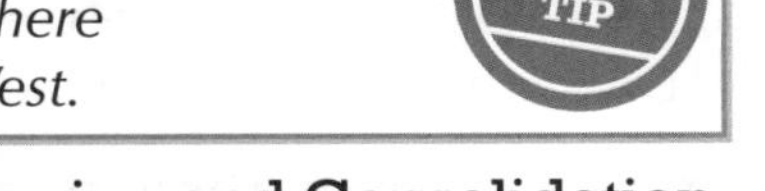

Wagons Roll

Settlers faced many challenges on their journey to the west coast — it was a long way and it was hard work.

The journey to the west coast was Difficult

1) It took around 5 months to complete the 2000 mile overland journey to the west coast. The journey had to be completed before winter. People travelled in wagons and formed wagon trains with other settlers.
2) The journey was dangerous — as many as 10% would die on the way.

- There were mountains and rivers to cross — this was difficult with heavy wagons.
- People suffered from food and water shortages, and diseases such as typhoid and cholera.
- Accidents were common, such as falling under wagon wheels and accidental shootings.

3) Travellers were wary of Native Americans — some killings did occur, but conflict was rare. Native Americans traded food with travellers and offered them guiding services, but they became more hostile with the rise in settlers in the 1850s (see p.13). Travellers also had disputes among themselves.
4) Women did all of the domestic chores at this time, and this was made harder by trail life. Some women had to give birth on the journey, while children were vulnerable to accidents, e.g. falling off wagons.

About half of the estimated 100,000 people who went to California during 1849 did so by sea. This journey also took around 5 months and had its own difficulties — crowded conditions, sickness and storms.

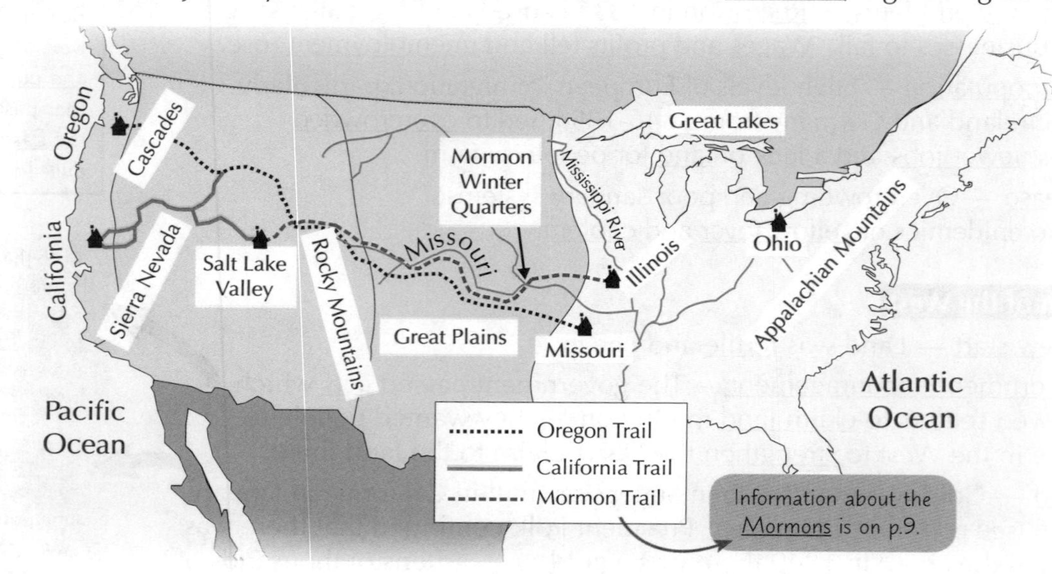

Information about the Mormons is on p.9.

The Donner Party had a Disastrous journey

- In 1846 the Donner Party, heading for California, tried to take a shortcut, but they ended up trapped in deep snow in the Sierra Nevada mountains.
- They had to camp in the mountains over winter. Supplies were low and many of the party starved to death.
- Of the 87 migrants, less than 50 survived till the next spring — by eating those who had died.

'Still snowing; now about three feet deep; wind west; killed my last oxen today.'

Extract from the diary of Patrick Breen, 27th November 1846.

The Donner Party had to kill and eat the animals which pulled their wagons because they ran out of food.

Once settlers had reached the west coast, life was still hard — they had to create farms and homes by hand from scratch. However, the fertile land meant that a good living could be made.

For the settlers, heading west was a big risk...

EXAM QUESTION

Give a brief description of the difficulties settlers faced on their journey to the west coast. [4]

The Mormons

Another group of settlers were the Mormons — members of 'The Church of Jesus Christ of Latter Day Saints'.

The Mormons were Persecuted because of their beliefs

1) This religion was started by Joseph Smith, who published the Book of Mormon in 1830. It claimed that Jesus had visited America and that Native Americans were descended from the lost tribes of Israel.
   - Mormons separated themselves from American society and called non-Mormons 'gentiles'.
   - Some Mormons formed a militia called the Danites and there was violence against non-Mormons and dissenters (Mormons who questioned or abandoned the Mormon faith).
   - Mormons were against slavery and they also tried to convert Native Americans to Mormonism.
2) Many US citizens disliked the Mormons, and repeatedly drove them out of their homes. They didn't agree with the Mormon practice of polygamy (having more than one wife), feared the expansion of the Mormon faith and felt threatened by the Mormons' political and economic power.

Ohio, 1831: The Mormons first settled in Kirtland, Ohio. They faced violence — Joseph Smith was tarred and feathered in 1832. The bank which Smith founded collapsed in 1837 — users of the bank were angry and drove the Mormons to Missouri.

Missouri, 1837: The Mormons' anti-slavery stance annoyed slave-owners, and the Danites were suspected of plotting with Native Americans. Many leaders were arrested, so Brigham Young led the Mormons to Illinois.

Illinois, 1839: The Mormons created their own city called Nauvoo, with its own army and laws. Joseph Smith declared his candidacy for President. Smith was eventually killed in jail by an angry mob and Brigham Young took over as leader.

They moved west and settled in Salt Lake Valley

1) Brigham Young decided to move the Mormons further west. He wanted to create an independent Mormon state where they could live freely. He chose Salt Lake Valley — conditions there were dry and harsh, but he believed that nobody else wanted to live there and it was part of Mexico, not the US.
2) The Mormons planned to leave Illinois in the spring of 1846, but due to an increase in anti-Mormon violence they had to leave in February. This rushed departure meant that they left supplies behind and were disorganised. Conditions were hard — it was a cold winter and there was deep mud.
3) Their progress was very slow, which meant they couldn't complete the journey that year. They stayed in Winter Quarters by the Missouri River over winter (see map on p.8) — by the spring of 1847, around 400 Mormons had died from disease, the cold and lack of supplies.

Although the journey was hard, the Mormons planted crops and built way stations along the trail to feed and help later travellers.

4) They set off again in April 1847 and organisation improved. They were divided into groups led by captains under the strict overall command of Young. They finally reached Salt Lake Valley in July.
5) The conditions in Salt Lake Valley were tough, but Young led the Mormons in solving their problems:

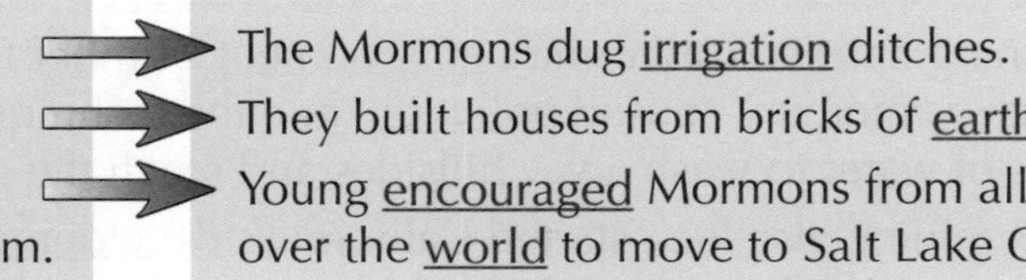
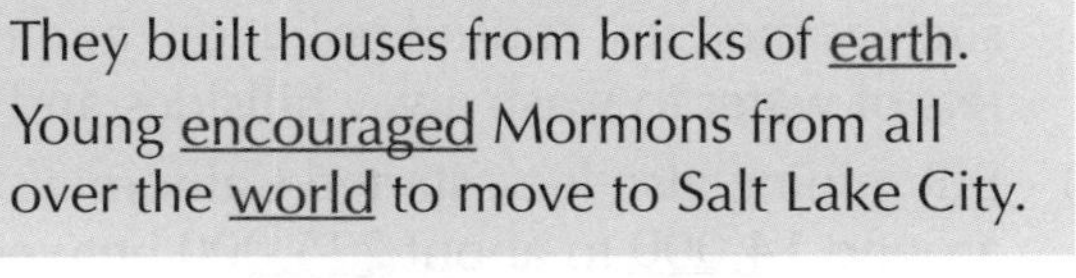

Problem	Solution
There was little rain or other water sources.	The Mormons dug irrigation ditches.
There were no trees to use for wood.	They built houses from bricks of earth.
They needed to become economically self-sufficient, but there weren't enough of them.	Young encouraged Mormons from all over the world to move to Salt Lake City.

6) Life was hard at first, but the Mormons were eventually successful in creating thriving communities.
7) But in 1848 Mexico gave Salt Lake Valley to the US — it became the territory of Utah and was subject to American laws. Conflict followed between Mormons and the US government (see p.20).

Comment and Analysis

The Mormons successfully settled in Salt Lake Valley, but they didn't achieve the independence they wanted.

The Mormons are important to the history of the West...

EXAM TIP

If you get an exam question on why early settlers went west, make sure your answer includes the Mormons. They had very different reasons for going west to other settlers.

Gold Miners

Migration to the west coast during the 1840s was gradual, with most people heading to Oregon. But the California Gold Rush changed this — in just a few years, huge numbers of travellers journeyed to California.

Gold was found in California in 1848

A miner panning for gold.

1) James Marshall found gold while working at John Sutter's sawmill in January 1848. News of this spread slowly to the east coast, until President Polk made a speech in December confirming that gold had been found. As a result, tens of thousands of people made the journey west during 1849.
2) People were excited at the prospect of making their fortune. Many hoped to find gold and then return home.
3) People came to California from all over the world — e.g. China, Mexico and South America, as well as from other parts of North America.

James Carson, an army sergeant in California, abandoned his post to look for gold, writing later that he had 'a very violent attack of gold fever.'

The California Gold Rush presented many Challenges

1) Life as a miner was hard, even before reaching California. There were many deaths from cholera on the journey to California between 1849 and 1853.
2) Only a lucky few found gold in California. Surface gold (found using the simple method of panning) was limited and soon grew scarce. Some miners returned home, but others couldn't afford to.
3) Living and working conditions were poor. There was little hygiene, disease was common and nutrition among miners was poor. Miners who couldn't find gold worked for mining companies in dangerous conditions for low wages. When not working, people turned to drinking and gambling which often led to trouble in mining towns.
4) The rapid migration of mostly male gold seekers and the quick development of mining towns meant that society was unstructured — there were no stable families or communities. There were no laws at first — miners had to enforce the law themselves but their justice wasn't always fair.
5) There was frequent racial conflict. White Americans considered themselves superior to foreign miners and more entitled to the gold, especially when it began to grow scarce.

Some people ran service industries, e.g. stores and saloons. Unsuccessful miners often stayed on in California as farmers and merchants and started families.

Native American tribes living in California suffered as a result of the Gold Rush. The Native American population in California dropped from around 150,000 to less than 30,000 during 1845-1870. This was the result of violent attacks, epidemics and being driven off their land.

California and the US as a whole felt the effects of the rush

1) Mining harmed California's environment. Timber for mine supports used up forests, chemicals such as mercury caused pollution, and the technique of hydraulic mining (the use of high powered jets of water to wash away hillsides and reach the gold beneath) destroyed the landscape.
2) But mining also kick-started California's development. The non-Native American population rose from around 14,000 to about 225,000 between 1848-1852. Mining towns such as Sacramento and Stockton expanded. San Francisco became the economic centre of California.
3) The Gold Rush accelerated the economic growth of the US. The wealth generated by gold mining gave America an important role in world trade. Settlement in California increased the need for better links between the east and west of the country, leading to improved mail services and a transcontinental railroad (see p.24).

Comment and Analysis

Mining had a negative impact on many individuals, especially the Native Americans, but it played an important role in the expansion of the US.

It's interesting how things panned out, isn't it...

Write a quick summary of all of the positive and negative impacts of the Gold Rush.

REVISION TASK

Lifestyle of the Native Americans

While many US citizens viewed the Great Plains as undesirable, a number of Native American tribes called the Plains home — they're known as the Plains Indians. They led very different lifestyles to the settlers.

The Plains Indians lived in different groups called Tribes

1) The Plains Indians weren't a single group with a single culture — there were many different tribes, such as the Sioux, the Comanche and the Apache.

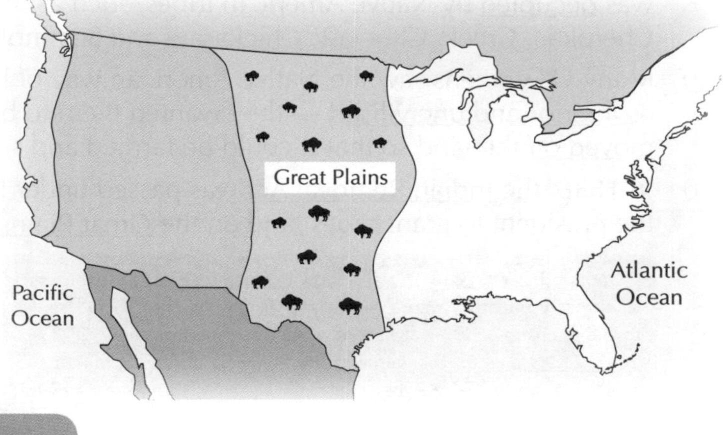

2) Many tribes were nomadic, hunting the millions of buffalo that lived on the Plains. Other tribes were more settled and lived in one place, farming the land.

E.g. The Lakota Sioux led a nomadic lifestyle, regularly moving from place to place. In contrast, the Mandans farmed and lived in permanent villages.

3) Tribal warfare was common. The aim wasn't necessarily to kill or seize land, but to perform acts of bravery such as stealing horses and counting coup (getting close enough to an enemy to touch him).

The Arapaho and the Kiowa often fought each other.

The Plains Indians led Very Different Lifestyles to white settlers

1) Tribes were usually split into bands, and each band had a chief and a council of elders. The chief didn't have complete control, but he would have earned loyalty over the years by demonstrating courage and generosity — this gave him influence over the tribe.
2) The Native Americans didn't see land as something that could be bought and sold — land belonged to everyone. Even for more settled tribes, agricultural land belonged to the tribe as a whole.
3) Medicine men and medicine women were spiritual leaders of tribes. Native American religion was closely linked with nature — humans were believed to be part of nature, not masters over it. Most tribes believed in a Great Spirit which created the world, and that everything in nature contained spirits which they needed to keep on their side — ceremonies and dance rituals were performed to contact the spirits.
4) Women did most of the work in the village or camp, while the men hunted and fought. Although men were head of the family, women owned the tipi (the family tent) and its contents, which gave them status.
5) Buffalo were vital for the Plains Indians. They used almost every part of the animal — meat for food, skin for clothing and tents, and bones for weapons and tools.

Many tribes practiced polygamy because the dangers of hunting and warfare meant there were often more women than men in tribes.

Hunting became easier when the Plains Indians began to use horses, which were brought over by the Europeans in the 16th century.

Comment and Analysis

Settlers failed to understand the culture of the Plains Indians because it was so different to their own. This led to tension and conflict.

I don't think they're going to get along, do you...?

Make a list summarising the different features of the Plains Indians' way of life. For each of the points you make, think about how it's different from the lifestyle and beliefs of the settlers.

The Permanent Indian Frontier

Some Native American tribes lived in the East. As US citizens settled more of the land in the East, these tribes were moved on to the Great Plains. But this arrangement was soon put under strain.

Tribes living in the East were Moved on to the Plains

1) Some of the land that settlers wanted to farm in the East was occupied by Native American tribes, such as the Cherokee, Creek, Choctaw, Chickasaw and Seminole.
2) Many US citizens saw the Native American way of life as inferior and uncivilised — they wanted them to be moved off the land so that it could be farmed and settled.

> Before 1830, the government had pursued a policy of assimilating Native Americans in the East into white society — this means making them change their lifestyle to fit in with that of whites. Tribes such as the Cherokee had taken on aspects of white culture as a result — but people still didn't see them as equal.

3) In 1830, the Indian Removal Act was passed under President Andrew Jackson — this authorised the president to grant tribes land on the Great Plains in exchange for their land in the East.

> Some tribes resisted removal. The Cherokee tried to resist through legal means, but they were eventually forcefully marched by US soldiers to the Plains in 1838 — it has been estimated that around 4000 out of 15,000 died on the journey. The Seminole of Florida fought US soldiers from 1835-1842, but eventually surrendered and moved west.

4) By 1840, most of the eastern tribes had been moved onto the Plains — around 70,000-100,000 people in total.
5) The intention was that Native Americans would live on the Great Plains, while settlers farmed land in the East — the Plains would be like one large Indian reservation. The boundary between the two regions was known as the Permanent Indian Frontier.
6) At this point, settlers viewed the Plains as 'The Great American Desert' (see p.6) — they didn't want to settle there themselves because they thought the conditions on the Plains were unsuitable for living and farming.

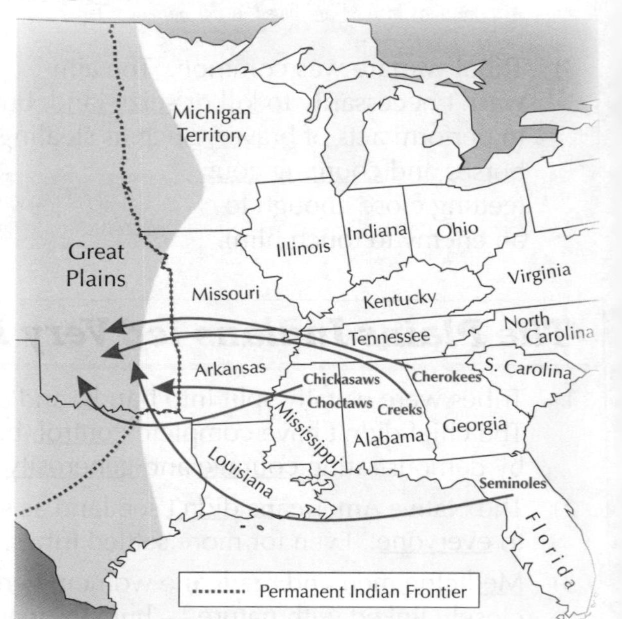

Comment and Analysis

The government gave the Native Americans the Great Plains, but only because white settlers didn't want the land themselves. This shows the attitude of many white people towards the Native Americans — they saw them as inferior, so felt it was acceptable to give them land they themselves didn't think was fit to live on.

Settlers began to Encroach on the Plains

Gradually, settlers began to use the Great Plains — land that had been promised to the Native Americans.

- Settlers moved across the Great Plains on their way to the west coast.
- In the 1850s, people began to see the possibility of settling on the Plains — it wasn't quite the 'Great American Desert' they had thought. In 1854, the government opened up Kansas and Nebraska for settlement.

> The adventurer John Charles Fremont, who mapped out the Oregon Trail in 1843-44, painted a more positive picture of the Plains than Stephen Long (see p.6).

'Here you are, you can have all this lovely desert to live in...'

EXAM TIP

Although you're studying the period from 1840, make sure you know about earlier events like the Indian Removal Act for the exam — it's an important part of the wider narrative that you're studying.

The Clash of Cultures

As more settlers started to cross the Great Plains, tension grew between them and the Plains Indians.

There was a Lack of Understanding between settlers and Indians

1) To settlers, it seemed that the Plains Indians had no system of government, that their warfare was cowardly and their religion just superstition (see p.11).
2) They had different views on land ownership. Native Americans believed that the land was for everyone, but settlers wanted to own, farm and exploit land.
3) Settlers thought that the Plains Indians' nomadic lifestyle was uncivilised and that they wasted the land. Native Americans thought that the settlers ruined the land.

Horace Greeley, a newspaper editor, wrote in 1859 that 'God has given this earth to those who will subdue and cultivate it.'

Native Americans and settlers Increasingly came into Contact

1) Significant numbers of settlers moved beyond the Permanent Indian Frontier and across the Plains to reach lands in the west from 1843. Many more came with the California Gold Rush of 1849.
2) The settlers disrupted buffalo herds which the Plains Indians relied on, and polluted water sources, bringing diseases such as cholera.
3) As a result, Plains Indians became more hostile. They sometimes attacked wagon trains, which increased the settlers' fear and distrust. The settlers also felt threatened by the Indians' inter-tribal conflict.

The Reservation System replaced the Permanent Indian Frontier

1) The government wanted to reduce conflict on the Plains. It decided to pursue a policy of concentration — the Plains Indians would be concentrated onto specific areas of the Plains called reservations.
2) The Fort Laramie Treaty (1851) was the government's first attempt to concentrate the Plains Indians in certain areas. It defined the territory of each tribe to try to minimise inter-tribal conflict.
3) Tribes agreed to remain in their territory, allow settlers to cross the Plains, and allow the government to build roads and forts along the trails. In return, the government promised the tribes that they would have permanent rights to their lands, and that tribes would receive $50,000 of goods a year for 50 years.
4) Neither side kept to the treaty. Not all tribes agreed with it and many didn't even know it existed. The US government didn't keep its side of the deal either — it couldn't ensure settlers kept to the agreement, and in 1852 it reduced the yearly payments from 50 years to 10.

The government never allowed existing treaties to prevent settlement it was in favour of — it simply negotiated new ones. For example, thousands of people encroached on Cheyenne land in Colorado during the Pike's Peak Gold Rush (1858-1861). The government then negotiated the Fort Wise Treaty, reducing Cheyenne land to make room for white settlers, and moving the Cheyenne to poor quality land on the Sand Creek Reservation. Some Cheyenne later claimed that they didn't understand the terms of the treaty when they signed it.

5) The treaty had a large impact:
   - Settlement increased in California and Oregon.
   - Restricting Native Americans to reservations threatened their way of life, as did the building of roads and forts in their territory.
   - Broken promises increased Native American resentment towards government and settlers.

Comment and Analysis

The Fort Laramie Treaty is significant because it marked the end of the Permanent Indian Frontier — the Native Americans could no longer live freely on the Plains. It paved the way for further treaties in the 1850s and 1860s which resulted in tribes losing land, e.g. in 1853 treaties were made with tribes in Kansas and Nebraska to make room for settlers in those areas (see p.12) — these tribes lost nearly 17 million acres.

Native Americans had been given the Great Plains when they were considered uninhabitable. This changed when settlers decided that they wanted the land.

'Well, when we said you could have all this lovely desert'...

It can be difficult to keep track of all the important events and treaties like Fort Laramie — start a timeline, noting down key developments and keep adding to it as you read through this section.

Increasing Tensions on the Plains

The Plains Indians felt increasingly threatened as more people settled on the Plains.

Railroads, Ranching and Gold angered the Plains Indians

Railroads

- Railroad companies often clashed with the Plains Indians. They encouraged the settling of the Plains as they expanded their networks.
- They frequently built railroads through Native American lands, even if it violated treaties.
- Railroad companies also encouraged the hunting of buffalo — both to feed the railway construction gangs, and to make money by transporting hunters.
- Buffalo were a hugely important resource for Native Americans (see p.11). So some tribes derailed trains and ambushed workmen. In response, the military built forts to protect the railroad.

Sioux raiding a train on the Great Plains.

Buffalo hunting became a popular sport (see p.27).

Ranching

- Ranchers clashed with the Plains Indians when they drove cattle through Indian land and when they built ranches on Indian territory.
- Again, this disrupted buffalo herds and the buffalo had to compete with cattle for grass.
- Indians attacked ranchers and cattle drives. The famous rancher and cattle driver Oliver Loving died in 1867 after a fight with Comanches.

Gold

- Gold discoveries led to further encroachments on Native American land.
- When gold was discovered in Montana in 1862, miners arrived in the area and prospected on Indian reservation land, breaking the treaties which had promised this land to the Native Americans.

Many Plains Indians were Unhappy with the Reservation Policy

1) More Indians were moved onto reservations as more settlers came to live on the Plains.
2) Life on reservations varied. The Navajos achieved peace and prosperity after 1868, when a treaty with the US allowed them sufficient reservation area in their homeland.
3) Other tribes were moved off their homeland and onto unfamiliar territory. They were encouraged to farm the land, which went against their culture and nomadic lifestyle.
4) Often reservation lands were insufficient and unsuitable for farming — some tribes faced starvation.
5) If the lands were good, they were likely to be grabbed by settlers, despite the promises in the government treaties. Many chiefs also lacked the authority to make their tribes keep to the agreements.

Many Plains tribes were still able to hunt buffalo, but only within certain areas.

Many tribes wanted peace, but the situation had become intolerable. They were forced into conflict during the 1860s in a series of Indian Wars (see p.15).

Comment and Analysis

It isn't surprising the Native Americans went to war. They had been promised the Great Plains when the Permanent Indian Frontier was created, but the government repeatedly broke their promises and forced the Native Americans onto ever-smaller areas of land.

'Turns out this desert is pretty useful isn't it?'...

Make sure you understand government policies towards the Native Americans and why they failed. The policy of concentration failed as more and more settlers began to use the Plains.

Early Conflicts on the Plains

The Indian Wars were a series of conflicts during the 1860s between the US army and Native American tribes.

Little Crow's War was an uprising in Minnesota — 1862

The first major Indian War was Little Crow's War:

1) Little Crow was chief of the Santee Sioux (known as the Dakota) who lived on a Minnesota reservation.
2) They were peaceful and accepted reservation life. But they nearly starved as a result of Civil War shortages, a delay in their yearly payment from the government, cheating by traders and a poor harvest.
3) In August 1862, four Dakota returning from an unsuccessful hunt murdered five settlers for a dare. Fearing retaliation on the entire tribe, Little Crow reluctantly led his warriors in an uprising. Hundreds of settlers and about 100 soldiers were killed, and the town of New Ulm was burned.
4) The uprising was ended when the Dakota were defeated at Wood Lake in September. 38 Dakota prisoners were hanged and most of the Dakota were expelled from what was left of their land.

The Cheyenne Uprising and the Sand Creek Massacre — 1864

1) In 1863, the Cheyenne faced starvation because they couldn't grow enough food on their infertile reservation land at Sand Creek (see p.13) or find any buffalo. They decided to raid settlers' wagon trains for food.
2) In April 1864, after a dispute over cattle, many Cheyenne began raids on ranches and stagecoaches, committing atrocities which outraged settlers.
3) In August, the governor of Colorado territory issued a statement urging the hunting of hostile Indians. Volunteers shot any Cheyenne they saw.
4) The Cheyenne chief, Black Kettle, wanted peace and a safe winter camp. Army officers promised his band protection if they moved to Sand Creek. But in November 1864, Colonel John Chivington attacked the camp while most of the band's men were out hunting. Of the 500 people left in the camp, at least 163 were killed — mostly women and children. This atrocity is known as the Sand Creek Massacre.
5) The Cheyenne, Arapaho and Sioux retaliated by attacking ranches and other settlements and killing those inside, including women and children. The central Plains erupted into war.

Comment and Analysis

Atrocities were committed by both whites and Native Americans — this increased the distrust and hatred on both sides and led to even more violence.

Red Cloud's War and the Bozeman Trail — 1866-1868

1) The Bozeman Trail was established to link the gold fields in Montana with the Oregon Trail. However, the trail passed through the hunting grounds of the Sioux, which had been guaranteed to them by the Fort Laramie Treaty of 1851.
2) The Sioux attacked travellers who used the trail, so the army wanted to build forts to protect them. Talks were held with Red Cloud, a Sioux chief, to negotiate the building of these forts, but they were abandoned when the Sioux saw soldiers marching out to begin building before any deal had been made.
3) The Sioux began to attack the army. In a major incident known as Fetterman's Trap, the Sioux ambushed Captain W.J. Fetterman and his troops — Fetterman and all 80 of his men were killed.
4) As a result, the US army surrendered and abandoned the forts. This was a major defeat for the army.

Red Cloud.

Relations between the Native Americans and settlers would continue to deteriorate — there's more on this on pages 26-29.

The Indian Wars soured relations ever further...

'Settlers and the Plains Indians were equally to blame for the conflict on the Plains in the period 1849-1870'. Explain whether you find this interpretation convincing or not. [8]

The Civil War: Background

The North and South of the USA developed in different ways and had different attitudes towards slavery.

The North and South had Different Economies

1) In the early 19th century, the South's economy was heavily based on cotton exports. Cotton was produced cheaply using slave labour on plantations.
2) Slavery wasn't as important in the North — it had a more diverse economy that was based on lots of different industries and agricultural crops.
3) By 1804, all of the northern states had abolished slavery (banned it). This created a division between southern 'slave states' and northern 'free states'.
4) As time went on, the North became even more industrialised, while the South relied more and more on cotton growing. By the 1860s, the North had six times as many factories as the South.
5) The North was more wealthy than the South as a result of its diverse and industrialised economy.

The North didn't necessarily want racial equality. They were more worried about the South gaining political power and spreading slavery into new territories (see below).

Comment and Analysis

Some historians point out that the South didn't need to industrialise, because they made lots of money out of plantation agriculture. This might be true, but it was a bad idea to rely on one industry (cotton) to keep the economy going.

Not all southerners were slave owners — in 1860, only about 5% of southerners owned slaves. Less than 1% of these slaveholders had large slave plantations with 200 or more slaves. However, because the southern economy was based on slave labour, southerners saw it as part of their way of life — they called it their 'peculiar institution'.

The North had a Bigger Population than the South

1) The North's population was bigger than the South's. A big proportion of the South's population were slaves — by 1860, there were almost 4 million slaves in the South compared to 8 million free white Americans.
2) The North's population gave it more political power, as states with a bigger population could have more representatives in the lower house of Congress.
3) The South still had lots of political power, though. Each state had two representatives in the Senate (the upper house of Congress). Each new state that applied to join the Union (the USA) chose whether to allow or ban slavery. If the number of free and slave states in Congress stayed balanced, the South could use its votes in the Senate to protect slavery.

Slaves were counted as three-fifths of a person. This gave southerners more power than they would've had if only free people were counted.

Westward expansion Increased the Tension over Slavery

1) Slavery became so important in the South that many southerners believed there would be economic and social chaos if it was abolished. They were keen to protect their way of life.
2) As westward expansion continued, northern senators tried to stop new states becoming slave states. They wanted to use land in the West for their own economic development.
3) This caused tension between the North and South, which came to the surface when new states requested admission to the Union.

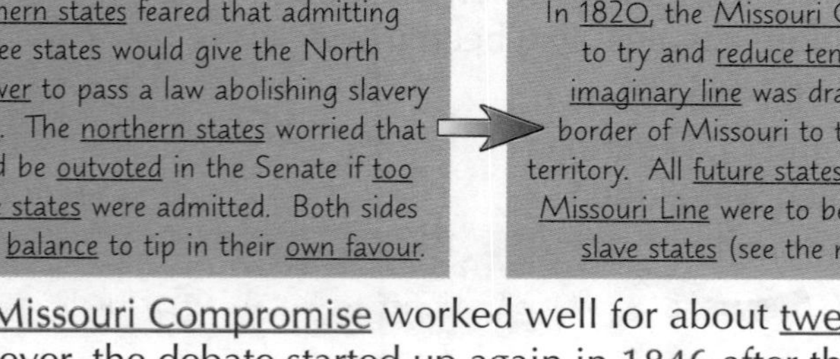
The southern states feared that admitting more free states would give the North enough power to pass a law abolishing slavery in all states. The northern states worried that they would be outvoted in the Senate if too many slave states were admitted. Both sides wanted the balance to tip in their own favour.

In 1820, the Missouri Compromise was created to try and reduce tension over slavery. An imaginary line was drawn from the southern border of Missouri to the western edge of US territory. All future states that formed north of the Missouri Line were to be banned from becoming slave states (see the next page for a map).

Comment and Analysis

As the differences between the North and South grew, both worried more about protecting their own interests, especially when it came to slavery. Politicians focused on their own state, even if it harmed national unity. This attitude is called sectionalism.

4) The Missouri Compromise worked well for about twenty years and Congress stayed balanced. However, the debate started up again in 1846 after the USA gained more territory in the West.

And I thought the UK had a North/South divide...

Write down all of the main differences between the North and South that you can think of.

The Civil War: Background

The tension between the North and South got worse when slavery started to spread into the West.

The Compromise of 1850 was meant to Settle the Tension

In 1846, the USA took control of more territory in the north-west after making a treaty with Britain. The USA also got lots of new land from Mexico in 1846 during the Mexican War. These territories weren't covered by the Missouri Compromise, so northerners and southerners argued over what to do about them.

Northerners wanted to ban slavery in all territories won from Mexico, but southerners said that these territories belonged to every state. They said that if the government tried to stop them from taking slaves there, then southern states could leave the Union (this was called secession).

Secession was based on the idea that states had the power to formally leave the Union if they wanted to, as each state had sovereign power (see p.23 for more on state powers).

In 1848, gold was discovered in California (p.10) — settlers there applied to join the Union as a free state in 1849. This angered the South and they considered secession, so the Compromise of 1850 was proposed.

1) California joined the Union as a free state, but the people of New Mexico and Utah were allowed to decide if their states would be slave or free. This was based on the idea of popular sovereignty, where settlers had the final say.
2) The Fugitive Slave Act was passed, requiring all Americans to return runaway slaves to their owners, even if the slaves reached free states.

Neither side was happy with this — the South resented that the North had gained prosperous California, while the North was angry that more slave states could be created. However, the Compromise did stop the South from seceding in 1850.

The Missouri Compromise was Broken in 1854

1) In 1854, a northern senator called Stephen Douglas wanted Nebraska to enter the Union so its land could be developed. The South wasn't keen on this idea, as Nebraska was above the Missouri Line.
2) The Kansas-Nebraska Act of 1854 was created as a compromise — Kansas and Nebraska were given popular sovereignty to decide to become slave or free states.
3) This undermined the Missouri Compromise. There was a sectional struggle in Kansas, as pro-slavery and anti-slavery settlers tried to take control.

Douglas thought the act would reduce tension, but it made things worse. Many in the North saw it as a concession to the South.

Free State Abolitionists wanted Slavery to End

Some in northern free states campaigned for slaves to be freed — they were called abolitionists. At first, abolitionists wanted slavery to be ended slowly and for owners to be compensated for losing their slaves.

1) The abolitionist movement became more organised when the American Anti-Slavery Society was formed in 1833 — its members included many evangelical Christians, women and freed slaves.
2) Abolition gained some support in the North. However, many northerners didn't support abolition — they worried about the impact of freed slaves coming to the North in big numbers. Southerners felt that their way of life was being attacked, so there was little support for the movement in the South.
3) In 1852, abolitionist Harriet Beecher Stowe attacked slavery in her novel 'Uncle Tom's Cabin'. It sparked support for abolition by making many in the North more aware of the immorality of slavery.

You can't always get what you want...

Write down a quick summary of the 1850 Compromise and explain why both northerners and southerners were unhappy with it.

The Civil War

In the 1860s, the tensions that had been brewing between the North and South caused some serious conflict.

John Brown tried to start a Slave Uprising in 1859

The abolitionist John Brown believed that peaceful attempts to end slavery would never work. He led an attack on a pro-slavery settlement in Kansas in 1856 as revenge for a southern attack on a free settlement.

1) In 1859, Brown led an armed raid on a government arsenal (weapon store) at Harper's Ferry in Virginia. He wanted to arm slaves in the South and start an uprising against southern plantation owners.
2) Some of the men led by Brown were African American — one was a fugitive slave. The Fugitive Slave Act had made it illegal to aid escaped slaves, so Brown was taking a big risk by leading the raid.
3) The raid was a failure — Brown was captured and hanged for treason. After the raid, the tension between the North and South intensified.

In the South, Brown's raid caused fear and anger towards abolitionists. Many northerners saw Brown as a hero, even if they didn't agree with his methods.

Lincoln's Election as President in 1860 triggered Secession

After the Missouri Compromise was undermined by the Kansas-Nebraska Act, the Republican Party was formed in the North to stop slavery advancing. By 1856, the Republicans had gained lots of support in the North, but the Democrats stayed popular in the South. This created more sectional tension.

1) In 1860, Republican Abraham Lincoln won the presidential election. He was a minority president — he only got 40% of the overall vote and he didn't get any votes in 10 of the southern states.

Before the election, one of Lincoln's opponents had said that Lincoln supported abolition and wanted racial equality. Southerners feared Lincoln's motives, and saw him as a symbol of abolitionism.

Many southerners felt that they didn't owe any loyalty to a man who threatened their way of life. His election triggered the secession of South Carolina and six more southern states.

Lincoln thought slavery was immoral, but he didn't actually want to interfere with it in the South. He made that very clear in his inaugural speech in March 1861.

'I have no purpose, directly or indirectly, to interfere with the institution of slavery in the States where it exists. I believe I have no lawful right to do so, and I have no inclination to do so.'

2) In February 1861, the seven states that had seceded from the Union formed the Confederate States of America with Jefferson Davis as their president.
3) When Lincoln was sworn in as Union president in March 1861 he said that he wouldn't accept secession. There were still some US government troops at Fort Sumter in South Carolina — Lincoln refused to withdraw this garrison. He sent more supplies to the fort, but said that he would only attack if the South did so first. In April 1861, Confederate troops attacked the fort.
4) This triggered a civil war between the Union and the Confederates. By August 1861, 11 southern states had seceded from the Union. Lincoln declared that the Confederate states were in rebellion.

Jefferson Davis wanted to create a New Nation

Davis joined Congress in 1845 as a senator for Mississippi. Before this, he'd been an officer in the Army, and he owned a cotton plantation.

1) Davis thought that states had the right to secede, but he didn't want the Union to break up. However, he also believed in the South's freedom to own slaves.
2) After being elected Confederate President, Davis tried to make the Confederacy into an independent country based on slavery. Lincoln's refusal to remove the Fort Sumter garrison was seen as a lack of respect for the Confederacy's independence, which is why Davis attacked it.

'We have entered upon the career of independence... As a necessity, not a choice, we have resorted to the remedy of separation; and henceforth our energies must be directed to the conduct of our own affairs, and the perpetuity of the Confederacy which we have formed.'
Extract from Davis's inaugural speech, February 1861.

In 1863, Lincoln declared the Emancipation Proclamation to blackmail southern states into returning to the Union. All slaves in states that were in rebellion were to be freed.

Comment and Analysis

Lincoln went back on his earlier declarations on slavery and turned the war into a battle over slavery. After this, it was less likely that the South would negotiate a peaceful end to the war, as their new nation was based on slavery.

The South really didn't like Lincoln...

Was Lincoln's election or slavery the more important reason for the outbreak of the US Civil War? Explain your answer, referring to both reasons. [12]

Impact of the Civil War

The Civil War had a big impact on the lives of civilians — things were especially tough for southerners.

The War had a Negative Impact on the South's Economy

1) In 1861, the South introduced a ban on cotton exports to force Europe to side with them in the war. Europe had more cotton than they needed, so the ban failed and the South lost valuable income.
2) Southerners were cut off from northern markets during the war and the blockade made it hard to import food. Also, lots of farmland was destroyed by fighting. Things got worse in 1864 when the North started to target southern transport and civilian property to deliberately cause economic hardship.
3) Food shortages led to inflation (when prices go up and money loses value) — black markets formed and made inflation worse. In 1863, the Confederacy introduced new ways of collecting tax to help cover the costs of the war effort.
4) The Confederate government issued paper money in 1861. Once it became obvious that the South was losing the war and had printed too many notes, the value of the notes fell quickly and inflation increased.

Lincoln knew the value of cotton exports, so he ordered a blockade of ships to be put in place. By July 1861, all Confederate ports were surrounded by Union ships. Even after the South ended their ban, they struggled to export cotton because of the blockade.

Comment and Analysis

Some historians criticise Davis's government for taking over the economy and then failing to protect it — its handling of paper currency and interference in the cotton industry made things worse.

The Economy in the North actually Benefited from the War

1) The North suffered from inflation too, but its economy was in a stronger position to deal with it. During the war, northern agricultural and industrial production increased, as the army needed a good supply of food and weapons. This created job opportunities and increasing prosperity for northerners.
2) Northerners were also taxed, but only those with incomes above a certain amount had to pay. The government borrowed a lot of money from richer northern citizens to fund the war.

The Social Impact of the War was Serious

Around 260,000 Confederate soldiers and 360,000 Union soldiers died during the war. Historians reckon that about 50,000 southern civilians died because of the war too, though no one knows the full death toll.

1) Most of the fighting happened in the South — some areas were occupied by Union soldiers. Lots of property was destroyed, so many southerners became refugees. There was guerilla warfare too, where armed civilians fought against Union soldiers, raided their bases and cut their lines of communication. However, some guerilla groups also robbed and attacked other civilians.
2) People who weren't close to the fighting still knew quite a lot about what was going on — soldiers wrote letters to their families and newspapers ran stories about the war.
3) Civilians in both the North and South lost civil liberties during the war.

Conscription (forcing civilians into the army) was introduced in the South by Davis in 1862 and in the North by Lincoln in 1863.

Both sides suspended the right to a trial and introduced martial law (where a military commander takes control).

4) As men were fighting in the South, jobs were created for women and freed slaves in the North. This caused social tension — some felt that freed slaves were taking 'white jobs'.
5) In 1863, there were riots against conscription in New York. A lot of anger was directed at black citizens.

During the 1864 election, a northern Democrat stirred up fears of mixed-race marriage as part of a racist campaign that played on this social tension.

An engraving from the Illustrated London News, August 1863. A black man is hung by rioters during the New York Draft Riots in July 1863.

The war was bad news for the South...

If you're writing about the impact of the war, think about how the differences between the North and South might have influenced the way that civilians experienced the war.

EXAM TIP

Coming to Terms with the Mormons

In the 1850s, there was a conflict between the Mormons and the government over who should govern Utah.

The Mormons fought the US Government in the Utah War

Utah was a territory of the US government, which meant that it had to stick to US laws. Brigham Young (p.9) was made governor of Utah in 1851. What he really wanted to do was create an independent Mormon state.

1) In 1851, three government officials left Utah because they disapproved of Mormon polygamy. They felt unable to work with Young, who supported polygamy (he had 55 wives in total). The government and the Mormons eventually got into a serious conflict over the issue of polygamy.

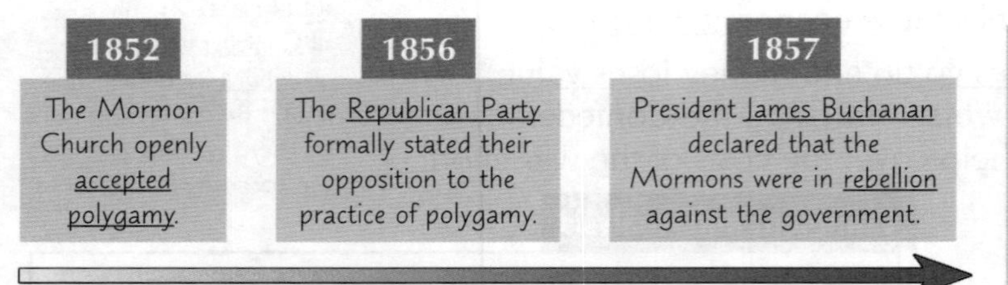

May 1857

Buchanan appointed a new governor to replace Young and sent troops to force the Mormons to accept the government's authority. This sparked a conflict between the Mormons and US troops called the Utah War. In the autumn of 1857, more than 140 non-Mormon migrants were killed in the Mountain Meadows Massacre. The Mormons blamed Native Americans, but Mormon militia were suspected of carrying out the attack.

2) The Utah War ended in 1858 when Congress urged Buchanan to solve the conflict. He gave peace terms to Young — he pardoned the Mormons for their acts during the war, as long as they agreed to obey government authority.
3) Young accepted the terms, but he said the Mormons had never been rebellion. Government troops stayed in Utah until the Civil War broke out in 1861.

Tensions existed between the Mormons and Native Americans who lived in Salt Lake Valley — there were violent clashes over resources.

More Attempts to End Polygamy were made after the Civil War

1) Congress attempted to outlaw polygamy during the Civil War — in 1862, the Morrill Anti-Bigamy Act was passed. However, the Act wasn't enforced and Lincoln basically gave Young permission to ignore it as long as the Mormons stayed out of the Civil War.
2) In 1882, tougher measures were taken — polygamy was declared a serious crime in the Edmunds Act. Polygamists were banned from voting, holding political power and sitting on juries.
3) In 1887, the government introduced the Edmunds-Tucker Act to finally put an end to polygamy among the Mormons. The act dissolved the Mormon Church and the Perpetual Emigrating Fund Company.
   - Polygamy was banned — those who were caught could be fined and put in jail for up to five years. Marriage licenses were also made compulsory in Utah to make it easier to prosecute people for polygamy.
   - Mormon Church property worth over $50,000 was taken over by the federal (national) government.
   - The federal government and authorities in Utah were given powers to appoint judges and gather information on Mormons attending and working in schools in Utah.

This organisation was set up by the Mormon Church in 1849 to fund emigration to Salt Lake Valley.

4) Utah wasn't allowed to become a state while it still practised polygamy. The Mormons eventually abandoned polygamy in 1890 after the Supreme Court said their property could be legally confiscated.

The president of the Mormons, Wilford Woodruff, knew that the Mormon Church would lose lots of property if the Mormons resisted the Edmunds-Tucker Act after the Supreme Court decision. He stated that the Mormons would not teach polygamy or allow anyone to begin the practice. Having ended polygamy, Utah finally became a state in 1896.

I haven't got 55 friends, never mind 55 wives...

Scribble down a quick description of the events that led up to the Mountain Meadows Massacre in 1857. Explain why the Mormons might have blamed Native Americans for the attack.

Aftermath of the Civil War

After the Civil War, efforts were made to rebuild the United States — this is known as the Reconstruction Era.

Slavery was Formally Abolished after the War

After the Union won the war in 1865, over four million slaves were freed and the South's plantation economy was destroyed. Politicians started to rebuild the South and help freed slaves to become part of free society.

1) Securing freedom for African Americans was a key part of Reconstruction. Many slaves in the South had already been freed by the Emancipation Proclamation in 1863, but slavery still existed in the border states (the slave states of Delaware, Kentucky, Maryland and Missouri which remained loyal to the Union).
2) The 13th Amendment to the US Constitution was introduced by Lincoln when he was re-elected in 1864 — it abolished slavery in all states. It was ratified by most northern and border states, and some southern states in December 1865.

> Lincoln was assassinated in April 1865, but it was his government that laid the groundwork for the 13th Amendment.

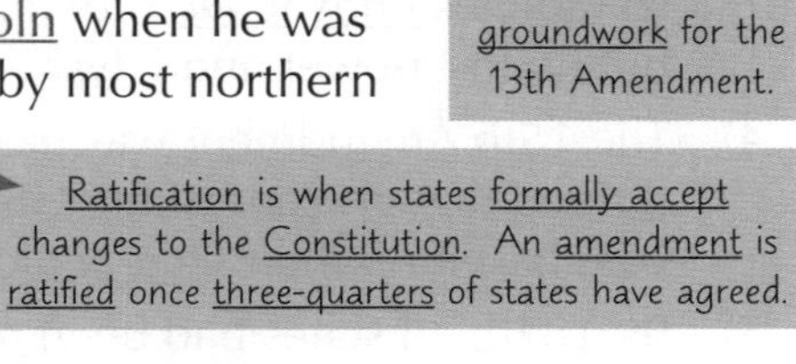

> Ratification is when states formally accept changes to the Constitution. An amendment is ratified once three-quarters of states have agreed.

> The 13th Amendment freed slaves, but it didn't give them equal rights. There was a debate over how far African Americans should be given civil rights during the Reconstruction Era.

3) The Freedmen's Bureau was set up in March 1865 to help freed slaves and poor southerners to rebuild their lives. It provided food and shelter, and legal and medical aid. It also helped communities to establish new schools. But it was poorly funded and limited by political issues — it closed in 1872.

Andrew Johnson began Presidential Reconstruction in 1865

1) Andrew Johnson took over as President in April 1865 after Lincoln was assassinated. He took a lenient approach to the South.

> Andrew Johnson was a Democratic senator from Tennessee. He was pro-slavery but strongly disagreed with southern secession.

- He pardoned all white southerners except Confederate leaders and wealthy planters, but many later received individual pardons.
- Property was returned to its original owners instead of being redistributed. Many African Americans rented land from white people (sharecropping) — sometimes they rented from their former masters.
- Some of the southern elite regained power — many had been in the Confederate government and army.
- Some southern states created the Black Codes, which limited the freedom of African Americans. For example, South Carolina made black people pay a tax if they were not farmers or servants.

2) Johnson didn't support equal rights for African Americans, so he did nothing to stop the Black Codes.
3) In 1866, he tried to veto (reject) the Civil Rights Act. However, his veto was overturned (see below), and the Civil Rights Act became law in 1866.

> The Civil Rights Act gave citizenship and equal rights to all who were born in the US — it excluded Native Americans and people who were under the control of a foreign power. The act was designed to protect the rights of African Americans.

Some Republicans disagreed with Johnson's Approach

1) Some radical Republicans wanted racial equality and greater punishment of Confederate leaders.
2) Moderate Republicans didn't agree with Johnson's veto of the Civil Rights Act. They created an alliance with the radicals and overturned his veto to ensure that the Act became law.
3) Congress passed the 14th Amendment in 1868 — Johnson opposed it and the southern states refused to ratify it. Many in the North began to think that a tougher approach was needed in the South.

> The 14th Amendment had a 'Citzenship Clause', which guaranteed citizenship to all males born in the US regardless of race. It also had an 'Equal Protection Clause', which gave black people the same rights as white people to state protection.

If only you could abolish exams...

When you're writing about Reconstruction, think about how the North and South's different attitudes to slavery might have influenced the way that they wanted the South to be rebuilt.

Aftermath of the Civil War

Radicals won the 1866 elections — they decided Congress should control Reconstruction, not the President.

Radical Republicans took over Reconstruction in 1867

1) The First and Second Reconstruction Acts were passed by Congress in March 1867. These acts placed the South under military rule. Before rebel states could rejoin the Union, they were forced to ratify the 14th Amendment (p.21) and rewrite their state constitutions to allow black people to vote.
2) Congress's approach to the South was more forceful than Johnson's — they sent troops to the South to keep the peace and protect freed slaves and their right to vote. Leading rebels were removed from office.
3) Johnson tried to obstruct Radical Reconstruction — he vetoed both Reconstruction Acts, so radicals impeached him (put him on trial). He wasn't convicted, but he lost power and Ulysses Grant was elected President in 1869.
4) The 15th Amendment was passed in 1869 and ratified in 1870 — it ruled that citizens of the USA could not be denied to the right to vote based on their 'race, colour, or previous condition of servitude'.
5) By 1870, all states had been re-admitted to the Union. The southern states had Republican governments made up of white southerners who supported Reconstruction, northerners, and African Americans.
6) Three Enforcement Acts were passed between 1870 and 1871. They made it illegal to use terror, force or bribery to stop black people from voting, and they gave the government powers to quickly suppress the Ku Klux Klan.

Northerners who went to carry out the government's Reconstruction policies in the South were called 'carpetbaggers' by southerners. They were accused of being corrupt and exploiting the South.

The Ku Klux Klan was a white supremacist group that formed in 1865. They murdered, lynched, beat and threatened African Americans, white republicans and their supporters. They also burned churches, homes and schools. Many Klan members were arrested and put on trial under the Enforcement Acts.

Comment and Analysis

Radical Reconstruction was a period of hope and idealism for many, in spite of southern grievances. Radicals believed that equality could be achieved.

The Reconstruction Era ended in 1877

1) By 1873, political support for Reconstruction had weakened in the North. Economic depression in 1874 caused high unemployment, so northerners lost interest in the South.
2) Supreme court decisions also weakened the power of the 14th Amendment to protect black civil rights.
3) The depression, and corruption and scandal under President Grant, meant that Republicans lost support. The Democrats won control of the lower house of Congress in 1874 for first time since the Civil War.
4) Republican Rutherford B. Hayes was elected President in 1876, but the election results were disputed. In return for recognition of his election, he accepted the Democrats' control of the South and ended federal military involvement there. The Reconstruction Era was over.

In 1876, the Supreme Court ruled that only states, not the federal government, could prosecute people under the Enforcement Acts — this resulted in many violent crimes going unpunished in the South.

The Reconstruction Era improved rights for African Americans, but many issues were unresolved by 1876:

- More than 700,000 black people were registered to vote and over 1500 were elected to state and national offices. However, while they had representation, it wasn't in proportion to their population.
- Some southerners ignored laws like 15th Amendment — they tried to stop black people from voting using literacy tests and poll taxes.
- Many Ku Klux Klan members were fined and let off with a warning. Other violent groups emerged, like the Rifle Clubs and the Red Shirts, who carried on murdering and threatening southern Republicans.

Comment and Analysis

A key barrier to the success of Reconstruction was that the attitude of many southern whites didn't change. African Americans had more independence than under slavery, but in many ways, their rights were still limited.

Some southerners found ways to get around the law...

Write down a description of what these acts or amendments did to protect African Americans — the First and Second Reconstruction Acts, the 15th Amendment and the Enforcement Acts.

Federal and State Powers

A lot of the conflict that happened before, during and after the Civil War was to do with how much power the government should have over individual states — there was a lot of debate over the issue of states' rights.

The Union of States was founded on the Idea of Federalism

Federalism is the idea that individual states hold political power — each state decides how to govern itself.

1) Each state had state laws, but there were also federal laws that everyone had to obey — the government created and enforced these laws. If state law conflicted with federal law, then federal law took priority.
2) As sectionalism increased in the North and South (p.16), people in the South began to question how much control the government should have over the states, and their right to practise slavery. They argued that the power of the government was limited by states' rights.
3) The idea of states' rights was laid out in the 10th Amendment of the Constitution, which was ratified in 1791. It said that, unless the government was given a certain power by the Constitution, that power belonged to individual states.

The 10th Amendment

'The powers not delegated to the United States by the Constitution, nor prohibited by it to the states, are reserved to the states respectively, or to the people.'

John Calhoun used the idea of States' Rights to Protect Slavery

John Calhoun, a politician from South Carolina, strongly defended states' rights.

1) Calhoun argued that, since it was the states that wrote and ratified the Constitution, they had the right to interpret it. If they thought the government was going beyond its constitutional powers, then the states had the right to block whatever law the government was trying to impose. They could even leave the Union.
2) In 1850, the government's Fugitive Slave Act required free states to return escaped slaves to their owners, even though those states opposed slavery.

Comment and Analysis

This didn't mean that Calhoun wanted secession (p.17) — he was using the fact that the South could leave the Union to stop the government attacking slavery.

In 1857, the Dred Scott case weakened the power of the government to stop slave owners from bringing slaves into free states. Dred Scott was a slave who tried to apply for freedom through the Supreme Court, as he'd lived with his master in a free state. The court denied Scott's bid, since black people weren't US citizens at this time and couldn't bring a case to the court. The ruling also weakened the popular sovereignty of states that had chosen to ban slavery, since slave owners could bring slaves to those states anyway.

States' Rights were Strengthened after the Reconstruction Era

During Reconstruction, government acts were passed to protect African American rights. The Equal Protection Clause of the 14th Amendment gave black people equal rights to state protection (p.21), but the government's power to enforce this clause was weakened by some key Supreme Court cases, which upheld states' rights.

1) In 1873, white Democrats attacked black Republicans — many black Republicans were killed. A government judge convicted several of the white Democrats, but the Supreme Court reversed their convictions in 1876.
2) In 1883, the government's ability to protect black people from assault and murder was weakened. The Supreme Court argued that it was up to individual states, not the government, to deliver justice for these crimes.

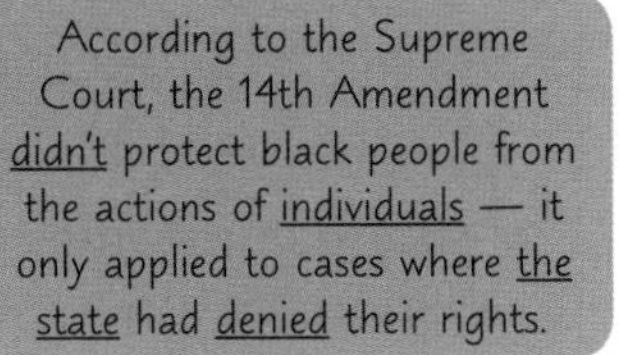
According to the Supreme Court, the 14th Amendment didn't protect black people from the actions of individuals — it only applied to cases where the state had denied their rights.

3) There was a series of civil rights cases in 1883 where private individuals were sued for discriminating against black people. The Court repeated its claim that the 14th Amendment didn't apply to the actions of individuals, which destroyed the power of the Civil Rights Act of 1875.
4) This decision led to the growth of segregation (where white and black people were forced to use separate facilities), as the government had no power to stop southern states from discriminating against black people.

This act had given black people equal rights to use public places (like theatres) and public transport, and to rent or buy a home.

The Supreme Court kept putting a spanner in the works...

Explain how states' rights were used to discriminate against African Americans between 1840 and 1895. [8]

EXAM QUESTION

Homesteaders and the Railways

After the Civil War, large numbers of settlers began to move on to the Great Plains — an area once seen as unsuitable for living. The US government did a lot to encourage homesteaders and the building of the railways.

Different Groups of people moved to the Plains

Many settlers had previously viewed the Plains as a 'desert' (see p.6). More began to move there in the 1850s (see p.12), but after 1865, thousands followed — this was a big change in attitude. This included:

- Migrants from eastern states who moved because of growing population and high land prices.
- Immigrants who'd come to America to escape poverty and religious and political persecution.
- Slaves who had been freed after the Civil War and ex-Civil War soldiers who wanted a new start.

After the end of the Reconstruction era in 1877 (see p. 22-23), African Americans faced growing oppression in the South. As a result, thousands moved west — e.g. approximately 20,000 black migrants known as exodusters moved to Kansas in 1879.

The Government encouraged people to Settle on the Plains

1) The government encouraged people to move west and settle on the Plains by promoting the idea of 'Manifest Destiny' (see p.7).
2) They moved Indians onto reservations, which freed up land for settlement (see p.12-13).
3) In 1862, they passed the Homestead Act, which gave each settler 160 acres of free land if they farmed it for five years. This opened up 2.5 million acres for settlement and was open to everyone, including immigrants, freed slaves and single women. Between 1862 and 1900, around 600,000 people claimed land under the Act.
4) The condition of farming the land for five years was meant to discourage speculators — those aiming to make a short-term profit on rising land prices rather than settling and living on the land. However, the Act was still affected by speculators and corruption.

Before the US Civil War, southerners in Congress opposed acts which encouraged non-slave-owning settlers to move into new areas — southerners were worried that this would result in these areas eventually becoming free states (see p.16). When the South seceded, the North was able to pass these acts.

Comment and Analysis

The Act was important because it opened up land ownership to ordinary people. Although there were problems, it helped to establish settlement on the Plains.

Railway Companies also encouraged homesteading

The Pacific Railroad Act of 1862 approved the construction of The First Transcontinental Railroad — a railway which ran across the US from east to west. The government believed it would make migration into unsettled land easier and create national unity by connecting the West and the East.

1) Railway companies were granted huge areas of land on the Plains by the government — they sold this land cheaply to settlers to help fund their railway building.
2) These companies produced advertising posters which made exaggerated claims about the 'good life' on the Plains. They knew that settlers would become customers for their railways.

'**The Location is Central**, along the 41st parallel, the favorite latitude of America. Equally well adapted to corn or wheat; free from the long, cold winters of the Northern, and the hot, unhealthy influences of the Southern states... **The Soil** is a dark loam, slightly impregnated with lime, free from stone and gravel, and eminently adapted to grass, grain and root crops; the subsoil is usually light and porous, retaining moisture with wonderful tenacity. **The Climate** is mild and healthful; the atmosphere dry and pure. Epidemic diseases never prevail; Fever and Ague are unknown. The greatest amount of rain falls between March and October. The Winters are dry with but little snow... **Timber** is found on the streams and grows rapidly.'

Extract from a Union Pacific Railroad advertisement for farming lands in Nebraska, 1870.

Was Long wrong, or were the railways telling porkies...

How does the image of the Plains in the Union Pacific Railroad advertisement above differ from Major Long's view of the Plains (see p.6)? Why do you think this is? [8]

EXAM QUESTION

Farming on the Great Plains

Unfortunately, homesteaders found that the Plains weren't quite as delightful as they'd been promised. But as more people faced the difficulties of living and farming on the Plains, they found ways to survive.

Life on the Plains was Hard for homesteaders...

- The soil was fertile, but the thick top layer of earth (known as sod) was too hard for light ploughs.
- There was little or no wood for building or fuel.
- Lack of water meant crops like maize failed and deep wells had to be dug.
- Wind, extremes of weather, grasshopper plagues and prairie fires often destroyed crops.

...but the Plains were eventually Successfully settled

1) New developments in technology, crops and techniques helped:

- Better machinery — John Deere developed a stronger steel plough in the 1830s which could break through the tough soil. Windpumps increased the supply of water by pumping underground water to the surface. The introduction of barbed wire in 1874 meant that farmers could cheaply fence off their land to keep animals off their crops.
- New crops — Turkey Red Wheat was a hardy crop brought over from Russia in around 1874 which was well-suited to growing on the Plains.
- New Techniques — Farmers learned techniques to cope with the low rainfall and retain the moisture in the soil, e.g. 'dry farming' involved turning the soil after rain.

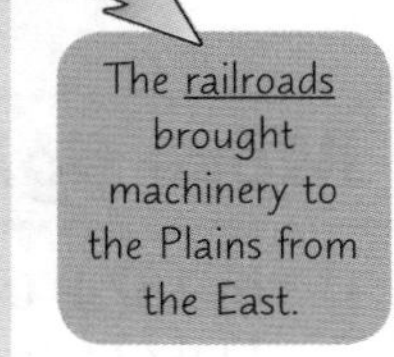

2) Government acts helped. The Timber Culture Act of 1873 and the Desert Land Act of 1877 gave more land to settlers living in less fertile areas.

People had started to move onto the even drier High Plains by 1880.

3) People adapted to the conditions:
   - Because of the lack of wood, people made houses out of sod.
   - Women were responsible for housework and their children's education. They had to collect buffalo dung for fuel and made a lot of what they needed, such as clothes and soap. They also nursed the sick and helped each other in childbirth. There weren't many doctors on the Plains.
   - Isolation was a constant problem for early settlers, as towns and neighbours were often far away. Women formed church groups and other social networks to combat the loneliness.
   - As more settlers arrived, communities formed. This eventually led to the building of schools and shops.

Comment and Analysis

Improved technology and knowledge meant that settlers were now able to cultivate the Great Plains — an area once seen as uninhabitable.

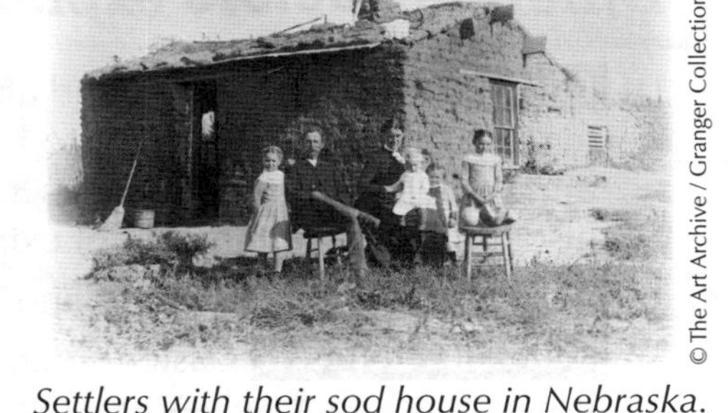

Settlers with their sod house in Nebraska.

1) Even though the failure rate for new farms was high, the Great Plains emerged as the 'breadbasket' of the nation. The railways made the boom possible by linking producers to wider markets.
2) There were 10 million immigrants to America during 1865-90 — many of these helped settle the West, such as the Scandinavians in North and South Dakota.
3) The Homestead Act failed to discourage speculators and poverty from eastern cities, but it did achieve the settlement of the West. By 1900 there were 500,000 farms on the Plains.

Life on the Plains was... well... plain difficult...

Fold a piece of paper in half, and on the first half make a list of hardships faced by homesteaders. On the second half jot down how they tried to overcome them.

War and Peace on the Plains

The government attempted a more 'peaceful' approach to Native Americans, but it only led to more conflict.

Policies of Separation and Assimilation were tried

1) The Indian Wars (see p.15) led to differing views on how the Native Americans should be handled:

Many settlers and army officers thought the Native Americans should be destroyed. The people who took this view are known as 'exterminators'.

Many politicians believed that violence towards Native Americans would only make them more hostile. Instead they wanted to help assimilate them into society by teaching them to live like white people. The people who took this view are known as 'humanitarians'.

2) The government decided to follow a small reservations policy. Treaties such as Medicine Lodge (1867) and Fort Laramie (1868) put tribes onto smaller areas of land away from settlers. It was hoped that this would minimise conflict.
3) This policy failed to bring peace. Native Americans didn't want to assimilate and settlers continued to encroach on Indian land. While Red Cloud kept to the Fort Laramie Treaty, other Sioux chiefs such as Crazy Horse and Sitting Bull opposed it.

Red Cloud signed the 1868 Fort Laramie Treaty after Red Cloud's War (see p.15) — it created a Sioux reservation on an area that included the sacred Black Hills of Dakota. The government agreed not to rebuild forts on the Bozeman Trail and Red Cloud promised never again to make war on the settlers.

More fighting occurred at the battle of Little Bighorn

1) In 1874, troops under Lt. Col. George Custer confirmed the presence of gold in the Black Hills of Dakota and a gold rush began. The US government tried to buy the Black Hills from the Sioux, but they refused — the hills were sacred and belonged to them under the 1868 Fort Laramie Treaty.
2) The government ordered the Sioux back to their reservation, but they refused. By the start of 1876, Sitting Bull and Crazy Horse had raised the largest Native American force ever seen (several thousand men).
3) The army was sent to oppose the uprising. Army commanders Sheridan and Terry planned an attack on the Sioux village at Little Bighorn, but Custer and his men arrived first and decided to attack alone.
4) Custer split his men into three groups — the other two were led by Reno and Benteen. When Custer approached the village with around 220 soldiers, they were surrounded by Indians — he and all of his men were killed. This was the greatest Native American victory in battle against the US army.

Different Factors explain the Defeat of the US army

1) **Custer** He was ambitious and after personal glory. He marched his men through the night and arrived at Little Bighorn a day early, so his men were tired. He ignored orders to wait for the rest of the army and warnings from his Indian scouts that the Sioux village was too large for them to fight alone. He also turned down the offer of extra men and guns, and weakened his force by splitting it into three.
2) **Custer's commanders** Terry and Sheridan didn't try to find out how many Indians were in the village.
3) **Reno and Benteen** Custer ordered them to come to his support but they didn't. They were under attack themselves and later argued that this was why they were unable to help Custer.
4) **Bad luck** Quicksand stopped Custer from crossing the river to attack the village — he and his men were forced onto higher ground, where they were seen by the Sioux.
5) **Native Americans** The Sioux were determined to save their territory. Instead of fleeing, which was their usual tactic, they stood and fought — Custer wasn't expecting this. He also wasn't expecting the Indians to have superior weaponry — many had repeating Winchester rifles, while Custer's soldiers had single shot Springfields. Sioux leaders such as Crazy Horse were experienced warriors, and they joined forces with their traditional enemies, the Cheyenne and Arapaho, to greatly outnumber the US army.

I don't get it — was it a little or a big horn?

Was Custer's ambition or the Indians' determination the more important reason for the US army's defeat at Little Bighorn? Explain your answer, referring to both reasons. [12]

A Way of Life Destroyed

Although the Indians won against the US army at the battle of Little Bighorn, it was too little too late.

The Indians Won at Little Bighorn but it made things even Worse

- The army launched a winter campaign against the Sioux in 1876-77. Facing hunger and the loss of their horses, the Sioux surrendered and were forced onto reservations. Crazy Horse surrendered in May 1877 and was later killed by a US soldier while resisting arrest.
- Sioux reservations were put under military control and, in 1877, the Black Hills were opened to white settlement.
- Sitting Bull retreated to Canada, but returned and surrendered in 1881.

Comment and Analysis

Little Bighorn was only a short-term victory for the Native Americans. It wasn't enough to turn their fortunes around and the US army's determination to defeat them increased following the battle.

Buffalo Slaughter forced Native Americans to accept Reservations

1) Millions of buffalo had once roamed the plains. They were vital to the Native Americans' survival (see p.11) and were sacred to them.
2) Buffalo were slaughtered in large numbers by white settlers (see p.14). They were killed to feed soldiers and railroad construction workers. People also killed them for their skins — there was a demand for buffalo robes in the East from the 1850s, and from 1871 a process was developed to make buffalo hides into leather. Others just killed them for sport — men would shoot the animals from the windows of trains.
3) As a result of this, buffalo numbers decreased rapidly — it has been estimated that there were 13 million buffalo on the Plains in 1865, but by the end of the century they were almost extinct.
4) The effect on the Plains Indians was devastating — their main source of food was gone, as well as a major part of their culture. This forced many Indians to accept life on the reservations — they feared starvation.
5) It isn't clear whether there was an official policy to exterminate the buffalo, but many people recognised that destroying them would help defeat the Native Americans.

General Sheridan is said, 'let them kill, skin and sell until the buffalo is exterminated as it is the only way to bring lasting peace and allow civilisation to advance'.

A buffalo skinner. Buffalo skins were much in demand. The rest of the animal would be left to decay on the plains.

Reservations destroyed the Indians' Culture

1) The formerly nomadic Plains Indians, now confined to smaller areas, could no longer feed or clothe themselves without government aid. Living on hand-outs, they became demoralised and there were high rates of alcoholism.
2) Many tribes were moved off their ancestral lands and on to reservations elsewhere. Hostile tribes were sometimes placed next to each other.
3) Reservations were run by Indian agents, appointed by the government. This weakened the influence of chiefs and undermined tribal structures.
4) The government deliberately targeted Indian culture. Polygamy and religious practices, such as the Sun Dance, were banned. Many children were taken away to be educated, e.g. at the Carlisle Indian School in Pennsylvania. The threat of withholding rations was used to make them cooperate.

Comment and Analysis

The government had always wanted the Indians to assimilate. As Indians living on the reservations were now dependent on the state, there was a way to force them to abandon their own culture.

The Native Americans couldn't bring the buffalo back...

If you're writing about how the Native Americans were defeated, make sure you mention the impact of the destruction of the buffalo — the buffalo were crucial to their survival.

Assimilation of the Native Americans

America's population was still growing — increasing the pressure on reservation land.

The government decided to Break Up reservation land

1) Government policy from the 1850s had been to move Native Americans onto reservations away from settlers. In the late 1880s, the government decided to split up the reservations into smaller units. These would be given out to individual tribe members to own and farm — the aim was to convert tribesmen into independent farmers.
2) It was believed that this would help destroy tribal bonds and the power of tribal leaders — and that this would finally lead to the assimilation of Native Americans into white society.

Comment and Analysis

Native Americans could no longer be separated from white society on reservations — there was no more land to move them onto as settlers continued to claim more and more.

- Some reformers believed that assimilation was necessary to save the Indians from extermination. They wanted to stop the suffering of Native Americans on reservations and believed that their lives would improve if they assimilated.
- Some people thought that reservation life encouraged idleness because Native Americans were reliant on government hand-outs. If they could make their own living and become prosperous, then the government would no longer have to oversee the reservations.
- Others just wanted to open up reservation lands to settlers.

The Dawes Act (1887) Parcelled Out tribal lands

1) The Dawes Act broke reservations up into allotments. Heads of family were assigned 160 acres, single adults 80 acres, and children 40 acres. They also got US citizenship.
2) When all the inhabitants of a reservation had been assigned their holdings, the remaining land was thrown open to white settlement. Indian schools were established from the sale of this surplus land.

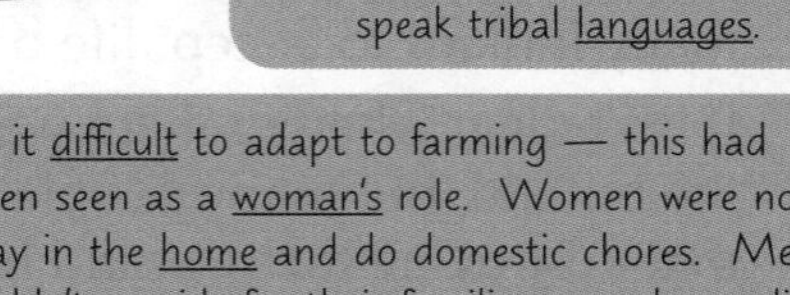

3) The Act was a disaster for the Native Americans:
   - Their tribal communities were broken up and their culture almost destroyed — the idea of land ownership went against Native American tradition.

     Men found it difficult to adapt to farming — this had traditionally been seen as a woman's role. Women were now expected to stay in the home and do domestic chores. Men who felt they couldn't provide for their families were demoralised.
   - The sale of surplus land led to Indians losing a lot of their land — down from 138 million acres in 1887 to 78 million acres in 1900. They also lost land granted to them under the Act (nearly two thirds of it between 1887 and 1934) as a result of being cheated by land speculators.
   - Lands belonging to the five eastern tribes that had been moved onto the Plains in the 1830s (see p.12) were exempt from the Dawes Act. But through forced sales they too were eventually lost. For example, in the Oklahoma land rush of 1889, the government opened up two million acres of this land to settlers. In 1893, another 6 million acres was opened up.
   - In 1934, the government cancelled the Dawes Act and encouraged tribal identities. But by that time, Native Americans had lost over 60% of their original reservation lands and were suffering from high rates of poverty, alcoholism, illiteracy and suicide.

Comment and Analysis

The Dawes Act was devastating for Native Americans — it helped destroy their culture. While many reformers may have believed they had good intentions, their actions were based on their prejudiced belief that Native Americans were inferior and needed to be introduced to Christianity and Western civilisation to improve themselves.

The Permanent Indian Frontier seems like a long time ago...

The Dawes Act continued the process of the Native Americans being squeezed onto an ever smaller area of the land. Summarise the Dawes Act and the impact it had on the Native Americans.

The End of the Frontier

A lot had changed by 1895. Native American resistance had ended and settlers had claimed so much land that the American frontier — the line separating settlements from unsettled land — no longer existed.

The Battle of Wounded Knee was the End of Indian Resistance

1) Some armed resistance continued during the 1880s, but it was finally suppressed in 1890 at the Battle of Wounded Knee. This was to be the last confrontation between Native Americans and the US army.
2) A Native American spiritual leader named Wovoka taught that a special Ghost Dance could raise the dead and bring a new world, free from the settlers. He was opposed to violence, but ghost dances built the dancers up into a frenzy — this unsettled whites who feared that the dance would lead to rebellion.
3) Tensions peaked at the Pine Ridge Reservation in Wounded Knee Creek, South Dakota. Troops tried to disarm a band of Sioux led by Chief Big Foot, but when a warrior fired a shot, the troops fired back, killing 52 people. Survivors went on to fight by hand.
4) The battle escalated when more warriors from nearby heard the gunfire and swarmed out, shooting at the soldiers, then disappearing into the prairie.

- The Battle of Wounded Knee cost the lives of some 150 Sioux (about 60 of them women and children) and 25 soldiers.
- It marked the final suppression of Native Americans by armed force. By mid-January 1891, the dispersed warriors had all surrendered.
- Some Sioux followers of the Ghost Dance movement had believed that special shirts would protect them from the bullets of the Americans. The sight of Ghost Dance shirts pierced by bullets after the battle destroyed the Indians' faith in a magical restoration of the old way of life. The reservation was reluctantly accepted as home.

Native Americans were Unable to fight back Successfully

It's debatable whether the Plains Indians could ever have protected their traditional way of life. There were many factors at work against them:

1) The US army usually had better weapons than the Native Americans — repeating rifles, machine guns and cannons.
2) The system of forts gave the US army control on the Plains. The railroads and telegraph system provided fast transport and communication.
3) Divisions between Native American tribes meant that it was almost impossible for them to organise their resistance. Reservation life also made it increasingly difficult for them to resist.

Comment and Analysis

It seems that nothing could halt the tide of white settlers — and broken government promises failed to protect the Indians from it.

Americans became aware of the End of the Frontier

1) In 1890, census results revealed that, unlike in 1880, there was no longer a definable Western frontier of settlement. The frontier was declared officially closed.
2) This didn't mean that there was no more land available for settlers, but what remained was in isolated pockets and the best areas had been taken.
3) Settlers occupied land from the East all the way to the West. 'Manifest Destiny' had been fulfilled.

The Native Americans were no longer a barrier to settlement — they'd been subdued and were in the process of being assimilated into white society.

The frontier closed — and the West is history...

To sum up — settlers in, Indians out. It's all very well knowing all the little facts about this period of American history, but to write a good answer you've got to know how they fit together too.

Revision Summary

Now you've absorbed all of that lovely knowledge, here are some revision questions to get your teeth into.

- Try these questions and tick off each one when you get it right.
- When you've done all the questions for a topic and are completely happy with it, tick off the topic.

Expansion: Opportunities and Challenges (p.5-12)

1) Make a list of the geographical obstacles someone travelling from east of the Mississippi would face on a trip to California in the 1840s.
2) Explain why many people viewed the Plains as the 'Great American Desert' before the 1860s.
3) What factors made early migrants travel to the west coast?
4) Give a brief description of 'Manifest Destiny'.
5) Give two examples of how Mormons overcame problems they faced in Salt Lake Valley.
6) How did the expectations of miners compare with the reality of life in California?
7) Summarise the Plains Indians' beliefs about land and nature.
8) Why were the buffalo important to the Plains Indians?
9) What was the Permanent Indian Frontier? Why was it created?
10) Why was the Permanent Indian Frontier put under threat?

Conflict Across America (p.13-20)

11) Give a brief summary of the 1851 Fort Laramie Treaty.
12) Give three examples of settler activity on the Plains which caused tension with the Plains Indians.
13) Why did many Native Americans dislike life on the reservations?
14) Describe the events of the Cheyenne Uprising and the Sand Creek Massacre.
15) Give two reasons why westward expansion increased tension over slavery.
16) Briefly explain how the Kansas-Nebraska Act undermined the Missouri Compromise.
17) a) What was the abolitionist movement?
    b) Why were some northerners against abolition?
18) Why did John Brown's raid at Harper's Ferry anger southerners?
19) Give two reasons why the South's economy suffered during the Civil War.
20) What was the Mountain Meadow Massacre?

Consolidation: Forging the Nation (p.21-29)

21) Give two examples of Andrew Johnson's lenient approach to the South during Reconstruction.
22) Explain why some Republicans disagreed with Johnson.
23) What were the Enforcement Acts?
24) Briefly explain the idea of states' rights.
25) What was the Homestead Act?
26) List three things which helped settlers live and farm on the Plains.
27) Explain three factors which led to the defeat of the US army at Little Bighorn.
28) Why did the government break up the Indian Reservations in the late 1800s?
29) What happened at Wounded Knee in 1890?
30) In what year was the American Frontier declared officially closed?

Kaiser Wilhelm II

The German Empire was created in 1871 and lasted until 1918. It was ruled by Kaiser Wilhelm II from 1888.

The Constitution made the Kaiser very Powerful

When the German Empire was created in 1871, its constitution made the Kaiser the most powerful figure in government. A German parliament called the Reichstag was also created, but in reality it held little power.

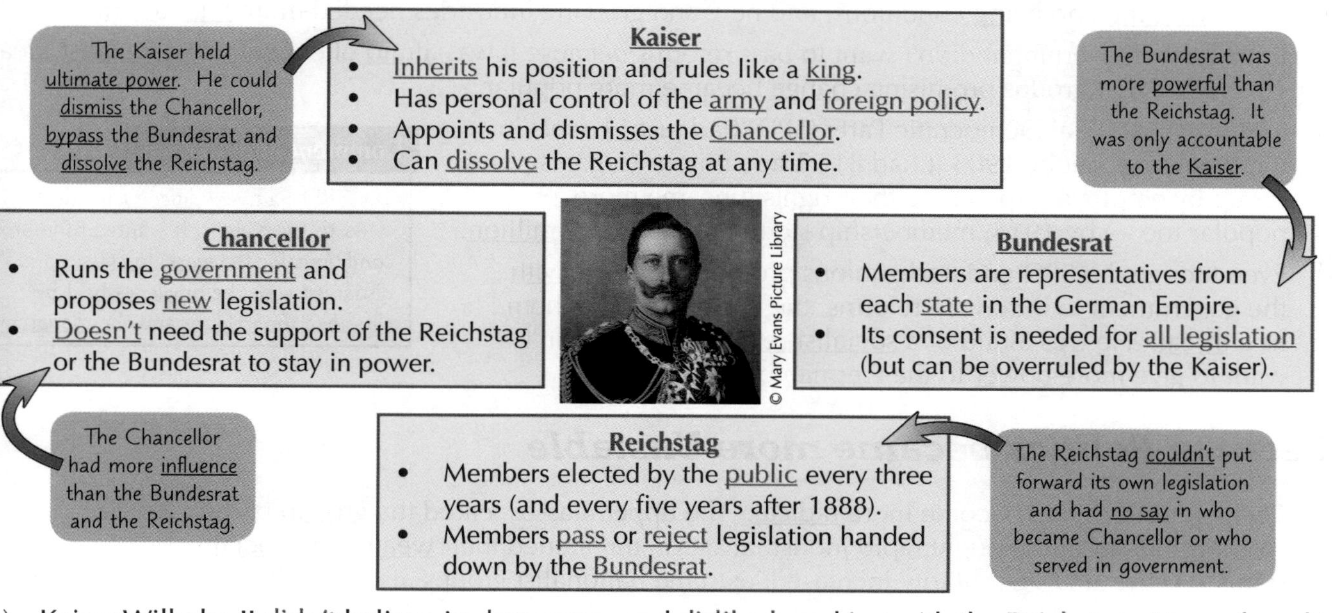

1) Kaiser Wilhelm II didn't believe in democracy and disliked working with the Reichstag. He preferred to place his trust in the army, and often relied on military advisors to help him make important decisions.
2) The Prussian army played an important role in Germany's unification in 1871. Wilhelm II was strongly influenced by its prestige and power, and adopted a system of militarism — this meant strengthening Germany's military (e.g. its army and navy) and using it to increase Germany's influence.
3) Wilhelm II wanted to make Germany a world power. He also believed in Germany's traditional class system, where the upper classes held the most power.

Before 1871, Germany was made up of lots of independent states — one of these was called Prussia.

Germany experienced Economic and Social change

In the early 20th century, Germany's economy was modernised and the working classes grew.

1) Germany's economy expanded massively between 1890 and 1914. Production of iron and coal doubled, and by 1914 Germany produced two-thirds of Europe's steel. It was also successful in new industries like chemical manufacturing.
2) As a result of industrialisation, new jobs were created and the population in Germany's cities grew. The working classes expanded and the upper classes had less economic power.
3) The working classes played a larger part in German society, but their working conditions were poor. They had a growing sense of identity and wanted better representation.
4) This contributed to a rise in socialism — a political ideology promoting equality, and public ownership of industry. This led to a growth in support for the Social Democratic Party (SPD) in Germany (see p.32).

Comment and Analysis

The German aristocracy and Kaiser Wilhelm feared the growth of socialism — Wilhelm was worried that the SPD wanted a revolution to overthrow the monarchy and destroy the German class system.

Social and economic change shifted the balance of power...

EXAM TIP

Even though the Reichstag was elected by the people, it didn't have much power. The Kaiser thought his authority was secure, but Germans wanted more of a say in how the country was run.

The Monarchy Under Threat

Social and economic changes were good for industry, but bad for German politics. The growth of the working classes and the rise of socialism made ruling Germany increasingly difficult for Kaiser Wilhelm II.

Social problems Increased and Germans wanted Reforms

1) The growing population in cities and towns created new social problems. The working classes wanted better working and living conditions, and new and growing industries needed more regulation.
2) Initially, the government didn't want to pass reforms because it was afraid of encouraging socialist ideas. This meant that groups promising change became more popular.
3) In 1887, the Social Democratic Party (SPD) had just 11 seats in the Reichstag, but by 1903 it had 81. Trade unions (organisations set up by employees to defend their rights) became more popular too — by 1914, membership stood at around 3.3 million.
4) Even though the SPD and trade unions promised to work with the government to introduce reforms, the Kaiser still saw them as a threat. He was afraid of a socialist revolution and didn't want to give more power to the German public.

Comment and Analysis

The SPD had very different political views to the Kaiser. It wanted to improve conditions for the working classes and disagreed with the privileges held by elites like the military and the monarchy.

German Politics became more Unstable

1) German politics had become more radical. The upper classes feared the growth of the working classes and thought rapid industrialisation threatened their wealth and social status. As the SPD's popularity increased, extreme nationalist groups also grew.
2) This made it harder for the Kaiser to govern Germany. He was under pressure to introduce socialist reforms, but knew that doing so would risk angering his supporters.
3) To make matters worse, the popularity of the SPD made it more difficult for the government to get legislation passed in the Reichstag.

Chancellors found it hard to get support in the Reichstag, so they struggled to pass new laws. The Reichstag had more influence over German politics than it had ever had before.

Wilhelm tried to Divert Attention away from Socialism

1) The Kaiser tried to reduce discontent among the working classes by introducing some limited social reforms, e.g. in 1891 the Workers' Protection Act was introduced to improve safety in the workplace.
2) In 1897, the Kaiser adopted a foreign policy called 'Weltpolitik' — this focused on expanding Germany's territory and boosting the size of Germany's army and navy.
3) The Kaiser hoped this would distract attention from socialism and increase support for the monarchy and the military. It would also help to make Germany a world power.

The Navy Laws made people feel patriotic...

- In 1898, the first Navy Law was passed. Its eventual aim was to build up Germany's navy to rival Great Britain's. It increased Germany's fleet to include 19 battleships.
- In 1900, the Reichstag passed another Navy Law, which put a 17 year navy expansion programme into place.

The government used propaganda (see p.45) to promote the Navy Laws and inspire patriotism among the German people. The laws were popular, and socialist opposition to them was seen as unpatriotic. In the elections of 1907, the SPD lost 36 seats in the Reichstag.

Comment and Analysis

Despite the Kaiser's best efforts, by 1912 the SPD was the largest party in the Reichstag. The Kaiser had managed to keep his power, but the growth of the SPD showed an increasing desire for democracy amongst the German people.

Even with the Navy Laws, ruling wasn't plain sailing...

Fold a piece of paper in half. Jot down all the problems the Kaiser faced between 1890 and 1914 on one half, and write how he tried to solve them on the other.

The War Ends

World War I lasted from 1914-1918. During the war, political parties agreed to support the government. However, by 1918 Germany was experiencing widespread unrest, which eventually resulted in a revolution.

World War I had a Devastating Impact on Germany

1) Towards the end of the war, people in Germany were undergoing severe hardship. The Allies had set up naval blockades which prevented imports of food and essential goods — by 1918, many people faced starvation.
2) Public opinion had turned against Kaiser Wilhelm II and there were calls for a democracy. Germany's population were war-weary — they were tired of fighting and wanted an end to the war. There was widespread unrest.

A British cartoon from 1917. German civilians queue for food as an over-fed official walks past them. The cartoonist is highlighting the difference between the lifestyle of Germany's rich officers and that of the rest of its struggling population.

- In November 1918, some members of the German navy rebelled and refused to board their ships.
- In Hanover, German troops refused to control rioters.
- A Jewish communist called Kurt Eisner encouraged a general uprising, which sparked mass strikes in Munich.

Social Unrest turned into Revolution

1) By November 1918, the situation in Germany was almost a civil war. A huge public protest was held in Berlin, and members of the SPD (Social Democratic Party) called for the Kaiser's resignation.
2) Kaiser Wilhelm abdicated (resigned) on 9th November 1918. On the same day, two different socialist parties — the Social Democratic Party and the Independent Social Democratic Party (USPD) — declared a republic.
3) On November 10th, all the state leaders that had been appointed by the monarchy left their posts. New revolutionary state governments took over instead. The monarchy had been abolished and Germany had the chance to become a democracy.

A republic is a country ruled without a monarch (king or queen) — power is held by the people via elected representatives.

Germany was made up of 18 states, and each had its own government. The national government decided national affairs, and state governments dealt with more local affairs.

The signing of the armistice

- On 11th November 1918, a ceasefire to end the First World War was agreed. The Allies (Britain, France and the USA) signed an armistice (truce) with Germany.
- The new republic was under pressure to sign. The government didn't think Germany could continue fighting — its people were starving and military morale was low.
- The armistice wasn't supported by some right-wing Germans, who saw the truce as a betrayal. They believed Germany could still win the war.

The Socialists set up a Temporary Government

1) After the abdication of the Kaiser, Germany was disorganised. Different political parties claimed control over different towns.
2) A temporary national government was established, consisting of the SPD and the USPD. It was called the Council of People's Representatives.
3) It controlled Germany until January 1919, when elections were held for a new Reichstag (parliament) — see p.34.

Revolutions pop up in history over and over and over again...

EXAM QUESTION

Give two reasons for the German revolution in 1918. [4]

The Weimar Republic

The Weimar Republic was the first time Germany had ever been governed as a democracy. It was designed to give the German people a voice. However, there were major flaws in its constitution that made it weak.

The Weimar Republic was formed

1) The Council of People's Representatives organised elections in January 1919 to create a new parliament. Germany was now a democracy — the people would say how the country was run.
2) Friedrich Ebert became the first President, with Philip Scheidemann as Chancellor. Ebert was leader of the SPD, a moderate party of socialists.
3) In February 1919, the members of the new Reichstag met at Weimar to create a new constitution for Germany.
This was the beginning of a new period of Germany's history that historians call the Weimar Republic.

The constitution decided how the government would be organised, and established its main principles.

The Weimar Constitution made Germany More Democratic...

The new constitution reorganised the German system of government.

Proportional representation is where the proportion of seats a party wins in parliament is roughly the same as the proportion of the total votes they win.

President
- Elected every 7 years.
- Chooses the Chancellor and is head of the army.
- Can dissolve the Reichstag, call new elections and suspend the constitution.

The President was elected by the German people, and so were the parties in the Reichstag. The President had the most power, but the Chancellor was in charge of the day-to-day running of government.

Reichstag
- The new German Parliament.
- Members are elected every 4 years using proportional representation.

Reichsrat
- Second (less powerful) house of parliament.
- Consists of members from each local region.
- Can delay measures passed by the Reichstag.

1) The new constitution was designed to be as fair as possible. Even very small political parties were given seats in the Reichstag if they got 0.4% of the vote or above.
2) The constitution allowed women to vote for the first time, and lowered the voting age to 20 — more Germans could vote and the German public had greater power.

...but the Consitution had Weaknesses

Even though the new constitution was more democratic, it wasn't very efficient.

1) Proportional representation meant that even parties with a very small number of votes were guaranteed to get into the Reichstag. This meant it was difficult to make decisions because there were so many parties, and they all had different points of view.
2) When a decision couldn't be reached, the President could suspend the constitution and pass laws without the Reichstag's consent.
3) This power was only supposed to be used in an emergency, but became a useful way of getting around disagreements that took place in the Reichstag. This meant it undermined the new democracy.

The President's ability to force through his own decision was known as 'Article 48'.

The Weimar Republic was vulnerable from the beginning...

When you're writing an answer in the exam, make sure you develop the points you make. For example, don't just say that Weimar Republic was weak — explain why it was weak.

Early Unpopularity

The Treaty of Versailles was signed in June 1919. The treaty was very unpopular in Germany and many Germans resented the new government for accepting its terms — not exactly a great start for the Republic.

President Ebert signed the Treaty of Versailles

1) After the armistice, a peace treaty called the Treaty of Versailles was imposed on Germany.
2) The terms of the treaty were mostly decided by the Allied leaders — David Lloyd George (Britain), Georges Clemenceau (France) and Woodrow Wilson (USA).

Comment and Analysis

Since the President had signed the Treaty of Versailles, the Weimar Republic became associated with the pain and humiliation it caused.

The new German government wasn't invited to the peace conference in 1919 and had no say in the Versailles Treaty. At first, Ebert refused to sign the treaty, but in the end he had little choice — Germany was too weak to risk restarting the conflict. In June 1919, he accepted its terms and signed.

The Terms of the Versailles Treaty were Severe

1) Article 231 of the treaty said Germany had to take the blame for the war — the War-Guilt Clause. → Many Germans didn't agree with this, and were humiliated by having to accept total blame.
2) Germany's armed forces were reduced to 100,000 men. They weren't allowed any armoured vehicles, aircraft or submarines, and could only have six warships. → This made Germans feel vulnerable.
3) Germany was forced to pay £6600 million in reparations — payments for the damage caused by German forces in the war. The amount was decided in 1921 but was changed later. → The heavy reparations seemed unfair to Germans and would cause lasting damage to Germany's economy.
4) Germany lost its empire — areas around the world that used to belong to Germany were now called mandates. They were put under the control of countries on the winning side of the war by the League of Nations — an organisation which aimed to settle international disputes peacefully. → People opposed the losses in territory, especially when people in German colonies were forced to become part of a new nation.
5) The German military was banned from the Rhineland — an area of Germany on its western border with France. This left Germany open to attack from the west.

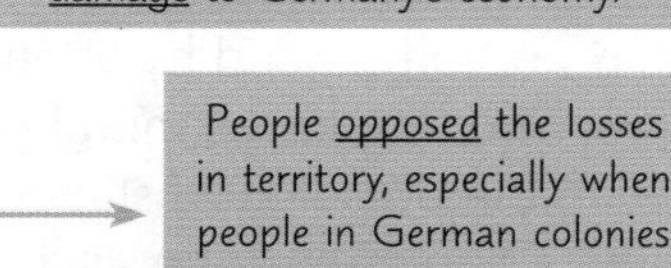

Germany Felt Betrayed by the Weimar Republic

The Treaty of Versailles caused resentment towards the Weimar Republic.

1) Germans called the treaty a 'Diktat' (a treaty forced upon Germany), and many blamed Ebert for accepting its terms.
2) Some Germans believed the armistice was a mistake and that Germany could have won the war. They felt 'stabbed in the back' by the Weimar politicians, who brought the Treaty of Versailles upon Germany unnecessarily.

The Weimar politicians involved in signing the armistice became known as the 'November Criminals'.

Comment and Analysis

The Treaty of Versailles played an important part in the failure of the Weimar Republic. It harmed the Republic's popularity, and created economic and political unrest that hindered the government for years.

This German cartoon demonstrates Germany's feelings towards the Treaty of Versailles. The Allies are shown as demons, out for revenge.

Germans felt 'stabbed in the back' by the government...

Scribble down as much as you can remember about the terms of the Treaty of Versailles. Include how Germans felt about it and its consequences for the Weimar Republic.

Years of Unrest

The first four years of the Weimar Republic (1919-1923) were dominated by political, social and economic unrest. This unrest created hardship for the German people, and fuelled criticism of Ebert's government.

There was Widespread Discontent in Germany

1) By 1919, thousands of Germans were poor and starving, and an influenza epidemic had killed thousands.
2) Many Germans denied they had lost the war and blamed the 'November Criminals' who had agreed to the armistice and the Treaty of Versailles.
3) Others who were blamed for losing the war included communists and Jews.
4) The government was seen as weak and ineffective — the Treaty of Versailles made living conditions worse.

Soon there were Riots and Rebellions

The government faced threats from left-wing and right-wing political groups.

The extreme left wanted a revolution...

- In January 1919, communists led by Karl Liebknecht and Rosa Luxemburg tried to take over Berlin. They took control of important buildings like newspaper headquarters, and 50,000 workers went on strike in support of the left-wing revolution. This became known as the Spartacist Revolt.
- Ebert asked for help from the right-wing Freikorps (ex-German soldiers) to stop the rebellion. Over 100 workers were killed. The Freikorps' use of violence caused a split on the Left between the Social Democratic Party and the communists.

The right also rebelled against the Weimar government...

- In March 1920, some of the Freikorps themselves took part in the Kapp Putsch ('Putsch' means revolt) — led by Wolfgang Kapp. They wanted to create a new right-wing government.
- The Freikorps marched into Berlin to overthrow the Weimar regime. But German workers opposed the putsch and staged a general strike. Berlin was paralysed and Kapp was forced to give up.
- Even after the putsch failed, threats to the government remained. In 1922, some former Freikorps members assassinated Walter Rathenau — he'd been Foreign Minister and was Jewish.

As Germany's economic problems got worse after the war, anti-Semitic (anti-Jewish) feelings increased.

In 1923 Germany Couldn't Pay its Reparations

1) By 1923, Germany could no longer meet the reparations payments set out by the Treaty of Versailles.
2) France and Belgium decided to take Germany's resources instead, so they occupied the Ruhr — the richest industrial part of Germany. This gave them access to Germany's iron and coal reserves. The occupation led to fury in Germany, and caused a huge strike in the Ruhr.
3) German industry was devastated again. Germany tried to solve her debt problem by printing more money, but this plunged the economy into hyperinflation.
4) In 1918, an egg cost ¼ of a Mark. By November 1923, it cost 80 million Marks.

Hyperinflation happens when production can't keep up with the amount of money in circulation, so the money keeps losing its value.

The consequences of hyperinflation

- Germany's currency became worthless. Nobody wanted to trade with Germany, so shortages of food and goods got worse.
- Bank savings also became worthless. The hardest hit were the middle classes.

By 1923, even basic necessities were hard to get hold of. The German people were undergoing immense hardship, which they'd now come to associate with the rise of the Weimar Republic.

Hyperinflation — sounds good for blowing up balloons...

EXAM QUESTION

Give two problems faced by the Weimar Republic between 1919 and 1923. [4]

Early Stages of the Nazi Party

Hitler entered German politics around the time the Weimar Republic was formed. By the time the Nazi Party was founded in 1920, he was growing in influence. In 1923, he tried to overthrow the Weimar government.

Adolf Hitler became the Voice of the German Workers' Party

Hitler began his political career in the German Workers' Party — a nationalist party led by Anton Drexler.

1) Hitler joined the German Workers' Party in January 1919, when he was still in the German army. He became known for his talent as a passionate and skilled speaker, and crowds gathered to hear him talk.
2) In 1920, the party was re-branded as the National Socialist German Workers' Party (the Nazi Party). In July 1921, Hitler became its leader.

In 1919, the party had around 60 members. By the end of 1920, it had around 2000.

The Nazi Party Developed its Identity

As the Nazi Party grew in popularity, it established an identity that appealed to as many people as possible.

1) In February 1920, the Nazi Party promoted its policies in the 'Twenty-Five Point Programme'. The Programme stressed German superiority and promoted anti-Semitism (prejudice against Jews).
2) The party wanted to raise pensions, and improve health and education — but only for Germans. It also rejected the Treaty of Versailles. Promoting German greatness gave the party a nationwide appeal.
3) In 1921, Hitler founded his own party militia called the SA ('storm troopers'). The SA were political thugs — they carried out violent anti-Semitic attacks and intimidated rival political groups. Many people were scared of them, but some Germans admired them. It also gave many ex-soldiers a job and a purpose.

Hitler tried to Overthrow the Government in the Munich Putsch

In 1923, the Weimar Republic was in crisis:

Hitler thought the time was right to attempt a putsch (revolt)...

- In 1923, things were going badly for the Weimar Republic — it seemed weak.
- Hyperinflation was at its peak and there were food riots.
- Many Germans were angry at the French and Belgian invasion of the Ruhr (see p.36). When the government stopped resisting by ending the strike there in 1923 (see p.38), discontent increased.

In November 1923, the Nazis marched on Munich...

- Hitler's soldiers occupied a beer hall in the Bavarian city of Munich where local government leaders were meeting. He announced that the revolution had begun.
- The next day Hitler marched into Munich supported by his storm troopers. But news of the revolt had been leaked to the police, who were waiting for Hitler. The police fired on the rebels and the revolt quickly collapsed.

1) Hitler was imprisoned for his role in the Munich Putsch and the Nazi Party was banned. However, his trial gave him valuable publicity.
2) He wrote a book in prison called 'Mein Kampf' ('My Struggle') describing his beliefs and ambitions.
3) Mein Kampf was vital in spreading Nazi ideology — millions of Germans read it. It introduced Hitler's belief that the Aryan race (which included Germans) was superior to all other races, and that all Germans had a right to 'Lebensraum' (more space to live).

The ban on the Nazi Party was lifted in February 1925.

Hitler was charismatic and stood for German greatness...

Some historians interpret the Munich Putsch as a failure for the Nazi Party, but others think it ended up helping Hitler. Jot down a couple of reasons in support of each view.

Recovery

In 1923, Gustav Stresemann became Chancellor of the Weimar Republic. His domestic and international policies helped the German economy to recover, resulting in the 'Golden Years' of the Weimar Republic.

Stresemann introduced a New Currency

1) Gustav Stresemann was Chancellor of the Weimar Republic between August and November 1923. He made important changes to help Germany to recover from its economic crisis.
2) In September 1923, he ended the strike in the Ruhr. This reduced tension between Germany, France and Belgium, and meant the government could stop compensation payments to strikers.
3) In November 1923, Stresemann replaced the German Mark with the Rentenmark to stabilise Germany's currency.
4) Stresemann created the 'great coalition' — a group of moderate, pro-democracy socialist parties in the Reichstag who agreed to work together. This allowed parliament to make decisions more quickly.

Stresemann wanted International Cooperation

In November 1923, Stresemann became Foreign Minister. He tried to cooperate more with other countries and build better international relationships. Germany's economy prospered as a result.

1) **The Dawes Plan** was signed in 1924. Stresemann secured France and Belgium's withdrawal from the Ruhr and agreed more realistic payment dates for the reparations. The USA lent Germany £40 million to help it pay off its other debts.
2) **The Young Plan** was agreed in 1929. The Allies agreed to reduce the reparations to a quarter of the original amount, and Germany was given 59 years to pay them.
3) **The Locarno Pact** was signed in October 1925. Germany, France and Belgium agreed to respect their joint borders — even those created as a result of the Treaty of Versailles.
4) **The League of Nations** (see p.35) allowed Germany to join in 1926. Germany was re-established as an international power.
5) **The Kellogg-Briand Pact** was signed by Germany in 1928, alongside 65 other countries. They promised not to use violence to settle disputes.

The Dawes Plan helped Germany's economy, but meant its success was dependent on American loans.

The Structure of the Dawes Plan

The USA could afford to loan out money to other countries.

The USA lent Germany money to help it pay off its debts.

Germany was able to pay its reparations to Britain and France.

Britain and France used the money they'd received to pay off their own debts to the USA.

Germany had begun to Recover — but Depended on US Money

1) Life was beginning to look better for Germany thanks to the work of Stresemann.
2) But he died in October 1929, just before the disaster of the Wall Street Crash — a massive stock market crash in the USA which started a global economic depression.
3) The plans he had agreed would only work if the USA had enough money to keep lending to Germany — but after the crash, it didn't. Things were suddenly going to get worse again (see p.40).

Comment and Analysis

Germany's economic recovery helped restore faith in the Weimar Republic — there was strong support for pro-Weimar political parties in the 1928 elections.

No need to Strese, mann — it's all under control...

Stresemann had a positive impact on the Weimar Republic and on the lives of many Germans, but he didn't solve all of Germany's problems — the economy was still very unstable.

Changes Under the Weimar Republic

Despite political, social and economic unrest, life did improve for some under the Weimar Republic.

Living standards Improved for the Working Classes

During the 'Golden Years', living standards improved in the Weimar Republic. This was a result of Germany's economic prosperity, but also of the reforms which took place throughout the 1920s.

What Improved	How It Improved
Unemployment	The unemployed were more protected. In 1927, the government introduced unemployment insurance. Workers could pay into the scheme and would receive cash benefits if they became unemployed.
Wages	The working classes became more prosperous. Wages for industrial workers rose quickly in the late 1920s.
Housing	The government launched mass housing projects. More than 2 million new homes were built between 1924 and 1931. This also provided extra employment.

Comment and Analysis

Not everyone benefited from higher standards of living. The middle classes felt ignored by the Weimar government and their resentment made it easier for the government's political opponents to gain support.

Despite these changes, some problems remained:

1) Higher living standards could only be maintained with a strong economy, and Germany's was fragile.
2) The changes mainly helped the working classes — the middle classes couldn't access the welfare benefits.

Women gained more Freedoms

Women were given more freedom and greater access to public life under the Weimar Republic.

1) Politically, women were more given more representation. They were awarded the vote and could enter politics more easily — between 1919 and 1932, 112 women were elected to the Reichstag.
2) Women showed that they were capable workers during the war, and the number of young women working increased.
3) The traditional role of women began to change. New female sports clubs and societies sprang up, and women had more opportunities.
4) Divorce became easier, and the number of divorces rose.

Comment and Analysis

These changes fuelled right-wing criticism — some German nationalists thought giving women more power and freedom threatened traditional family life and values in Germany.

The Weimar Republic had many Cultural Achievements

1) The Weimar Republic was a period of creativity and innovation in Germany. Freedom of expression generated new ideas. Artists began to question traditional forms and styles, especially ones that focused on authority and militarism.
2) There were advances in the arts — some developments were bold and new, like the drama of Bertholt Brecht. The Bauhaus School of design was highly influential, especially in fine arts and architecture.
3) There were also important changes in music, literature and cinema. German films were successful — e.g. 'Metropolis' directed by Fritz Lang.
4) The Weimar Republic encouraged new ways of critical thinking at places like Frankfurt University, and a cabaret culture developed in Berlin.

Not all Germans liked the rejection of traditional forms and values in Weimar culture. Some were afraid it symbolised a loss of German tradition.

It wasn't all doom and gloom...

EXAM QUESTION

Explain how the lives of Germans changed under the Weimar Republic. [8]

The Great Depression

In 1929, the Great Depression hit Germany. The desperation it caused in the 1920s and 1930s meant that the German people were willing to consider any political party that promised something different.

The Wall Street Crash Ended economic Recovery

In October 1929, the Wall Street stock market in America crashed. It sparked an international economic crisis (the Great Depression) and meant the USA couldn't afford to prop up the German economy any longer.

1) Germany's economic recovery between 1924 and 1929 was built on unstable foundations. The biggest problem was that it was dependent on loans from the USA, which had been agreed in the Dawes Plan (see p.38).
2) After the Wall Street Crash, the USA couldn't afford to lend Germany money anymore. It also wanted some old loans to be repaid.

- Germany's economy collapsed without American aid. Industrial production went into decline — factories closed and banks went out of business.
- There was mass unemployment. In October 1929 1.6 million people were out of work, and by February 1932 there were over 6 million.
- The government also cut unemployment benefits — it couldn't afford to support the large numbers of Germans out of work.

This made many Germans angry with the government.

Extremist parties became More Popular

Popular discontent with the Weimar government and economic instability created an opportunity for extremist parties to grow. The KPD (the Communist Party of Germany) increased in influence.

1) The KPD was founded in December 1918 and wanted a workers' revolution. The communists promised to represent workers' needs and make German society more fair.
2) This helped the KPD to gain a lot of support from unemployed Germans during times of economic crisis.

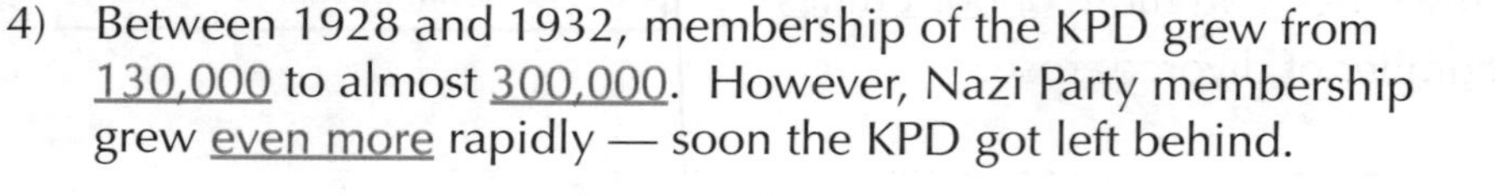

3) When the Great Depression hit Germany in 1929, the KPD competed with the Nazi Party for the support of Germans who had been hit hard by the economic crisis.
4) Between 1928 and 1932, membership of the KPD grew from 130,000 to almost 300,000. However, Nazi Party membership grew even more rapidly — soon the KPD got left behind.

Comment and Analysis

Some historians think the Nazi Party's rise to power wasn't guaranteed — in the 1930s, both left and right-wing political parties increased in popularity in Germany.

Revision couldn't get any cheerier...

Describe the changes in federal election results between 1928 and 1932.
What do they show about the changing popularity of the three different political parties?

The Nazi Rise

The Nazi party was able to take advantage of the discontent and anger created by the Great Depression.

The Nazi Party Appealed to many Different Groups in Society

The Nazis promised a more prosperous and less humiliating future, which was very popular among the German people — by 1930, membership had grown to over 300,000.

1) After the onset of the Depression, the Nazi Party's popularity soared. Hitler's promise to make Germany great again appealed to the growing ranks of unemployed and young people who wanted a brighter future.
2) Some people also supported the Nazis' anti-communist and anti-Jewish views. Communists and Jews were useful scapegoats for Germany's economic problems and gave Germans someone to blame.
3) Some wealthy businessmen who had lost out in the Great Depression turned to the Nazi Party. They approved of the Nazis' anti-communist stance and wanted the economic prosperity Hitler had promised.

Comment and Analysis

After the Depression hit Germany, more Germans began to vote. Participation in elections increased by around 10% between 1928 and 1932. Many of these new voters were attracted by the changes the Nazi Party promised.

The Nazi Party was well organised...

- Hitler's private army, the SA (see p.37), gave the party a military feel, which made it seem organised and disciplined. His authority over the SA and his undisputed role as head of the Nazi Party made the Nazis seemed strong in comparison to the Weimar government.
- Propaganda was very efficient. It often focused on regional issues and targeted specific groups. This made individuals feel valued by the Nazi Party and stole votes from smaller parties.

Hitler's Personality attracted Support

Interviews with Germans who lived through this period suggest that Hitler's personality was an important factor in the Nazis' popularity.

1) Hitler was patriotic and energetic, and was able to effectively get across his enthusiasm to his supporters. His speeches brought hope to those who listened.
2) In the 1932 election campaigns, Hitler was depicted as Germany's saviour. He stood up to the Weimar government and opposed communism.
3) He came across as a strong leader, which created a sharp contrast with the politicians of the Weimar governments. Hitler's authority over the SA and his undisputed role as head of the Nazi Party attracted support — many Germans had now lost faith in democracy.

© Thaliastock / Mary Evans

A Nazi election poster from April 1932. The text reads 'Our last hope: Hitler'.

Here are two different interpretations of Hitler's rise to power. There's evidence to support both opinions.

Interpretation 1: After the onset of the Great Depression, Germans were willing to support any strong extremist party as an alternative to the democratic Weimar government.

After the Great Depression, both the Nazi Party and the Communist Party became more popular, and support for moderate parties like Social Democratic Party dropped off.

Interpretation 2: There was only one credible party to turn to after the Great Depression hit — the Nazi Party. It was the only party with a charismatic leader who had mass appeal.

The Nazi Party grew more rapidly than any other party after 1928. Hitler's passion and energy made the Nazis stand out, and support for the KPD simply couldn't keep up.

Hitler's personality was magnetic — it attracted support...

In the exam you'll be given two interpretations. You'll need to say how their views are different and be able to explain why each view is valid. For more, see p.4.

Establishing a Dictatorship

As the Depression got worse, political instability grew. Several parties were competing for power in the elections of 1932 (see p.40). In 1933, the Nazis would emerge on top. Hitler's rise continued.

Hitler Gained Power in Elections... with the aid of a Political Deal

1) By April 1932, conditions had worsened. The country was desperate for a strong government.
2) President Hindenburg had to stand for re-election because his term of office had run out. He was a national hero, but Hitler decided to run against him. Despite claiming he'd win easily, Hindenburg didn't win a majority in the first election. In the second ballot he won 53%, beating Hitler's 36.8%.
3) In July 1932, the Nazis won 230 seats in the elections for the Reichstag — more than any other party. Hitler demanded to be made Chancellor, but Hindenburg didn't trust Hitler and refused to appoint him.
4) Then in the election of November 1932, the Nazis seemed to be losing popularity — they lost 34 seats.
5) But Hitler struck a deal with another politician, Franz von Papen — if Papen would persuade Hindenburg to make Hitler Chancellor, Hitler would make Papen Vice-Chancellor.
6) Hindenburg agreed to Papen's suggestion, thinking that he could control Hitler. But Hitler used his new powers to call another election in March 1933, hoping to make the Nazis even stronger in the Reichstag.

Comment and Analysis

Hindenburg hoped that Hitler would be less extreme once he was actually in power. He also hoped that Hitler wouldn't be able to repair the economy — meaning he (Hindenburg) might be able to regain popularity and power.

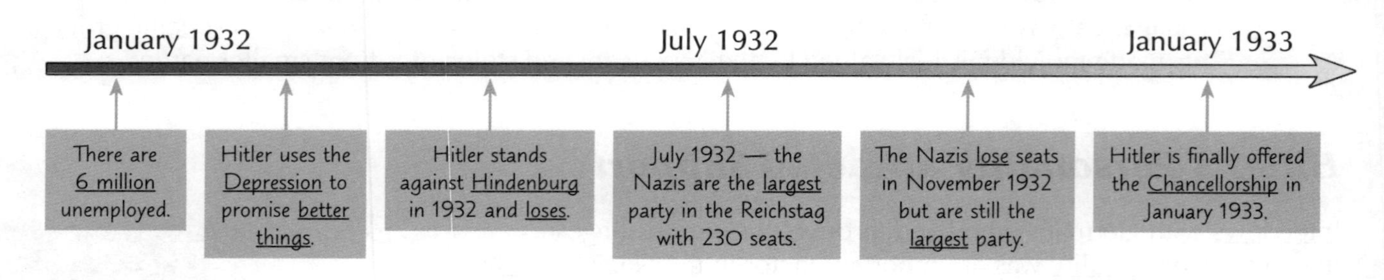

The Nazis used Dirty Tricks to Win in 1933

1) In the elections of 1933, the Nazis took no chances:
   - They controlled the news media, and opposition meetings were banned.
   - They used the SA to terrorise opponents.
   - When a fire broke out in the Reichstag building, Hitler blamed the communists. He used the fire to claim that communists were a threat to the country and to whip up anti-communist feelings. Hitler was even given emergency powers to deal with the supposed communist threat — he used these powers to intimidate communist voters.
2) The Nazis won 288 seats but didn't have an overall majority. So Hitler simply made the Communist Party (who had 81 seats) illegal.
3) This gave him enough support in parliament to bring in the Enabling Act, passed with threats and bargaining in March 1933. This let him govern for four years without parliament.
4) Trade unions were banned in May 1933. Then in July 1933, all political parties, apart from the Nazi party, were banned. Germany had become a one-party state.

Comment and Analysis

The emergency powers granted to Hitler were a turning point — they mark the first step towards making Germany a dictatorship. Hitler justified them by saying that they were necessary to protect the German people. This meant he faced little opposition from the German public.

The Nazis — gaining power...

When answering exam questions, consider the circumstances of people and what they could have known at the time. For example, no one knew the horror that World War II would bring.

Achieving Total Power

Hitler was more powerful, but he still had enemies. He wanted to remove them to secure his dictatorship.

The SA was a Threat to Hitler

1) The SA had helped Hitler come to power, but Hitler now saw it as a threat.
2) Its members were very loyal to Ernst Röhm, the SA's leader. Hitler was worried that Röhm was becoming too powerful — by 1934 the SA had more members than the German army.
3) The SA was also unpopular with the leaders of the German army and with some ordinary Germans.

The 'Night of the Long Knives' — Hitler removes his enemies

1) Ernst Röhm was the biggest threat to Hitler, but Hitler was also worried about other members of the Nazi Party who disagreed with his views.
2) On the 29th-30th June 1934, Hitler sent men to arrest or kill Röhm and other leaders of the SA. Hitler also used this opportunity to remove some of his political opponents. Altogether, several hundred people were killed or imprisoned.
3) Hitler claimed that those who had been killed had been plotting to overthrow the government, so he declared their murders legal.
4) This became known as the 'Night of the Long Knives', and was a triumph for Hitler.
5) It stamped out all potential opposition within the Nazi party and sent a powerful message to the party about Hitler's ruthlessness and brutality. It also showed that Hitler was now free to act above the law.

Comment and Analysis

Most Germans wouldn't have known exactly what had happened on the 'Night of the Long Knives' until a few days later, when Hitler declared the events legal. Even then, there was little outcry. It's likely that some people believed Hitler's claims that the violence was necessary to protect the country. Others were too scared to speak out.

Hitler took full control of National and Local government

1) In August 1934, Hindenburg died. Hitler used the opportunity to combine the posts of Chancellor and President, and also made himself Commander-in-Chief of the army.
2) He called himself Der Führer (the leader) — this was the beginning of the dictatorship.
3) At this point, Germany was reorganised into a number of provinces. Each province was called a Gau (plural: Gaue), with a Gauleiter (a loyal Nazi) in charge of each.
4) Above them were the Reichsleiters, who advised Hitler, e.g. Goebbels who was in charge of propaganda, and Himmler who was chief of the German police.
5) At the top and in absolute control was the Führer — Hitler.
6) Every aspect of life was carefully controlled, and only loyal Nazis could be successful.

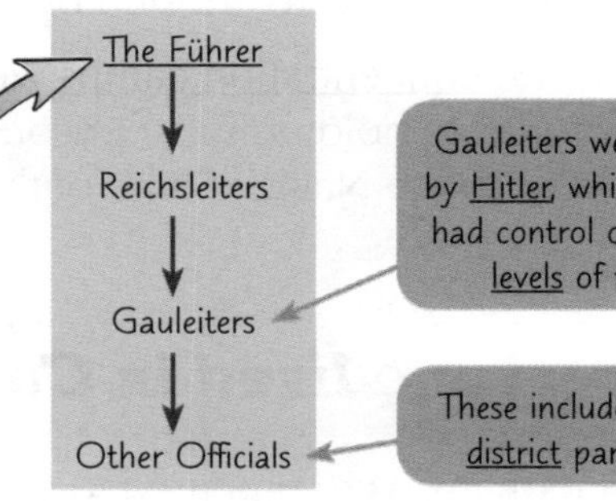

Gauleiters were appointed by Hitler, which ensured he had control over the lower levels of the party.

These included local and district party leaders.

Comment and Analysis

When the Nazis took over, some Germans were glad that someone was at last taking control after the chaos and political weaknesses of the Weimar years.

The army had to swear an oath of allegiance to Hitler, instead of pledging to protect Germany. Some German workers were also forced to take an oath of obedience, promising loyalty to Hitler. Those who refused could lose their jobs.

The Nazis — eliminating opposition...

You need to know how Hitler secured his power to become Führer. Write a summary of the steps he took to consolidate his position between January 1933 and August 1934.

The Machinery of Terror

The Nazis aimed to make Germany a totalitarian state (where the government controls all aspects of life).

Germany became a Police State

1) The Nazis wanted complete control over the machinery of government and people's lives.
2) Hitler's Enabling Act of 1933 (see p.42) allowed the government to read people's mail, listen in on their phone calls, and search their homes without notice.
3) The Law for the Reconstruction of the Reich (1934) gave the Nazis total power over local governments.
4) There were laws to sack civil servants who didn't support the Nazis and accept their rules.
5) The Nazis also made changes to the justice system. Judges didn't have to be 'fair' and unbiased. Instead, they were expected to make rulings that were in line with Nazi Party policy.
6) The Sicherheitsdienst (SD) was the Nazi intelligence service. It was initially run by Reinhard Heydrich — he aimed to bring every German under continual supervision.

The legal system was far from fair...

- In 1933, the Nazis set up special courts where the basic rights of those accused were suspended — they couldn't appeal or question evidence given against them.
- In 1934, Hitler established the People's Court in Berlin, which held trials for important political crimes. Defendants were nearly always found guilty.

People could be Terrorised into Conforming

The government was also prepared to use terror and even violence against the German people.

1) The SS (Schutzstaffel) began as a bodyguard for Hitler. It expanded massively under the leadership of Himmler during the 1930s. Its members were totally loyal to Hitler, and feared for their cruelty.
2) Himmler was also in charge of the secret police — the Gestapo. The Gestapo's job was 'to protect public safety and order', but their methods included harsh interrogations and imprisonment without trial.
3) Local wardens were employed to make sure Germans were loyal to the Nazis. Members of the public were encouraged to report disloyalty. Many were arrested by the Gestapo as a result.
4) After 1933, concentration camps were created across Germany and its territories to hold political prisoners and anybody else considered dangerous to the Nazis. Some of these were later turned into death camps.

Security Police search a car in Berlin on the orders of the Gestapo.

Not everyone lived in Constant Terror

1) Most Germans were prepared to go along with the new regime. Some people accepted the new rules out of fear.
2) Others went along with them because they believed in their aims, even if they didn't approve of the Nazis' brutal methods.

Comment and Analysis

For those that didn't fit in with the Nazi ideals (e.g. Jews), life under the SS and the Gestapo could be terrifying. But Hitler was supported, not feared, by many Germans.

The Nazis exercised control using any means necessary...

Turn this page over, then try to scribble down as much as you can remember about the Nazi police state. If you get stuck, think how you might've been treated if you were a political enemy.

Nazi Propaganda

The Nazis also used propaganda to help them control the German people's lives.

Propaganda aims to Control how people Think

1) Propaganda means spreading information that influences how people think and behave.
2) It gives only certain points of view and often leaves out important facts.
3) The Nazis used powerful propaganda to get the support of the German people. Dr Joseph Goebbels was in overall charge of the Nazis' 'propaganda machine'.

Nazi propaganda took Simple Ideas and Repeated them

1) Nazi propaganda was used to unite the German people and convince them that the Nazis would make Germany strong.
2) Germans were encouraged to hate the countries that signed the Treaty of Versailles. The Nazis said Germany should fight to get back the territory 'stolen' by the treaty.
3) Goebbels created the 'Hitler Myth', which made Hitler seem like a god and the saviour of Germany. This was the 'cult of the Führer'.
4) The Nazis' propaganda also said that Jews and communists were the biggest cause of Germany's problems. One Nazi paper claimed that Jews murdered children for the Passover Feast.
5) The Nazis encouraged a return to traditional German values and a revival of traditional German culture.

A popular slogan was 'One people, one empire, one leader'. Many Germans devoted their lives to Hitler.

The Government had to Approve all Artistic Works

1) Goebbels founded the Ministry of Public Enlightenment and Propaganda in 1933.
2) It had departments for music, theatre, film, literature and radio. All artists, writers, journalists and musicians had to register to get their work approved.

Nazis used the Media as a tool of Propaganda

1) The Nazis wanted to surround people with their propaganda. They used censorship to prevent Germans from seeing or hearing anything that gave a different message.
2) They sold cheap radios and controlled broadcasts. By 1939 approximately 70% of households had a radio, which gave the Nazis a voice in most people's homes.
3) In 1933, only 3% of German daily newspapers were controlled by the Nazis. By 1944, this had risen to 82%. This meant the Nazis could decide what was published in the papers.
4) The Nazis also produced hundreds of films. Many films showed the strengths of the Nazis and Hitler, and the weakness of their opponents. An important German director was Leni Riefenstahl.
5) Another method of spreading propaganda was through posters showing the evil of Germany's enemies and the power of Hitler. Propaganda also let Germans know what was expected of them.

According to Goebbels, radio was a 'weapon of the totalitarian state' — it was a way to control the German people.

Nazi propaganda poster, 1935. It states that 'the German student' fights for the Führer and for the German people.

Radio Nazi — broadcasting to you wherever you are...

In the exam, you might need to think about why propaganda had such a big impact on many Germans. Think about why it was attractive, who it targeted and how powerful it was.

EXAM TIP

Nazi Propaganda

Nazi propaganda was sophisticated and it was everywhere.

Nazi propaganda could involve Spectacular Displays

1) The Nazis used public rallies to spread their propaganda. The annual Nuremberg Rallies focused on speeches by leading Nazis, like Hitler and Goebbels. The 1934 Nuremberg Rally was recorded by Riefenstahl in her film 'Triumph of the Will'.

Hermann Göring at a Nuremberg Rally, as shown in 'Triumph of the Will'.

2) One million people attended the 1936 rally. There were displays of lights and flags to greet the arrival of Hitler. These made him look more powerful.
3) Sporting events like the 1936 Berlin Olympics were used to show off German wealth and power. But the success of non-Aryan athletes like African-American Jesse Owens (who won four gold medals) undermined Hitler's message.
4) Nazi power was also shown through art and architecture, and grand new buildings appeared in Nuremberg and Berlin.

Propaganda was used to change Culture and Society

1) The Nazis promised an empire that would last a thousand years — based on traditional values.
2) Modern art was banned, in favour of realistic paintings that fit with Nazi ideology. Modern art was labelled 'degenerate' and exhibitions were created to show people how 'bad' it was. The Nazis celebrated the works of 'German' composers, such as Wagner, but much modern classical music, works by Jewish composers, and jazz were all attacked.
3) School textbooks were rewritten to make Germans look successful. Children were taught to believe in Nazi doctrines (see p.50).
4) The 'Strength through Joy' programme sought to show ordinary workers that the Nazi regime cared about their living conditions (see p.49).

In the Weimar Republic, artists had started to use ideas that were new and experimental (see p.39).

Propaganda was most Effective when Reinforcing Existing Ideas

Surprisingly, it's quite difficult to tell how effective Nazi propaganda was.

1) Some historians say Nazi propaganda was better at reinforcing people's existing attitudes than making them believe something different.
2) Many Germans felt angry and humiliated by the Treaty of Versailles, so Hitler's promises to reverse the treaty and make Germany great again were very popular.
3) After the political weakness of the Weimar Republic, people found the image of Hitler as a strong leader appealing. So the 'Hitler Myth' was very effective and made Hitler an extremely popular leader.
4) Anti-Jewish and anti-communist attitudes already existed in Germany before the Nazis came to power.
5) The Weimar Republic was seen as too liberal by many — they thought standards in Germany had slipped. These people liked the promise of a return to traditional German values.
6) The Depression had left many German people in poverty. This made them easier to persuade, and the Nazis' promises of help extremely popular.

Comment and Analysis

However effective their propaganda was, the Nazis' control of the media made it almost impossible for anyone to publish an alternative point of view.

Nazi spin — sophisticated, but probably not 100% effective...

EXAM QUESTION

How did the Nazi Party try to change German culture and society using propaganda?
Focus on the period when the Nazis were in power (from 1933-1945). [8]

Nazis and the Church

The Nazi Party publicly supported religious freedom, but in reality saw Christianity as a threat.

Hitler wanted to Reduce the Church's Power

1) In the 1930s, most Germans were Christians and the Church was very influential. During the Weimar Republic, the state and the Church had worked closely together and the Church was involved in national matters like education.
2) Some prominent Nazis were anti-Christian and Nazi ideology disagreed with the role the Church had traditionally had in society.
3) Hitler thought religion should comply with the state and wanted churches to promote Nazi ideals. He was also worried that some members of the Church might publicly oppose Nazi policies.
4) The Nazi Party was careful to maintain support from the Catholic and Protestant Churches during its rise to power because they were so popular. However, as Hitler consolidated his totalitarian state, his control over churches increased.

The Catholic Church was Persecuted

1) In July 1933, an agreement called the Concordat was signed between the Pope and the Nazi government. Hitler promised not to interfere with the Catholic Church if the Church agreed to stay out of German politics.
2) The Catholic Church was now banned from speaking out against the Nazi Party, but Hitler soon broke his side of the deal.

Comment and Analysis

The Concordat reassured Christians that Hitler was consolidating ties with the Catholic Church, but he was actually restricting its power.

- The Nazi Party started to restrict the Catholic Church's role in education.
- In 1936 all crucifixes were removed from schools and by 1939 Catholic education had been destroyed.
- The Nazis began arresting priests in 1935 and put them on trial.
- Catholic newspapers were suppressed and the Catholic Youth group was disbanded.

3) In 1937, the Pope spoke out against Hitler in a letter to Catholic Churches in Germany. The view of the Church had changed, but many German Catholics were too scared to speak out against the Nazi Party.

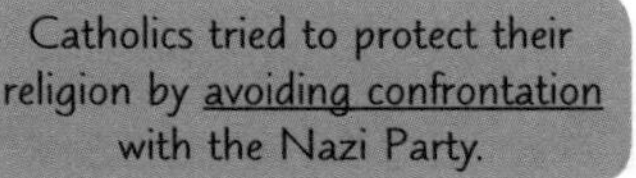

The Nazi Party Controlled the Protestant Church

The Protestant Church was reorganised and fell under Nazi control.

1) When Hitler became Chancellor in 1933, there were 28 independent Protestant Churches. These Churches were politically divided — some formed a group known as the 'German Christians'. They supported Hitler and favoured an anti-Semitic version of Christianity.
2) The Nazi Party backed this version of Christianity and believed all Christians should follow its principles. In 1936, all Protestant Churches were merged to form the Reich Church.

The Reich Church 'Nazified' Christianity...

The Reich Church replaced the symbol of a cross with the Nazi Swastika, and the Bible was replaced by 'Mein Kampf' (see p.37). Only Nazis could give sermons and the Church suspended non-Aryan ministers.

3) The Reich Church was an attempt to increase state control over the Protestant Church and make a National Socialist version of Christianity.

Comment and Analysis

Not everyone supported the Reich Church — it was opposed by a Protestant group called the 'Confessing Church' (see p.48).

The Nazis wanted the state to come first...

In the exam you'll be given two different interpretations. Think about the authors' experiences. For example, a German Catholic may have been more persecuted than a German Protestant.

Opposition to the Nazis

The Nazis had a tight grip on Germany, but some opposition remained.

The Political Left opposed Hitler, but was Divided and Weak

1) Once in power, the Nazis had banned other political parties, including those on the political left, such as the Communist Party (KPD) and the Social Democratic Party (SPD).
2) But members of these parties formed underground groups to try and organise industrial unrest (e.g. strikes). These networks were often infiltrated by the Gestapo, and party members could be executed.
3) Their impact was also limited because the different parties of the left were divided and didn't cooperate.

Some members of the Church Opposed the Nazis

There was little opposition to the Nazis in Germany from Christian groups. But a number of Church members did oppose the Nazis, even though they risked being sent to concentration camps (see p.44):

1) Martin Niemöller was a Protestant pastor, a former U-boat (submarine) captain, and a one-time Nazi supporter. He objected to Nazi interference in the Church, and was one of the founders of the Confessing Church. He used a sermon in 1937 to protest against the persecution of Church members, and as a result spent several years in concentration camps.
2) Another key member of the Confessing Church was Dietrich Bonhoeffer, a Protestant philosopher and pastor who opposed the Nazis from the beginning. He joined the resistance, helped Jews escape from Germany and planned to assassinate Hitler. He was caught and imprisoned, then executed just weeks before the fall of the Nazis.
3) Clemens August von Galen was the Catholic Bishop of Münster, who used his sermons to protest against Nazi racial policies and the murder of the disabled. His protests didn't stop the killing, but they did force the Nazis to keep them secret. Only the need to maintain the support of German Catholics stopped the Nazis from executing him.

The Confessing Church protested against Hitler's attempt to unite the different Protestant Churches into one Reich Church (see p.47).

The Edelweiss Pirates and Swing Kids were Youth Movements

1) The Edelweiss Pirates was the name given to groups of rebellious youths who rejected Nazi values.
   - They helped army deserters, forced labourers and escaped concentration camp prisoners.
   - At first the Nazis mostly ignored them, but cracked down after they started distributing anti-Nazi leaflets. Many members were arrested, and several were publicly hanged.
2) The Swing Kids (or Swing Youth) were groups of young people who rebelled against the tight control the Nazis had over culture, acting in ways considered 'degenerate' by the Nazi regime (e.g. listening to American music and drinking alcohol). They were mostly considered a nuisance rather than a threat, but some members were arrested and even sent to concentration camps.

Comment and Analysis

German opposition to the Nazis didn't really threaten their dominance, but it did mean the Gestapo was kept busy tracking down people who had distributed anti-Nazi leaflets, held secret meetings, committed acts of sabotage, etc.

Comment and Analysis

Other Germans expressed their dissatisfaction with the Nazi regime in 'low level' ways — e.g. by grumbling about the government or spreading rumours. Not everyone considers this genuine opposition, but even this was probably risky.

If you weren't with the Nazis, you were against them...

Write the headings 'political opposition', 'religious opposition' and 'opposition from youths' on a piece of paper. Cover this page, then jot down as much as you can remember about each one.

REVISION TASK

Work and Home

The Nazis encouraged women to be homemakers and tried to provide jobs for men.

Women were expected to raise Large Families

1) Nazis didn't want women to have too much freedom. They believed the role of women was to provide children and support their families at home.
2) Women were banned from being lawyers in 1936, and the Nazis did their best to stop them following other professions.
3) The League of German Maidens spread the Nazi idea that it was an honour to produce large families for Germany. Nazis gave awards to women for doing this and encouraged more women to marry by offering financial aid to married couples.
4) Women were expected to dress plainly and were discouraged from wearing make-up and smoking. At school, girls studied subjects like cookery. It was stressed that they should choose 'Aryan' husbands.

This didn't quite go to plan for the Nazis — after 1939, the war caused a shortage of workers, which meant lots of women had to go back to work (see p.52).

Public Works and Rearmament meant Unemployment Fell

1) Hitler started a huge programme of public works, which helped to reduce unemployment — e.g. from 1933 jobs were created as a result of the construction of autobahns (motorways).
2) All men between 18 and 25 could be recruited into the National Labour Service and given jobs. Industrial output increased and unemployment fell.
3) Hitler also brought in military conscription and encouraged German industry to manufacture more ships, aircraft, tanks and weapons for the military. This rearmament meant further falls in unemployment.
4) Trade unions were banned (see p.42), and workers had to join the Nazis' Labour Front instead. The Labour Front acted like one big trade union, but it was controlled by the Nazis. Workers couldn't go on strike or campaign for better conditions, and wages were relatively low.

Comment and Analysis

Although unemployment fell after the Depression, the Nazis fiddled with the statistics to make it look lower than it really was — e.g. they didn't count women or Jewish people without jobs in the official unemployment statistics.

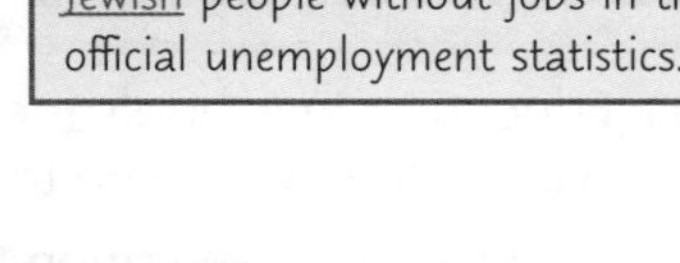

Many groups in society Felt Better Off

1) The Nazis made efforts to maintain the support of German workers. They wanted workers to feel important and believe that they were an essential part of the Volksgemeinschaft.

'Volksgemeinschaft' means a community of people working hard towards the same aims.

- The Nazis introduced the Volkswagen (the 'people's car') as a luxury people could aspire to own.
- They also introduced 'Strength through Joy' — a scheme which provided workers with cheap holidays and leisure activities.
- The 'Beauty of Labour' scheme encouraged factory owners to improve conditions for workers.

2) Many in the middle classes also felt better off, e.g. small-business owners were able to advance more in society than previously.
3) But even though many people felt better off, workers and small-business owners had lost out in some ways.
   - The cost of living rose by about 25% — but wages didn't go up.
   - Workers didn't have the right to strike or resign.
   - Small businesses had to pay high taxes.

Comment and Analysis

During the Depression, one third of all workers had been unemployed. Many Germans had been desperate, so life under the Nazis did feel genuinely better for them.

Hitler reduced unemployment — and gained popularity...

It's important to remember that for some Germans life really did get better under the Nazi Party.

EXAM TIP

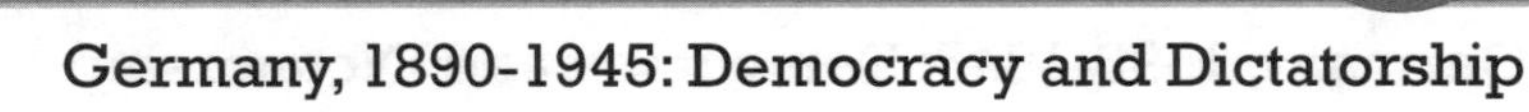

Young People

An important key to Nazi success was controlling the minds of German youth.

Youth Movements helped produce Committed Nazis

1) Hitler knew that loyalty from young people was essential if the Nazis were to remain strong.
2) Youth movements were a way of teaching children Nazi ideas — so they would be loyal to the Nazi Party when they grew up.

The Hitler Youth seemed exciting...

- The Hitler Youth was founded in 1926. Boys aged fourteen and over were recruited to the movement. It became compulsory in 1936 and lasted until 1945.
- Boys wore military-style uniforms and took part in physical exercise preparing for war. High-achieving boys might be sent to Hitler Schools to be trained as loyal Nazi leaders.
- They also went on camping trips and held sports competitions. Some of those who took part said the organisation was fun, made them feel valued and encouraged a sense of responsibility.

The League of German Maidens was for girls...

- The League of German Maidens was the female branch of the Hitler Youth, aimed at girls aged between fourteen and eighteen.
- Girls were trained in domestic skills like sewing and cooking.
- Sometimes they took part in physical activities like camping and hiking. This gave girls new opportunities that were normally reserved for boys.

Comment and Analysis

After 1936, children were obliged to join the Hitler Youth and all other youth organisations were banned. However, towards the end of the 1930s, attendance actually decreased as activities adopted an increasingly military focus.

Education across Germany was 'Nazified'

1) Education in schools meant learning Nazi propaganda. Most teachers joined the Nazi Teachers' Association and were trained in Nazi methods. Children had to report teachers who did not use them.
2) Subjects were rewritten to fit in with Nazi ideas. Children were taught to be anti-Semitic (prejudiced against Jews) — for example, Biology courses stated that Jews were biologically inferior to 'Aryans'. History courses explained that the First World War was lost because of Jews and communists.
3) Physical education became more important for boys to prepare them for joining the army. They sometimes even played games with live ammunition.
4) In universities, students burned anti-Nazi and Jewish books, and Jewish lecturers were sacked. Jewish teachers were also dismissed from public schools.

German children were always being bombarded with Nazi propaganda. Erika Mann, a German who opposed the Nazis, described Nazi education in Germany. 'Every child says 'Heil Hitler!' from 50 to 150 times a day...[it] is required by law; if you meet a friend on the way to school, you say it; study periods are opened and closed with [it]... [The Nazis'] supremacy over the German child...is complete.'

German Youth eventually became involved in Fighting the War

1) During the Second World War, members of the Hitler Youth contributed to the war effort — for example, helping with air defence work, farm work and collecting donations for Nazi charities.
2) Towards the end of the war, many Hitler Youth members ended up fighting alongside adults. They were known for being fierce and fanatical fighters.

The Nazis' attempts to impose their ideology on children weren't always effective. See p.48 for more about how unofficial youth movements resisted Hitler and the Nazis.

The Hitler Youth — not everyone's favourite youth group...

Imagine you're a teacher in Nazi Germany. Write an account of how your job might have changed after the Nazis gained power in 1933.

Nazi Racial Policy

The Nazi belief in the idea of a 'master race' caused a huge amount of harm.

Hitler wanted to 'Cleanse' Germany of 'Inferior' groups

1) Most Nazis believed that Germans were members of a superior ancient race called the 'Aryans'. Hitler thought people who were not pure Aryans (e.g. Jews) did not belong in Germany, and had no part to play in the new German Empire.
2) He wanted to 'cleanse' the German people by removing any groups he thought 'inferior'. Jews were especially targeted, but action was also taken against other groups.

Hitler always claimed the Jews were responsible for many of Germany's problems.

- Many Romani (gypsies) and Slavs (an ethnic group from central and eastern Europe) were sent to concentration camps. The Nazis believed that they were racially inferior.
- The Nazis practised eugenics policies — they wanted to create a strong race by removing all genetic 'defects' from its gene pool. Many people with mental and physical disabilities were murdered or sterilised. Many people of mixed race were also sterilised against their will.
- Homosexual people were sent to concentration camps in their thousands. In 1936 Himmler, Head of the SS, began the Central Office for the Combating of Homosexuality and Abortion.

Nazis Changed the Law to Discriminate against Jews

1) In 1933, the SA organised a national boycott of Jewish businesses, which resulted in Nazi-led violence against Jews. The violence wasn't popular with the German people, so the Nazis decided to use the legal system to persecute Jews instead.
2) Over time, the number of jobs that Jews were banned from gradually increased.
3) The Nuremberg Laws of 1935 were based on the idea that Jews and Germans were biologically different. They removed many legal rights from Jews and encouraged 'Aryan' Germans to see them as inferior.

- The Nuremberg Laws stopped Jews being German citizens.
- They banned marriage between Jews and non-Jews in Germany.
- They also banned sexual relationships between Jews and non-Jews.

Some Jews were given passports enabling them to leave Germany but preventing them from returning.

4) Jews were later forced to close or sell their businesses, and they were banned from all employment.
5) By 1938, all Jewish children had been banned from attending German schools and Jews were no longer allowed in many public places, including theatres and exhibitions.

Comment and Analysis

The Nazis' racial policies aimed to isolate Jews from the rest of society. 'Aryan' Germans were even encouraged to break off friendships with Jews and avoid any contact with Jewish people.

Kristallnacht — the 'Night of the Broken Glass'

1) In November 1938, a German diplomat was murdered in Paris by a Jew.
2) There was anti-Jewish rioting throughout Germany — thousands of Jewish shops were smashed and almost every synagogue in Germany was burnt down. In the days that followed, thousands of Jews were arrested and sent to concentration camps.
3) The Nazis claimed that the events of Kristallnacht were a spontaneous reaction by the German people to the Paris murder. In fact, they had been planned and organised by the Nazi government. Few ordinary Germans had participated.

Comment and Analysis

Kristallnacht was a turning point in the Nazi persecution of Jews — it was the first widespread act of anti-Jewish violence in Nazi Germany. After Kristallnacht, conditions for German Jews got even worse.

Nazi Germany — a climate of cruelty and fear...

REVISION TASK

Fold a piece of paper in half. On one side, jot down all the different types of people who were persecuted as a result of the Nazis' racial policies, and on the other list how they were treated.

Germany's War Economy

Hitler had always planned a war to provide Lebensraum (more space to live) for the German people. But Germany wasn't at full strength when the Second World War broke out in 1939.

The Nazi Economy had to Prepare for War

1) Hitler transformed the German economy to prepare the country for war.
2) A Four-Year Plan was started in 1936, concentrating on war preparations. The Nazis needed to quickly build up industries making weapons and chemicals, and increase Germany's agricultural output.
3) Hermann Göring was put in charge of the economy. He aimed to make Germany self-sufficient — this meant producing enough goods to not need imports from other countries.
4) Many workers were retrained to do jobs that would help the war effort, such as producing weapons and working in chemical plants.
5) But Hitler knew that ultimately Germany would need to conquer new territories and capture their resources to become genuinely self-sufficient.

Supplies to Germany had been blocked during the First World War, causing severe shortages. By becoming self-sufficient, Hitler hoped to avoid this problem in future wars.

The Outbreak of War forced Changes in the Economy

1) When war broke out in 1939, the German economy wasn't ready. More changes were needed.
2) A quarter of the workforce was already working in war industries, especially weapons production. Two years later this had become three-quarters.
3) A lot of German workers were conscripted into the army, so the Nazis had to use foreign workers to keep the economy going. This included civilians from occupied territories, prisoners of war and slave labourers — see p.55.
4) Eventually, in 1942, after several years of fighting, Hitler put Albert Speer in charge of the war economy.

- Speer focused the economy completely on the war effort.
- He improved efficiency and greatly increased weapons production.
- Germany also used raw materials from occupied lands to support its production.

Daily Life in Germany was Affected by the War

Germans had to make sacrifices to help the war effort:

1) Wages were less than they had been before the Nazis took control and working hours increased.
2) Rationing affected people's quality of life. Food and clothes rationing began in 1939, but while Germany was winning the war, most goods could still be bought easily.
   - Rationing meant that some people ate better than they had before the war, though it soon became impossible to eat meat every day.
   - Later in the war, things became harder for ordinary Germans. By 1942, German civilians were living on rations of bread, vegetables and potatoes — these rations decreased as the war progressed (and were much less than British rations).
3) More women and children had to work, especially after 1941 when German forces suffered some heavy defeats in Russia.

Toilet paper and soap became difficult to get hold of too. And to save fuel, the use of warm water was restricted to two times per week. Germans also made use of 'ersatz' (or 'substitute') goods. For example, ersatzkaffee ('substitute coffee') was made from acorns or other types of seed.

By 1944, 50% of the German workforce were women (up from 37% in 1939).

Life under the Nazis got worse — even for Germans...

Explain how the German economy was affected by the outbreak of World War Two. [8]

The Impact of Total War

Food rationing was one thing. But the impact of total war on German civilians went way beyond that.

'Total War' involves Soldiers and Civilians

1) A lot of wars are fought between two armies. The term 'total war', on the other hand, is often used to describe conflicts where all of a country's resources are considered part of the war effort.
2) So a total war is also a battle between countries' economies, their scientists, their industries, and their civilians. World War II is usually considered to have been a total war.

Germans were More Heavily Affected later in the war

1) After some heavy defeats in 1942, Germany prepared itself for total war. In a speech at the Berlin Sportpalast (sports arena) in February 1943, Goebbels stated:

> 'Total war is the demand of the hour... The danger facing us is enormous. The efforts we take to meet it must be just as enormous... We can no longer make only partial and careless use of the war potential at home and in the parts of Europe that we control. We must use our full resources.'

Comment and Analysis

Hitler had hoped that the wars he was starting would be short (quick victories). This would have meant less disruption to normal life.

2) This meant that all of Germany's resources had to be directed to help with the war effort.
   - Non-essential production (production that wasn't vital to the war effort) stopped, and small non-essential businesses closed. Workers were used in war-related industries instead.
   - Civilian clothes and consumer goods were no longer manufactured.
   - Rationing was a fact of life in Germany from the very start of the war (see p.52). Food supplies for ordinary families became much more restricted later on.
   - More women were expected to work or join the army.
   - Eventually, males between the ages of 13 and 60 who weren't already serving in the military had to join the Volkssturm — a part-time defence force (a sort of German 'Dad's Army').

German women never fought on the front line — they took mainly clerical and administrative roles. However, many women did help to operate Germany's anti-aircraft defences and served in signals units on the front line.

Bombings Killed Thousands and left many more Homeless

1) From 1940, Germany rapidly prepared for bombing. Hundreds of community air raid shelters were built.
2) Auxiliary hospitals and emergency first-aid stations were also established to care for civilian injuries.
3) From 1942, the British and American air forces began bombing German cities more heavily. Around half a million German civilians were killed, and many more were made homeless.
4) Germany was later flooded with refugees from other German territories and from cities like Dresden, Berlin and Hamburg, which were all heavily bombed.
5) Germany struggled to deal with the growing number of refugees. There was little help for people displaced by the war — most struggled to find food and shelter.

German cities were attacked using incendiary bombs — these were designed to cause huge fires. Hamburg and Dresden were both fire-bombed.

Dresden, after an Allied air raid in February 1945.

Germany had to throw everything behind the war effort...

Remember, total war wasn't what the Nazis had wanted. They had hoped for short wars and prepared accordingly. But things hadn't gone at all as the Nazis had planned.

Growing Opposition

As the war went on, and especially as things started to go worse for Germany, opposition to Hitler grew.

There were some anti-Nazi Protest Movements

1) The Kreisau Circle was an anti-Nazi movement led by Helmuth von Moltke and Yorck von Wartenburg.
   - The group was against violence, so they didn't actively resist the Nazis. Instead they discussed how to make Germany a better country after the Nazis had fallen. Some members of the Circle tried to inform Allied governments about the dangers and weaknesses of Nazi control.
   - In 1944, members of the Kreisau Circle, including Moltke, were arrested and executed.
2) The Rosenstrasse protest took place in Berlin after the authorities had rounded up some of the last Jewish men left in the city — many of them married to 'Aryan' German women.
   - When the men's wives discovered what had happened, they went to the building in Rosenstrasse ('Rose Street') where their husbands were being held.
   - For several days, the women gathered outside the building and protested. Eventually Goebbels ordered the Jewish men to be released.

Comment and Analysis

This was one of the few successful anti-Nazi public protests. It's thought that the men were released because Goebbels saw it as the simplest way to quickly end the protest without attracting too much attention. He also thought the Jews would soon be killed anyway.

3) Underground networks of communists operated in Germany after 1941. They mostly gathered information about Nazi brutality and distributed leaflets.

Some young people joined the White Rose group

1) The White Rose group (active between 1942 and 1943) was an opposition movement of students and lecturers from Munich University. Among the leaders were brother and sister Hans and Sophie Scholl.
2) Some male members of the group had served in the army and had been horrified by the atrocities carried out by the German army, including the mass killing of Jews.
3) The group used non-violent methods to protest against Nazi discrimination against minorities — they wrote anti-Nazi graffiti and distributed anti-Nazi leaflets to encourage opposition. In 1943, the group organised the first public anti-Nazi demonstration.
4) Many of the group were later arrested by the Gestapo. Several were tortured and executed, including Hans and Sophie Scholl.

Comment and Analysis

At her trial, Sophie Scholl stated that everything she had written in the leaflets was also known by many others, but they didn't dare to say anything about it.

Resistance in the Army grew during the war

1) There had been plots against Hitler by army officers before the war. These became more serious when some became convinced Hitler was going to lead Germany to defeat.
2) One of the most famous army plots was the July plot of 1944. Claus von Stauffenberg (along with other German officers) planned to kill Hitler and install a moderate government, which would include members of the Kreisau Circle.
3) During a meeting, Stauffenberg left a bomb in a briefcase by Hitler's chair. However, someone moved the briefcase. The bomb exploded, but Hitler was unhurt.
4) Most of the plotters were quickly captured and executed.

It wasn't easy to stand against the Nazis...

Describe the increase in opposition faced by the Nazi Party during World War II. [4]

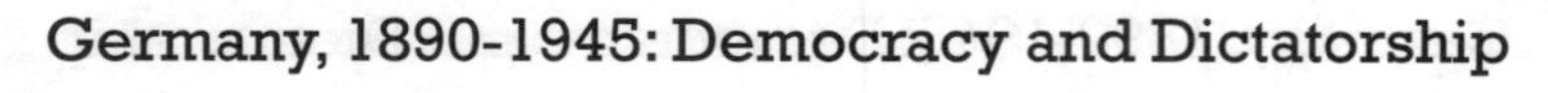

The Holocaust

The Holocaust is the name given to the mass murder of Jews by the Nazis.
The Nazis called their plan to kill Europe's Jews the 'final solution'.

The Final Solution was the Genocide of Europe's Jews

1) Large numbers of German Jews had been sent to concentration camps since the Nazis came to power. After the conquest of countries in western Europe, many more Jews had been deported to camps. When Germany invaded Poland and the Soviet Union, even more Jews fell under Nazi control.
2) The Nazis planned to deport them to a Jewish reservation in German-occupied Poland — but the idea was dropped because the area couldn't possibly hold all of Europe's Jews. Instead Jews were to be killed. This was described as the 'final solution to the Jewish question.'
3) As a temporary measure, the Nazis created ghettos — small areas of towns and cities where Jews were to be gathered together, away from the rest of the population.
4) Conditions in the ghettos were terrible. Many people died of disease or starved. Some were used for slave labour, e.g. in weapons factories.
5) After the Nazis invaded the Soviet Union, Einsatzgruppen followed the German army. These were units of SS soldiers whose job was to murder 'enemies' of the Nazi state in occupied eastern Europe. They were a key part of the final solution and killed in huge numbers, especially in Poland and the Soviet Union.

The largest ghetto was in Warsaw. In this picture, Jewish police are separating different members of the population.

Death Camps were built to Kill People on an Industrial Scale

1) To slaughter on the scale the Nazis required, death camps were built in Eastern Europe. Heinrich Himmler, head of the SS, was in overall charge of this operation.
2) The camps included gas chambers to carry out the mass murder, and crematoria to burn the bodies.
3) The plan was to kill around 11 million people — all of the Jews living in Nazi-controlled territory.
4) People were transported to the camps from all over Nazi-occupied Europe. They could take luggage and even paid for their own train tickets — the Nazis wanted to hide their intentions to prevent panic.
5) Mainly Jewish people were killed, but other groups were targeted as well, for example Slavs (e.g. Russians and Poles), Romani, black people, homosexuals, disabled people and communists.

It's Hard to understand How this Mass Murder happened

1) By the end of the war, the Nazis had killed approximately 6 million Jews and countless other people.
2) Before the war ended, orders went out to destroy the camps — but there wasn't time.
3) After the war, people around the world found it hard to believe that this inhuman, cold-blooded extermination had taken place, and that so many soldiers were involved. It has been argued that they might have gone along with the Nazi leadership for various reasons:
   - The Nazi guards felt they had to 'do their duty' and obey orders. They might have feared their leaders, or just felt that obeying orders was the right thing to do.
   - Jews may not have been regarded as fully human — so killing them didn't matter to guards.

Comment and Analysis

The world only discovered the horror of the death camps as the Allies advanced in 1945. Some historians claim there's evidence leaders like Churchill were told about the camps — but didn't believe the facts.

The Final Solution — the ultimate madness...

What was the most vital factor in the decision to kill Europe's Jews rather than segregate them?
a) Nazi racial policy b) the size of Europe's Jewish population [12]

Revision Summary

Well, that's Germany done and dusted — now have a crack at a revision summary to see how much stuck.

- Try these questions and tick off each one when you get it right.
- When you've done all the questions for a topic and are completely happy with it, tick off the topic.

Germany and the Growth of Democracy (p.31-39) ☑

1) Describe how the government of the German Empire was structured under Kaiser Wilhelm. ☑
2) Why did the Kaiser face difficulties ruling Germany between 1890 and 1914? ☑
3) Describe the events of the German Revolution in 1918. ☑
4) Name the three separate bodies of the Weimar government and describe what each one did. ☑
5) Give five terms from the Treaty of Versailles and explain why they were unpopular in Germany. ☑
6) Give two examples of unrest that occurred under the Weimar Republic between 1919 and 1922. ☑
7) What was the Munich Putsch? Why did it fail? ☑
8) How did Gustav Stresemann try to build better international relationships? ☑
9) How did life improve for the working classes and women under the Weimar Republic? ☑

Germany and the Depression (p.40-43) ☑

10) What was the Great Depression? ☑
11) Describe the trends in federal election results in Germany between 1928 and 1932. ☑
12) Give three examples of social groups that were particularly drawn to the Nazis and explain why. ☑
13) Describe how Hitler rose to the position of Chancellor. ☑
14) What was the Enabling Act? When was it introduced? ☑
15) What happened on the 'Night of the Long Knives'? ☑

The Experiences of Germans under the Nazis (p.44-55) ☑

16) Describe three powers the Nazis had that suggested Germany had become a police state by 1934. ☑
17) What were the aims of Nazi propaganda? ☑
18) What was the Reich Church? ☑
19) Name two members of the Church who opposed the Nazis. ☑
20) What expectations did the Nazi Party have of women? ☑
21) Describe one way in which daily life was affected by Nazi rule before the outbreak of war. ☑
22) How was education in Germany affected while the Nazis were in power? ☑
23) What were the Nuremberg Laws? Why were they important? ☑
24) Describe the events of Kristallnacht. ☑
25) What changes were made to the Nazi economy after the outbreak of World War Two? ☑
26) What is 'total war'? How did it affect German civilians? ☑
27) Who was Claus von Stauffenberg? What did he do to oppose Nazi rule? ☑
28) What is a ghetto? Describe the role of ghettos in the Holocaust. ☑
29) What was the role of Einsatzgruppen? ☑
30) Name four groups of people who were targeted for execution in the Nazi death camps. ☑

Exam Skills for the Depth Studies

These pages are about the wider world depth study and the British depth study sections of your exam.

Depth studies are about knowing a Short Period in Detail

1) The depth studies cover a short period of history (less than 100 years) in detail. They focus on understanding how the main features and events of the period affected one another.
2) You'll need to have a detailed knowledge of the period — this means knowing the main developments and important events that took place. It also means understanding how important features of the periods (e.g. political, social, economic, religious and military issues) helped to shape events.
3) You should know the causes and consequences of main events really well.

There are Two different Depth Studies

The Wider World depth study has Four basic types of exam questions

1) The first question will ask you to evaluate what a visual or written source is saying.

   Source A supports Britain. How do you know? Explain your answer by using Source A and your contextual knowledge. [4 marks]

2) The second question involves two more sources. You'll have to explain how useful each source is.

   How useful are Sources B and C to a historian studying attitudes towards the League of Nations? [12 marks]

3) The next question will ask you to write a narrative account of an event or development that took place during the period you've studied. It might focus on its causes or consequences.

   Write an account of how events in Abyssinia escalated between 1935 and 1936. [8 marks]

4) The final question will give you a statement about a feature of your period and ask you how far you agree with what it says.

   'Poor organisation was the main reason for the collapse of the League of Nations by 1939.' How far do you agree with this statement? Explain your answer. [20 marks]

   This question has 4 marks for spelling, punctuation and grammar (see p.137).

The British depth study has Three basic types of exam questions

1) One question will give you a written or visual interpretation, and ask you to think about how well it shows something — this could be an important event or development, or a certain group or individual.

   How convincing is Interpretation C about the treatment of the poor in Elizabethan England? Explain your answer. [8 marks]

2) The next question will ask you to explain something about a feature of the period you've studied. It could focus on its importance, its consequences or how it changed over time.

   Explain what was important about the Catholic plots against Elizabeth during her reign. [8 marks]

3) You'll also be asked to write a narrative account of a feature of your period. You might need to analyse its impact, its causes or look at how it developed.

   Write an account of the reasons why England and Spain went to war in 1585. [8 marks]

Exam Skills for the Depth Studies

Here's a bit more advice and a sample answer to a question from the depth study sections of your exam.

You'll need these Skills to answer the questions

1) When you're working with sources, it's not just a case of describing what you see or read. You need to analyse the source and draw conclusions from it — what is it trying to tell you?
2) To evaluate interpretations, you need to figure out what the author's saying by looking at the information they give. If the interpretation is visual, think about what's happening in the picture and what emotions are shown. Use your own knowledge to decide whether the interpretation is missing out any important details about the event, person or people it's describing.
3) Include specific information to show you have a good knowledge of the periods you've studied.
4) In the narrative account questions, don't just describe what happened — analyse every event that you talk about. Think about the impact that it had and show how different events were related.
5) When you're asked how far you agree with something, decide your opinion before you start writing and state it clearly at the beginning and end of your answer. Don't forget to include different sides of the argument, even if you don't agree with them — this shows that you've considered all of the evidence.

For some more general advice on answering exam questions, see p.136.

Here's a Sample Answer to help you

This sample answer will give you an idea of how to write a narrative account.
This question type comes up in both depth studies, so it's worth knowing how to answer it properly.

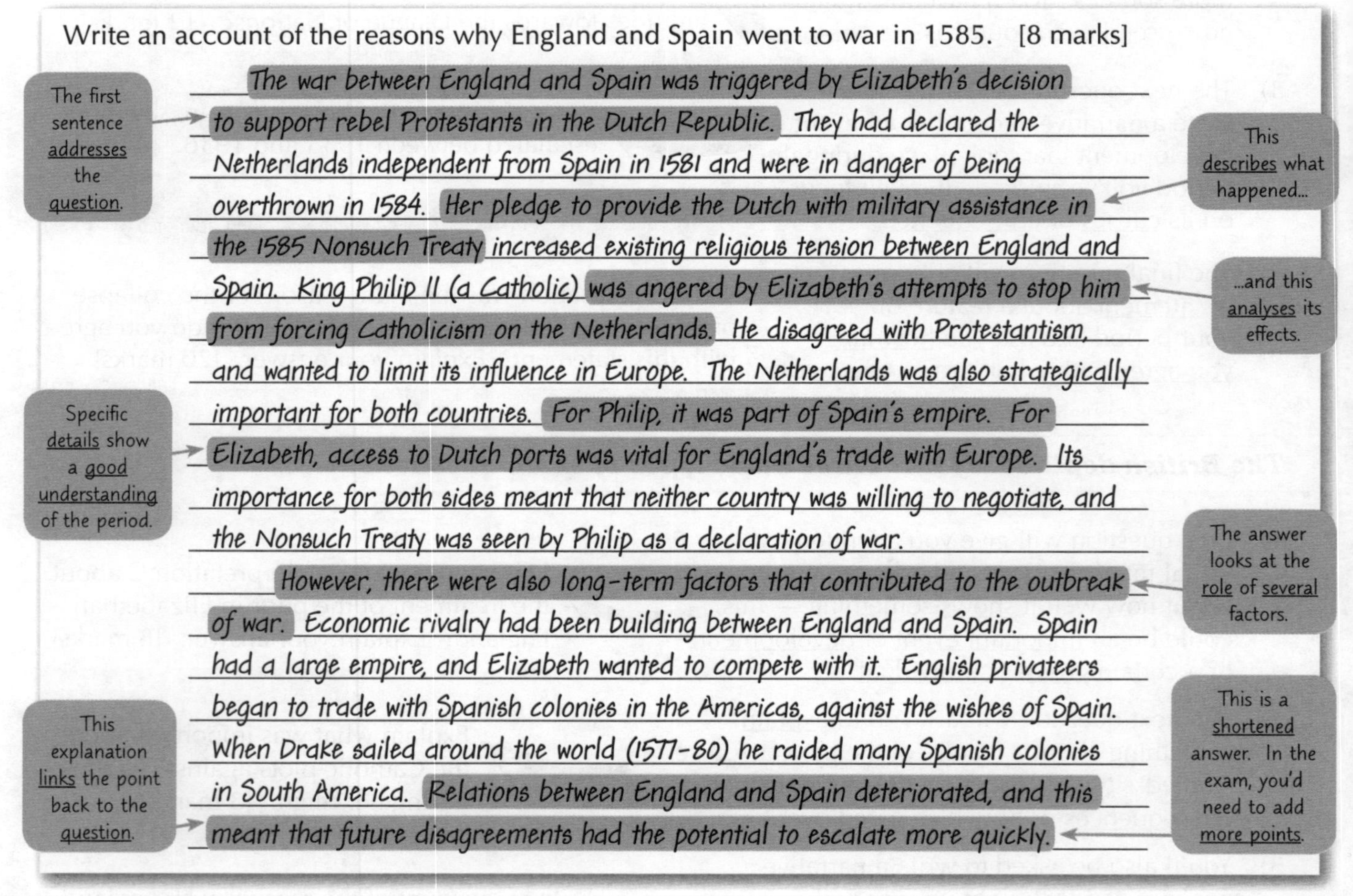

Write an account of the reasons why England and Spain went to war in 1585. [8 marks]

The war between England and Spain was triggered by Elizabeth's decision to support rebel Protestants in the Dutch Republic. They had declared the Netherlands independent from Spain in 1581 and were in danger of being overthrown in 1584. Her pledge to provide the Dutch with military assistance in the 1585 Nonsuch Treaty increased existing religious tension between England and Spain. King Philip II (a Catholic) was angered by Elizabeth's attempts to stop him from forcing Catholicism on the Netherlands. He disagreed with Protestantism, and wanted to limit its influence in Europe. The Netherlands was also strategically important for both countries. For Philip, it was part of Spain's empire. For Elizabeth, access to Dutch ports was vital for England's trade with Europe. Its importance for both sides meant that neither country was willing to negotiate, and the Nonsuch Treaty was seen by Philip as a declaration of war.

However, there were also long-term factors that contributed to the outbreak of war. Economic rivalry had been building between England and Spain. Spain had a large empire, and Elizabeth wanted to compete with it. English privateers began to trade with Spanish colonies in the Americas, against the wishes of Spain. When Drake sailed around the world (1577-80) he raided many Spanish colonies in South America. Relations between England and Spain deteriorated, and this meant that future disagreements had the potential to escalate more quickly.

These depth studies really get to the bottom of things...

The wider world depth study and British depth study are examined on separate papers, so make sure you revise the right one for the right exam. Don't forget about the historic environment, too — see p.104-106.

Peacemaking After the First World War

World War I started in 1914 and fighting ended with the armistice on November 11th 1918. The winners (Britain, France and the USA — known as the Allies) then had to agree a peace treaty with the losers.

The Allies and the Germans wanted Peace

1) As a result of the war, millions of people were dead or injured. Countries like Belgium and France were devastated by the fighting.
2) Both sides had spent a lot of money on the war.
3) The Allies knew that the German army was beaten and retreating.
4) Germany was in political chaos. Their troops were losing morale, and when sailors in the German navy mutinied on 3rd November 1918, it triggered a series of revolts across the country. There was a lot of uncertainty about how Germany would be governed — continuing the war was the last thing Germany needed.
5) Germany decided to ask for an armistice — an agreement to stop fighting for a period of time, often so that a more permanent peace can be negotiated. The Allies decided to allow it.

Comment and Analysis

The Allies could have rejected the request for an armistice, and forced the German army all the way back into central Germany, but it would have been difficult and costly. Supplying the Allied armies would also have been challenging, since so many roads and railways had been destroyed.

Wilson suggested Fourteen Points to ensure Peace

1) Woodrow Wilson was the President of the United States.
2) President Wilson had come up with his Fourteen Points in January 1918, when the Germans had first asked for a truce. Germany rejected them then, but they had changed their minds by November. Germany now wanted the armistice to be based on the Fourteen Points.

Wilson's Fourteen Points

1) No secret treaties
2) Free access to the sea for all
3) Free trade between countries
4) Disarmament by all countries
5) Colonies to have a say in their own future
6) Russia to be free of German troops
7) Belgium to be independent
8) Alsace-Lorraine to go to France
9) New frontier between Austria & Italy
10) Self-determination for people of Eastern Europe
11) Serbia to have access to the sea
12) Self-determination for people in Turkish Empire
13) Poland to be independent with access to the sea
14) League of Nations to settle disputes

(Point 1) A system of alliances between countries had been an important cause of the First World War.

(Point 4) Wilson wanted countries to disarm to the lowest possible level without risking their 'domestic safety'. There was no clear idea of how this could be measured, and it was unlikely in a time of war. This is one of the reasons that Wilson has been accused of being too idealistic.

(Point 8) Alsace-Lorraine was a region that had repeatedly changed hands between France and Germany.

(Point 10) Self-determination is the right for a nation to govern itself. This idea was very unpopular with countries like Britain, which had huge empires, and it became very difficult when put into practice (p.63).

(Point 14) Wilson had a vision for peace based on discussion rather than military action. The League of Nations was to become very important between the two world wars.

3) Wilson's main aim was to stop war from happening again. He wanted disagreements between countries to be settled by discussion rather than by force. He didn't want to be too harsh on Germany.

> 'We have no jealousy of German greatness, and there is nothing in this program that impairs it... We do not wish to injure her or to block in any way her legitimate influence or power... We wish her only to accept a place of equality among the peoples of the world — the new world in which we now live — instead of a place of mastery.'
> *Woodrow Wilson, January 1918*

Remember that Wilson was in a different position...

The United States had come into the war late, and hadn't been devastated by the war in the same way as France and Britain had. This made Wilson far more idealistic about peace.

The 1918 Armistice

Unfortunately for Wilson, Clemenceau and Lloyd George didn't like a lot of his Fourteen Points.

Lloyd George and Clemenceau had Different Ideas

Like Wilson, David Lloyd George (the British Prime Minister) and Georges Clemenceau (the French Prime Minister) also wanted to prevent a similar war from happening again. However, they disagreed about how to do this.

Clemenceau wanted Germany to be punished...

- France borders Germany. Clemenceau wanted the German army to be weakened so that it couldn't pose a threat to France.
- Clemenceau didn't support Wilson's Fourteen Points. For example, he wanted to keep his treaties with other nations, because he felt they protected France. He wanted to keep a naval blockade on Germany so he could control it.
- But he liked Wilson's idea that Alsace-Lorraine should be given to France — it would act as a barrier between the countries.

Lloyd George, Clemenceau and Wilson.

...and so did Lloyd George, but not as strongly

- Lloyd George didn't like Wilson's ideas of self-determination and colonial freedom — this would be a threat to Britain's empire.
- He wanted Germany to be punished, but not too harshly. Germany was also an important trading partner for Britain, so a very weak German economy could cause problems.
- Lloyd George also wanted to continue blockading Germany and to make private deals between nations.

Comment and Analysis

The French had suffered terribly during the war, and the British had also suffered badly. This helps to explain why they were more keen than the USA to punish Germany.

The Armistice was a Compromise for Everybody

1) Germany had hoped to negotiate. They had contacted President Wilson first, because of his Fourteen Points. But the final armistice terms didn't reflect them much at all — they were very strict on Germany.
2) The Kaiser abdicated on the 9th of November 1918. At this point, the German politicians sent to sign the treaty had to accept whatever terms were offered to them. This signing took place on the 11th of November. The armistice was in force for thirty days, but it was continually renewed until the Treaty of Versailles in 1919 (see p.61). The Allied leaders' aims were achieved to different extents:

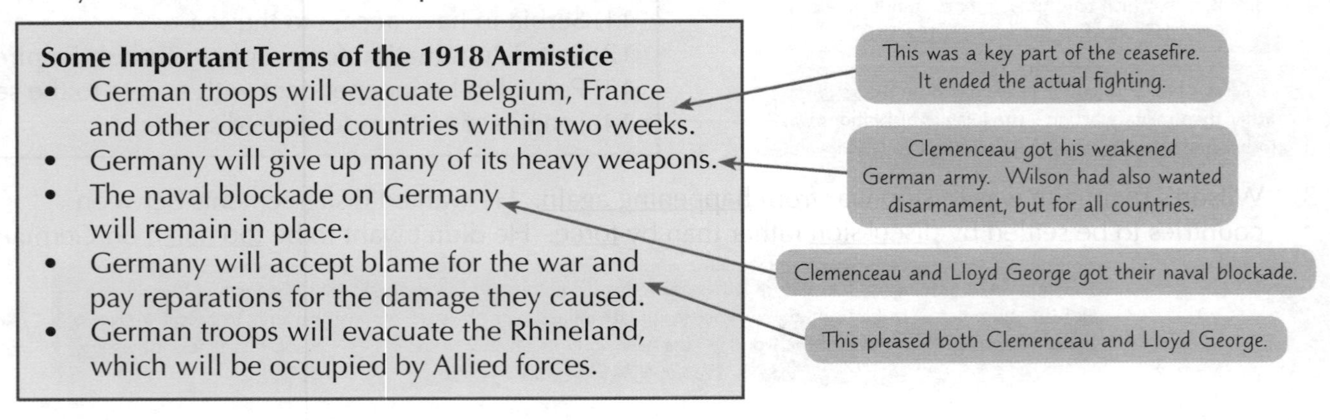

Some Important Terms of the 1918 Armistice

- German troops will evacuate Belgium, France and other occupied countries within two weeks.
- Germany will give up many of its heavy weapons.
- The naval blockade on Germany will remain in place.
- Germany will accept blame for the war and pay reparations for the damage they caused.
- German troops will evacuate the Rhineland, which will be occupied by Allied forces.

Think about the roles of the individual leaders...

EXAM QUESTION

Describe how the aims of Woodrow Wilson, Lloyd George and Clemenceau were different regarding the terms of the 1918 armistice. [8]

The Versailles Settlement

After the armistice was signed, negotiations could get underway for an official, lasting peace treaty.

The Peace Talks took place in Paris

1) Talks to replace the temporary armistice with a permanent peace treaty took place at the Versailles Palace, near Paris. These talks are known as the Paris Peace Conference. They began in January 1919.
2) Germany and Austria-Hungary (the losing nations) weren't invited.
3) There were delegates from about 30 countries at the Conference. However, it was dominated by the 'Big Three' — the leaders of Britain, France and the United States. (Italy was also an important member, but wasn't as powerful.)
4) These powerful men arrived with different aims, carried forward from the armistice. No-one wanted another war, but they couldn't agree on how to achieve this. Their disagreements meant that the talks lasted six months.

The Big Three had different priorities

Clemenceau — punish Germany (make them take the blame and weaken their economy and military)
Lloyd George — punish Germany, but not too harshly, and increase the power of the British Empire
Wilson — self-determination, disarmament and a League of Nations to ensure lasting peace in Europe

5) The final agreement was called the Treaty of Versailles. It was signed in June 1919. This treaty only dealt with Germany. Other defeated countries made separate treaties (p.65).

The Treaty of Versailles is also known as the 'Versailles Settlement'.

A lot of Land Changed Hands as a Result of the Treaty of Versailles

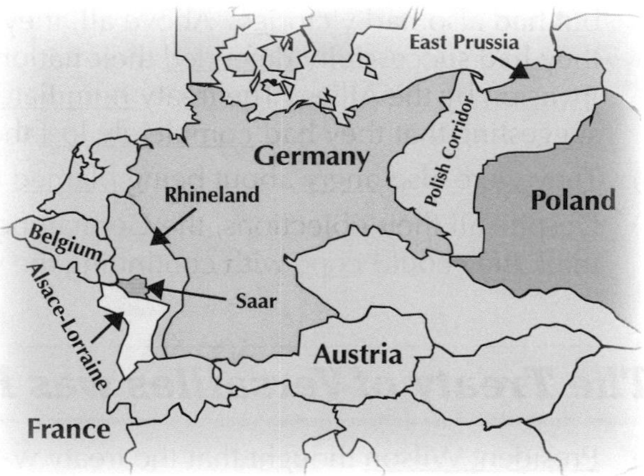

1) Germany had lost Alsace-Lorraine, a large piece of land to the west of Germany, as a result of the armistice. This was made permanent.
2) The Rhineland remained part of Germany, but it was demilitarised — Germany wasn't allowed to have troops there, as it bordered France and Belgium. This was aimed at decreasing Germany's ability to threaten those countries.
3) Parts of Poland had been seized by other countries before and during the war. The treaty rebuilt Poland as an independent country. Germany had to give up all of its territory in Poland.
4) Also, to give Poland free access to the sea (in line with one of Wilson's Fourteen Points), it was given a strip of land that became known as the 'Polish Corridor'. This divided the main part of Germany from East Prussia (its province in the east).
5) The Saar, a region of Germany with valuable coalfields, was taken from Germany for fifteen years, to be governed by the new League of Nations (p.66). Residents would then be allowed to vote on which country they wanted to belong to.
6) The city of Danzig was also to be put under the control of the League of Nations.

Comment and Analysis

Taking the Saar away from Germany was partly an act of French revenge, since so many of their coal mines were destroyed in the war.

Germany was being sliced up bit by bit...

Write a paragraph about the land that Germany lost as a result of the Treaty of Versailles. Then find a map of Europe and roughly mark these areas.

REVISION TASK

Reactions to the Versailles Settlement

Alongside Germany's land losses, there was a lot of resentment towards the treaty's other terms.

The Terms of the Treaty were Tough on Germany

1) Under Article 231 of the Versailles settlement, Germany had to accept blame for the war. This was known as the War-Guilt Clause.
2) The amount of reparations Germany was going to have to pay was vast — £6600 million. The amount was decided in 1921 but was changed later.
3) Germany's military was cut down severely. Only volunteers were allowed — a total of 100,000 men. It could have six warships, but couldn't have any armoured vehicles, aircraft or submarines.
4) Germany's empire was taken away — now the areas that it used to control would be handed over to the League of Nations.
5) The League was set up to keep world peace. At first, Germany wasn't allowed to join the League.

Remember that these terms went alongside a lot of lost territory (p.61). This would also harm Germany's economy, e.g. through reducing its access to raw materials.

The German People were Angered and Humiliated by the treaty

1) German politicians had hoped for a fair treaty based on Wilson's Fourteen Points. They were shocked by what they were asked to sign.
2) There was a mass protest outside the German parliament building (the Reichstag) in 1919.
3) In Germany, the treaty was often referred to as a 'Diktat' — a harsh settlement imposed on one country by another.
4) The Germans believed in the heroism of their troops, and didn't believe that they'd been properly defeated on the field of battle. They had suffered great losses, but had also had victories. Above all, they felt they had successfully defended their nation from invasion by the Allies. The treaty humiliated them by suggesting that they had completely lost the war.
5) They were also angry about being blamed for the war, making Article 231 extremely hard to accept.
6) Despite all their objections, the German politicians had little choice but to sign the treaty. They didn't think they could cope with continuing the war, and that even to try would risk an invasion of Germany.

Comment and Analysis

Rumours in Germany at the time claimed that the efforts of their troops had been ruined by German traitors. Pacifists, Jews and those involved in the revolts were all blamed. This kind of finger-pointing was later used and exaggerated by Hitler during his rise to power.

The Treaty of Versailles was Rejected by the US Senate

1) President Wilson thought that the treaty was far too harsh, and would risk further war.
2) He did get his League of Nations, but he faced opposition to it back home. Many politicians in the US Senate (the part of the US Government responsible for agreeing to treaties) objected to the League. They were worried it might force the USA to become involved in future wars, and end up being able to control the US military.
3) The US Senate refused to sign the Treaty of Versailles. They signed their own peace treaty with Germany in August 1921.

Comment and Analysis

Russia wasn't allowed to join the League. This left just Britain and France making sure the treaty was enforced. Some historians argue that splits between the winning powers after the war caused more problems in the long-term than the actual terms of the treaty.

No-one on this page is particularly happy about the treaty...

EXAM TIP

In the exam, don't just list the terms of the Treaty of Versailles. You need to analyse them, thinking about why they were included and how the reactions to them differed between countries.

Reactions to the Versailles Settlement

France and Great Britain also had problems with the terms of the treaty, though for quite different reasons.

Lloyd George was Worried that the treaty was Too Harsh...

1) Lloyd George was pleased that Britain had been given some German colonies. This expanded the British Empire, which would enhance Britain's trade, resources and military power.
2) The reduction in the size of the German navy was also important for Britain's power at sea.
3) But, like Wilson, Lloyd George thought that the treaty had been too harsh on Germany. He had suggested more lenient terms, such as allowing Germany to join the League of Nations. Lloyd George worried about the strictness of the treaty because:
   - Too much resentment in Germany could eventually lead to a future war.
   - Britain's trade would suffer if Germany was too weak.
   - If the German people became too disillusioned with their government, this might lead to a communist revolution (as had happened in Russia in 1917).
4) However, the British public wanted revenge on Germany — in this way, the treaty satisfied Britain.

'We shall have to fight another war all over again in 25 years time, at three times the cost.'
David Lloyd George, 1919

Lloyd George was thinking about how to create a peace that would last, rather than just about how to make Germany pay for the war. His fears that treating Germany too harshly would lead to another war turned out to be very valid.

Comment and Analysis

Lloyd George had to show that he represented public opinion, or risk losing political support at home. He needed to make sure that Germany was punished.

...but Clemenceau thought Germany Wasn't Weak Enough

1) Clemenceau's strict ideas about punishing Germany were shared by the French public. They were pleased that Germany was forced to take the blame for the war.
2) Reducing Germany's armed forces and demilitarising the Rhineland also gave France more security.
3) However, Clemenceau wanted the reparations to be even higher. He wanted Germany to be paying them back forever.

The French had seen a lot of their country destroyed by warfare.

Creating New Countries was Problematic

The key on this map shows which empires the new countries used to belong to.

1) Wilson's Fourteen Points included the right to self-determination — the right for people of different national or ethnic groups to rule themselves independently.
2) This was reflected in Versailles and other post-war treaties (p.65). Several new countries were created and given the right to self-determination.

In 1918 there had been uprisings across eastern Europe, with different national or ethnic groups (e.g. Poles, Austrians) demanding independence from large empires like Austria-Hungary. Making new countries was a way for the winning powers to solve these disputes and weaken the defeated nations (by taking bits of their land) at the same time.

3) However, these new countries were potentially unstable because many people from different national or ethnic groups were thrown together. These people had different cultures from one another and had different allegiances and resentments after the war.
4) This made self-determination difficult. The countries also started wars with one another for more land.

Lloyd George — a man who could predict the future...

Describe how David Lloyd George and Georges Clemenceau's reactions to the Treaty of Versailles were different. [8]

EXAM QUESTION

Reactions to the Versailles Settlement

Historians are still disagreeing about whether or not the treaty was the best one that could have been achieved. There might be different answers to this question today than there were at the time.

There is Debate about whether the Treaty was Fair and Sensible

You could argue that the treaty was fair and sensible...

1) Some people thought the treaty was fair because the war had caused so much death and damage. They believed that Germany was responsible for this, so it should pay for the war and take the blame.
2) The treaty that Germany had forced on Russia in 1918 was a lot harsher. For example, it took over a third of Russia's population — the Treaty of Versailles only took 12.5% of Germany's population.
3) The reparations were high, but they were only 2% of Germany's annual income.

This 1919 cartoon from a German satirical magazine shows how the Treaty of Versailles was seen in Germany — there would be no more sun for Germany.

The treaty can also be seen as unfair and unwise...

1) John Maynard Keynes, a British economist who attended the peace talks, believed the treaty was very unwise. He predicted that the restrictions and reparations imposed on Germany would contribute to an economic collapse in the country, which would damage the rest of Europe. (He was right.)
2) Some historians say that it wasn't sensible to exclude Germany, or powerful countries like Russia, from the talks, and that it'd be hard to keep the peace without them in the League of Nations.

'I believe that the campaign for securing out of Germany the general costs of the war was one of the most serious acts of political unwisdom for which our statesmen have ever been responsible.'
John Maynard Keynes, 1920

In hindsight, the treaty had a damaging long-term impact. The resentment felt in Germany stirred up hatred towards the winning countries, which Hitler used to gain popularity. He promised the German people revenge on those who had betrayed them in 1919 — the Treaty of Versailles is often seen as an important cause of the Second World War.

Comment and Analysis

Whether the treaty was actually fair or not, the important thing is that the German people strongly believed that it wasn't.

Gilbert White, an American peace conference delegate, wasn't surprised that the treaty turned out to be flawed. He was amazed that the Big Three had managed to make a peace treaty at all, given all of the issues they faced.

It Might have been the Best solution At The Time

1) The winning powers all had different aims, which made negotiations long and difficult. The treaty would always have to be a compromise.
2) The leaders were under a huge amount of pressure from their home nations. They had to make popular choices at the peace talks to maintain their political support. They were also trying to stabilise their countries, for example by resettling returning soldiers and rebuilding their economies.
3) There was also a lot of time pressure. Parts of Europe were now divided and ungoverned, with many new countries being formed and empires breaking apart. The leaders wanted to act quickly to stabilise Europe (partly because they didn't want communists to get involved).
4) People at the time just didn't know what we know now — e.g. the horrors that the rise of Hitler and the Second World War would bring. If they had known, they might have made different decisions.

Think about both sides of the argument...

Divide a piece of paper in half, then write why some people thought the treaty was fair on one side, and why some said it was too harsh on the other. List as many points as you can for each.

Other Treaties After the First World War

The Treaty of Versailles only dealt with Germany — separate treaties were made with other losing nations after the First World War. They largely followed the same pattern of taking away land and reducing the military.

Four more Treaties at the end of the war Caused Trouble

Treaty	Dealt With	Main Points
St. Germain 1919	**Austria**	Separated Austria from Hungary. Stopped Austria joining with Germany. Took land away, e.g. Bosnia. Made Austria limit its army. Created new countries (see p.63).
Trianon 1920	**Hungary**	Took land away, e.g. Croatia. Made Hungary reduce its army. Created new countries (see p.63).
Neuilly 1919	**Bulgaria**	Took away some land. Denied access to the sea. Made Bulgaria reduce its army.
Sèvres 1920	**Turkey**	Lost land — part of Turkey became new mandates, e.g. Syria. Turkey lost control of the Black Sea.

1) New countries like Czechoslovakia and Yugoslavia were formed out of Austria-Hungary.
2) Austria and Hungary's separation was important — and the fact that Austria wasn't allowed to join with Germany. Both Austria and Hungary suffered badly after the war.
3) The Turks hated Sèvres. Turkish nationalists like Mustafa Kemal resisted the treaty and forced some later changes at the Treaty of Lausanne in 1923. This reduced the amount of territory to be lost by Turkey and stopped all of its reparations payments.
4) The Arabs who fought alongside the Allies didn't gain as much as they'd hoped.

The Treaties had Similar Results

1) All the defeated countries lost land and had to disarm.
2) They were all punished, following the pattern of Versailles.
3) Versailles, St. Germain and Trianon were the harshest treaties — Germany, Austria and Hungary lost valuable industrial land. Bulgaria wasn't so badly treated because it hadn't played such a big part in the war.
4) Countries which were created or increased in size because of the treaties — like Czechoslovakia, Yugoslavia and Poland — were now governing people of many different nationalities.
5) Czechoslovakia, for example, had Germans, Slovaks, Hungarians, Poles, Ukrainians, and over 6 million Czechs. It would be difficult for people to work and live together when they spoke different languages and had different cultures.

Comment and Analysis

A lot of the consequences of these treaties would be long-term. For example, unstable new countries like Czechoslovakia and Poland would be easier targets for Hitler when he started expanding German territory in the 1930s (see p.75-80).

See p.63 for more on the problems these new countries faced.

Don't ignore these other treaties in the exam...

If you get a question that asks you to write about peacemaking after the First World War, don't forget to include these other treaties. Learn the details, and their effects.

Forming the League of Nations

The League of Nations came from Wilson's Fourteen Points. Lots of people admired its moral principles.

The League had Two Main Aims

1) **To maintain peace** — using three different methods:
   - Disarmament involved reducing the number of weapons that each country had.
   - Arbitration meant helping countries to talk about their disputes rather than fight.
   - Collective security meant that if one country attacked another, League members would act together to control the aggressor.
2) **To encourage cooperation** — and help solve economic and social problems, such as disease, slavery, and poor working and living conditions.

The League was made up of Various Parts

All the members of the League followed a Covenant (agreement) of 26 Articles (rules).
Articles 1 to 7 set up the structure of the League:

The Assembly
The Assembly met once a year. Every country in the League had one vote at the Assembly. Decisions could only be made if everyone agreed on them.

The International Labour Organisation
This part of the League discussed and made suggestions to improve working conditions. It was made up of government officials, employers and workers from different countries.

The Council
The Council met at least four times a year. It had permanent members (Britain, France, Italy, Japan and later Germany) and temporary members. All members had a vote, but permanent members could veto Council decisions.

The Permanent Court of International Justice
This was made up of fifteen judges from different member countries. They were asked to settle international disputes.

Everyone hoped this would avoid another major war.

The Secretariat
Carried out the work of the League, like a civil service.

1) 42 countries joined the League at the start. In the 1930s, about 60 countries were members. This made the League seem strong.
2) The League also had a range of agencies and commissions, which worked on specific humanitarian issues. These included a health organisation, a commission for refugees, and a commission for women's rights. These commissions did some valuable work (see p.68).

The League was intended to Police The World

1) The Covenant set out the moral guidelines for keeping peace that all members were supposed to follow. If this moral guidance wasn't enough, then the Permanent Court of International Justice (PCIJ) could:
   1) Decide which country was in the right.
   2) Tell a country it was doing wrong.
   3) Impose sanctions on an offending country.
2) The PCIJ could apply economic sanctions (penalties designed to damage the economies of misbehaving countries), then if necessary use military sanctions and send troops in.

The League didn't have its own army (see p.67), but it was hoped that collective security would mean it wouldn't need one. Collective security means that an attack against one country is seen as an attack against all — the armies of member nations would be used against aggressors.

The aims of the League of Nations are very important...

Divide a piece of paper in half, and write one aim of the League in each half. Below that, see if you can remember how the League intended to achieve the aim. (You'll need this again on p.73.)

REVISION TASK

The Weaknesses of the League of Nations

From the start, the League of Nations had some real problems.

The League had some Membership Problems

This British cartoon from 1919 shows the USA refusing to join the League, even though it's the 'keystone' of the organisation. The importance of the USA's refusal to join was recognised even at this early stage.

1) The United States didn't join the League of Nations. Wilson was very ill by this time, and the Senate rejected it:
   - The Senate disagreed with the Treaty of Versailles and had refused to sign it. They saw the League of Nations as connected to it.
   - Many thought that all people should live in democracies. They didn't want to be forced into wars to help countries like Britain and France keep undemocratic colonies.
   - Wilson's political enemies wanted to make him unpopular.
   - Many people wanted to keep American troops and money out of Europe, and wanted only to worry about American affairs. This attitude was called isolationism.
2) Germany wasn't allowed to join the League of Nations until 1926. The USSR wasn't allowed to join either, mainly because its communist government worried the other world leaders.
3) This meant that three of the most powerful countries in the world (the USA, Germany and the USSR) weren't involved in the League.

Comment and Analysis

This undermined the League's authority and strength. It also meant that the League didn't have access to the armies of these nations, and had to rely mostly on Britain and France instead — but both had been badly weakened by World War I.

The League Wasn't Powerful Enough

Britain and France were in charge...
...but neither country was strong enough after the war to do the job properly. Also, the fact that these two countries had the most power was unpopular with some countries, who saw the League as an extension of the harsh Treaty of Versailles.

The League could introduce sanctions...
...but these would only work if powerful countries applied them — three of these countries were missing from the League. Most member countries couldn't afford to apply sanctions, especially those still rebuilding after World War I.

The League relied on the armies of member states...
...but members didn't have to commit troops to the League, and most of them didn't want to. This made it difficult for the League to act on its threats.

It was a large organisation...
...but it was also terribly complicated. Everyone had to agree in the Assembly and Council before anything could happen, and the Court of Justice had no powers to make a country act. This made it very hard to get anything done.

It's like someone organising a party and not turning up...

Describe how the membership of the League of Nations affected its ability to achieve its aims. [8]

The Work of the League in the 1920s

Despite the problems with its membership and organisation, the League did have some success in the 1920s. It did some valuable humanitarian work, and managed to settle several territorial disputes.

The League made a Valuable Contribution to Social Issues

The League used its special agencies and commissions to achieve its aim of encouraging cooperation in solving economic and social problems. These bodies successfully improved the lives of many Europeans in the 1920s.

One commission helped refugees after the First World War. Millions of people had fled their homes during the fighting, and the League helped to resettle them. They also sent over 500,000 prisoners of war back home.

The Slavery Commission didn't wipe out slavery altogether, but it had success in many countries, e.g. it freed 200,000 slaves in places like Burma and Sierra Leone.

The health organisation worked to combat the spread of serious diseases such as leprosy, malaria and plague.

The International Labour Organisation also had lots of success, such as persuading member countries to introduce minimum wages, and limits on weekly working hours.

The League Resolved some Disputes in the 1920s...

The League resolved several difficult situations over territorial claims without fighting. These successes gave it a good reputation.

1) **UPPER SILESIA** was a region with valuable industry. A referendum was held for citizens to choose whether to be ruled by Poland or Germany, but the result was too close to be decisive. In 1921, the League suggested dividing the area between the two countries, which both sides (and most citizens) accepted.
2) **THE AALAND ISLANDS** sit almost exactly halfway between Sweden and Finland. They belonged to Finland, but most people there wanted to be ruled by Sweden. In 1921, the League decided that the islands should remain Finnish, and both sides accepted this.
3) **BULGARIA** was invaded by Greece in 1925 after border disputes. The League ordered Greece to withdraw, and it obeyed.

Comment and Analysis

None of these disputes threatened world peace, and they didn't involve any very powerful nations. Some historians say this means these successes aren't particularly impressive.

...but it Wasn't As Successful with Others

1) **CORFU,** a Greek island, was occupied by Italy in 1923 in response to an Italian diplomat being shot dead in Greece. At first, the League told Italy to leave and fined the Greeks. Italy ignored this and demanded compensation from Greece. The League changed its mind and agreed that Greece should give money to Italy and apologise. Greece obeyed and Italy then withdrew its troops.
2) **VILNA** was chosen as the capital of the newly-formed Lithuania after the First World War, but most of the population were Polish. Poland seized Vilna and refused to give it up when told to do so by the League. On this occasion, the League was powerless to stop military aggression.
3) **THE RUHR** (an industrial region of Germany) was invaded and occupied by France in 1923 after Germany had failed to keep up its reparation payments. The French began shipping its products back to France. The League of Nations didn't intervene. The USA helped resolve the situation with the Dawes Plan (p.69).

Comment and Analysis

Italy was a permanent member of the Council. The events in Corfu showed that powerful countries were able to ignore the League.

Remember that the League wasn't just for peacekeeping...

One of the League's aims was to encourage cooperation, but this wasn't just about solving arguments between countries. It meant making the world a better place, and they did OK on that.

Other Diplomacy in the 1920s

Countries also started making treaties between themselves in the 1920s, bypassing the League altogether. Either they were learning to get on together peacefully, or maybe they just had no confidence in the League.

Agreements were made in the 1920s...

1) Between 1921 and 1929, the political situation seemed to be improving as countries tried to cooperate.
2) There were many important agreements over arms reduction, borders and economic aid.

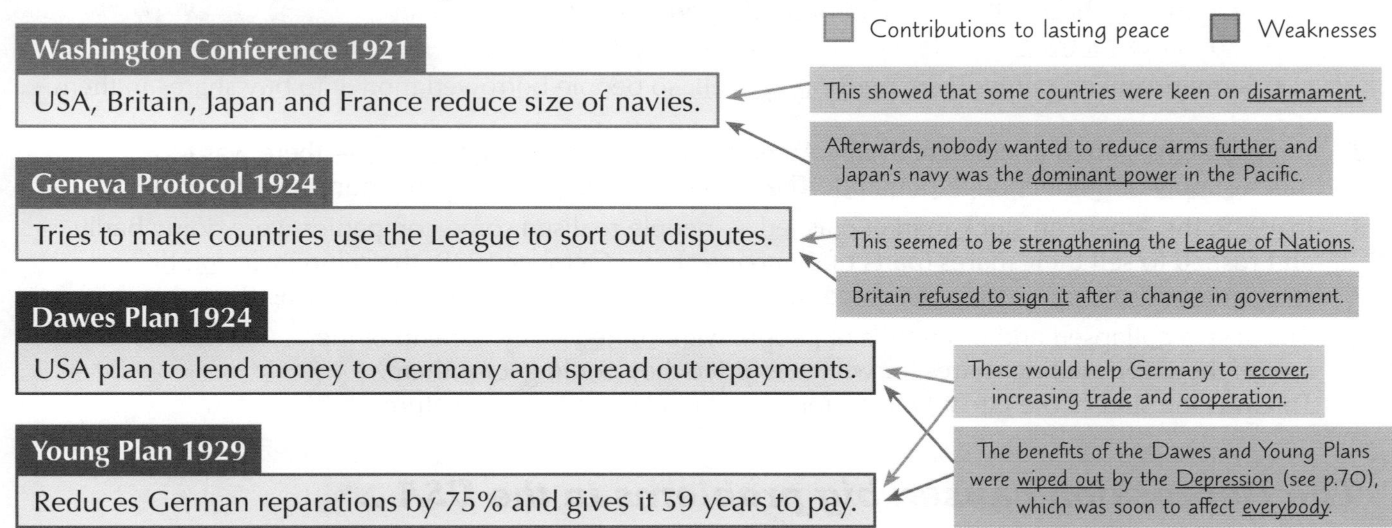

...including the Locarno Treaties and the Kellogg-Briand Pact

Locarno Treaties 1925

Germany's western borders set at Versailles should be permanent.

1) This suggested that Germany was at last prepared to accept the Treaty of Versailles.
2) The treaties were proposed by the German foreign minister, Gustav Stresemann, and signed voluntarily. Germany seemed to be moving on from feelings of resentment and could be treated more like an equal. This was a significant step towards peace.
3) The Locarno treaties also allowed Germany to join the League of Nations in 1926.
4) However, nothing was said about Germany's eastern borders, which worried Czechoslovakia and Poland.

Stresemann wanted Europe to trust Germany again. By pointing out that Germany played an active role in creating the Locarno treaties, Stresemann could show that Germany wanted to create a lasting peace. However, some were still suspicious that the Locarno treaties didn't cover Germany's eastern borders.

Kellogg-Briand Pact 1928

65 nations agree not to use 'aggression' to settle arguments.

1) One weakness of this pact was that it didn't define what 'aggression' actually meant, so countries could claim that they weren't guilty of it. Also, no one knew what would happen if a country broke the Kellogg-Briand Pact.
2) However, it was still one of the most significant steps of the entire decade towards a lasting peace. It showed that countries were truly committed to the idea of preventing future wars.
3) The USA signed it too, despite the isolationism that had kept them out of the League of Nations.

Comment and Analysis

The spirit of the League of Nations was strengthened by these treaties — especially when Germany joined. However, you could also argue that countries began to make agreements separate from the League because they didn't trust it to be effective.

This isn't the same Kellogg who makes the tasty cereals...

Write each treaty's name, date and basic details on a piece of paper, then cut them up so that the three things are separated. Mix up all the pieces and see how fast you can match them again.

REVISION TASK

The Great Depression

One of the things that really undermined the League of Nations was the Great Depression...

The American Stock Market Crashed in 1929

Wall Street is the main financial centre of the US, and is where the biggest stock exchanges are located. So the stock market crash of 1929 is often called the Wall Street Crash.

1) In the 1920s, the USA was the most prosperous country in the world:
   - Wages were high and there was mass production of goods.
   - During this boom, the USA lent billions of dollars to help European countries recover from the effects of the First World War.
   - American companies were performing well, so people borrowed money to buy shares in them.
2) But problems started to emerge. Many American companies overproduced — there was too much supply and not enough demand. There was also competition from countries like Japan.
3) In 1929, the American stock market crashed — people realised some companies were doing badly and rushed to sell their shares (parts of companies). By October 1929, the selling was frantic and share prices dropped — they lost value because no-one wanted to buy them during the panic.
4) Businesses collapsed and thousands of people were ruined — by the end of the month they were selling shares for whatever price they could get for them. This was the start of the Great Depression — a global economic downturn.

The Depression caused big problems in the USA...

1) In 1929, the USA stopped lending money abroad and asked for its loans to be paid back.
2) By 1930, nearly 2000 banks had collapsed as people rushed to withdraw savings.
3) Three years later there were over 12 million people unemployed in the USA.

...and also in Other Industrial Countries

1) Most industrial countries were affected — banks failed, industries struggled and trade ground to a halt. The least affected country was the USSR, which had a communist system.
2) Within three years there were over 2.5 million people unemployed in Britain, and more than 30 million unemployed in the industrial countries of the West.
3) Germany, which had relied on American loans, was particularly affected. German banks failed, exports suffered and unemployment rose to over 6 million by 1932.

Comment and Analysis

The Depression became a global problem because so many economies were linked to the economy in the USA (and to one another).

The Depression made the League's Work more Difficult

1) The Depression caused widespread poverty. In these circumstances, people were more likely to support extreme right-wing leaders, hoping they'd provide strong government. For example, Hitler was elected in Germany in 1933 — he wanted to defy the League of Nations and break the Treaty of Versailles (p.74).
2) Countries like Britain and France were also less willing to help the League by getting involved in resolving international conflicts. They wanted to concentrate on dealing with domestic problems like unemployment.
3) The economic downturn was also a factor in some political conflicts, e.g. the Manchurian Crisis (p.71).

The Nazis were also a nationalist party. Nationalism is the belief that your own country's interests should be prioritised above all others. It's often popular in times of economic crisis.

It's called the Depression — you know it's gonna be bad...

Describe the causes of the Depression in the 1920s and the effects it had on the work of the League of Nations. [8]

The Manchurian Crisis

One of the major crises for the League of Nations in the 1930s took place on the other side of the world.

Japan wanted to Expand its Territory

1) Japanese industries had grown while Europe was busy fighting World War I.
2) When the Depression wrecked Japanese industries, military leaders and business owners in Japan called for military expansion to strengthen the country.

Japanese Aggression led to the Manchurian Crisis

1) Japan had a large army and navy. Since 1905, it had controlled the territory of the South Manchurian Railway.
2) In September 1931, it used a disturbance as an excuse to capture the town of Mukden and send troops to take over the rest of Manchuria.
3) The Japanese pretended to give Manchuria independence. They put a weak leader in charge so they could control him.
4) The League of Nations sent Lord Lytton to assess the situation. He produced a report, which said the Japanese had been wrong, but the League didn't do anything else — it failed to stop Japan and end the crisis.

- Japan refused to accept Lord Lytton's report and withdrew from the League in 1933.
- In 1933, the Japanese invaded China's Jehol Province, which bordered Manchuria.
- Japan signed a treaty with Germany in 1936, and in 1937 started to invade China — again the League did nothing to stop it.

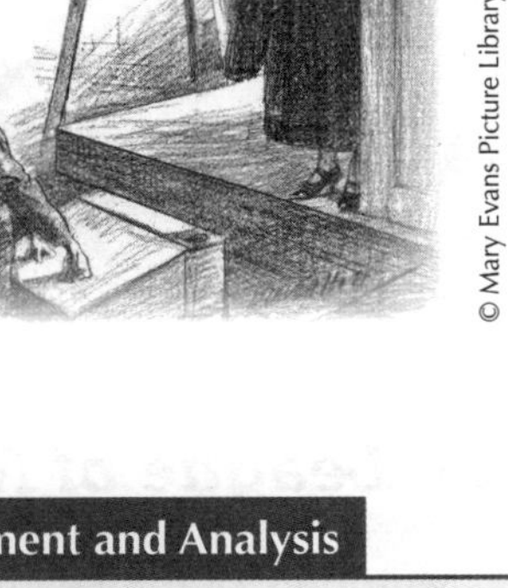

This cartoon from 1932 called 'The Ultimatum' shows Japan being treated like a misbehaving pupil by the League of Nations. The caption shows Japan saying 'If you go on saying I'm naughty, I shall leave the class.'

The League was Weakened

1) Japan was an important trading partner for many countries in the League. This made them reluctant to either put sanctions on Japan, or stop selling them weapons. This suggested that countries wouldn't support the League if it was against their own interests.
2) Countries like France and Britain were also reluctant to commit money and troops to stopping Japan because they were preoccupied with dictators like Hitler closer to home.
3) However, the League's failure to act just showed dictators like Hitler the obvious weakness of the League.

Comment and Analysis

This situation was worsened by the Depression — countries were trying to focus on their own economies.

In the first major challenge for the League, everyone saw it fail to confront Japanese aggression.

Focus on how the Manchurian crisis affected the League...

Look at the British cartoon source above. How useful would this source be for a historian who was studying the effects of the Manchurian crisis on the League's reputation? [12]

EXAM QUESTION

The Invasion of Abyssinia

Next it was the Italians who tested the strength of the League of Nations.

Italy was ruled by Mussolini's Fascists

1) Italy was under the control of Benito Mussolini and his Fascist Party.
2) Mussolini had been made Prime Minister in 1922 after threatening to take power by marching on Rome. He used his new position to change the voting rules, and in the 1924 election the Fascists swept to power.
3) From 1925, he began to establish a dictatorship in Italy.
4) Opposition political parties were banned. He used his harsh secret police against opponents.

In the early 1930s, Mussolini was on the side of France and Britain. He joined them at the Stresa Conference in 1935 to stand against a possible German invasion of Austria.

Mussolini Invaded Abyssinia for Three Reasons

- Italy had been defeated by Abyssinia in 1896 and the Italians wanted revenge.
- Success would divert people's attention from the Depression and boost Mussolini's popularity.
- Mussolini dreamed of making Italy a great empire again, and had seen Japan succeed in Manchuria in 1931.

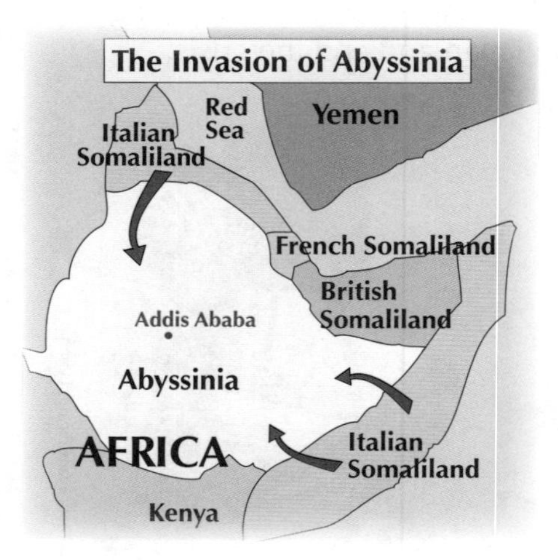

1) In October 1935, Mussolini sent troops with heavy artillery and tanks to invade Abyssinia.
2) The Abyssinian leader appealed directly to the League of Nations.
3) The League of Nations imposed economic sanctions, but delayed banning oil exports in case the USA didn't support them.
4) Britain and France didn't close the Suez Canal to Italian ships — so supplies got through despite the sanctions.
5) By May 1936, Italy had conquered all of Abyssinia.

Comment and Analysis

Mussolini had seen Japan get away with its Manchurian invasion despite the League of Nations' threats. This gave him more confidence to attack Abyssinia.

The League of Nations appeared Ineffective

1) Members of the League didn't want to go to war with Italy. Hitler was becoming powerful, and Britain and France wanted to save their resources.
2) Britain and France made a secret agreement (the Hoare-Laval Pact) to give Abyssinia to Mussolini. When the news got out, there was a public outrage.
3) Meanwhile, Italy became more confident — and eventually started making pacts with the fascist leader of Germany, Adolf Hitler (see p.77).
4) The League's reputation was ruined. Members were supposed to unite together against aggressors, but they didn't want to. The Covenant had been ignored, and the League was falling apart.

Comment and Analysis

These were exactly the kind of secret agreements that the League of Nations wanted to avoid. They undermined its core principle of all countries working together.

Abyssinia was one of the turning points of the period...

When you're writing about the years between the First and Second World Wars, make sure you point out any events that were definite 'turning points'. For example, many historians think that the invasion of Abyssinia signalled the beginning of the end for the League.

The Collapse of the League of Nations

The League of Nations lost most of its influence after the Abyssinia crisis and became largely irrelevant when the Second World War broke out in 1939. You need to know the different arguments for why it collapsed.

The League Didn't Achieve its original Aims

1) The League aimed to act against aggression, encourage nations to discuss their disputes, and work towards disarmament. These aims were all intended to prevent another war. The League failed to do this — the Second World War started in 1939.
2) The League did have some success in settling disputes in the 1920s, e.g. Upper Silesia (p.68).
3) It also managed to encourage cooperation on social issues (p.68). It helped to improve the lives of ordinary people around the world — but this wasn't its main purpose.

Some say the League was Doomed from the Start

1) The League of Nations had to defend the Treaty of Versailles, even though many of the members themselves thought the treaty was unfair. This associated the League with unpopular diplomacy from the start.
2) When the USA refused to join, Britain and France had a very difficult task — they had to support the League's finances and military, but they weren't very strong themselves. Germany and Russia weren't allowed to join the League at the start. This excluded two powerful nations which could have contributed to the League.
3) The League's organisation made decision-making complicated and lengthy. Britain and France didn't lead strongly, and were often very slow to do things.

Some say the League Failed because it made Bad Decisions

1) The League needed to show a strong response to aggressors, but didn't have the strength to do it. None of the members wanted to risk the lives of their troops after the First World War.
2) Ambitious members (e.g. Mussolini) weren't dealt with strongly enough.
3) Too many members didn't keep to the Covenant. When they were challenged, they simply left the League, e.g. Germany and Japan in 1933, Italy in 1937.
4) Instead of cooperation, the League let the old system of alliances creep back, even between members.
5) The Manchurian crisis was a turning point — the League failed to resist Japan. After that, countries began to increase their armed forces — they had lost faith in the League and expected war.

The League had to deal with Issues that it couldn't Control

1) In the 1930s, the Depression made the political situation tougher worldwide.
2) The Depression made the problems with the League's structure much worse — weakened countries were finding it hard to deal with their own problems, so they weren't able to respond to international problems.
3) You could argue that no organisation could have stopped leaders like Mussolini or Hitler peacefully.

Comment and Analysis

The League was founded on internationalism — the idea that countries should take collective action based on common interests. Instead of working together, the Depression made countries more isolated.

Time to find your (crumpled) piece of paper from page 66...

Write down as many bullet points as you can about what caused the League to fail. Which of these do you think is the most important?

The Rise of European Dictators

Dictators rose to power during a time of Depression and international tensions in Europe.

Problems and Fears aided the rise of Dictators...

Dictatorship might seem a scary idea, but for some people it solved a lot of worrying issues.

1) **THE LOCARNO TREATIES** had only settled the western borders of Germany. The borders on the east were vulnerable if Germany wanted to expand — people wanted strong leaders to protect them.
2) **THE DEPRESSION** still affected most countries, causing widespread unemployment and poverty. People welcomed strong governments who promised to put things right.
3) **DEMOCRACY** was often blamed for the bad conditions — democratic governments seemed unable to prevent them happening or to improve the situation.
4) **COMMUNISM** was seen as a threat to all of Europe after the Russian Revolution in 1917 — people looked to strong leaders to fight the threat of a worldwide communist revolution.
5) **FRANCE** was still suspicious of Germany and was building strong defences behind its border with Germany — many Germans felt they needed a strong leader against what they saw as a French threat.
6) **DISARMAMENT FAILED** — most countries refused to disarm to the same level as Germany in 1932. Germany saw this as unfair and became determined to rebuild its armed forces.

The situation wasn't made any easier by the continued isolationism of the USA. The USA stayed out of world affairs, and Britain and France weren't strong enough to oppose the large numbers of foreign dictators.

...including Adolf Hitler, who aimed to make Germany Great again

1) Adolf Hitler, the leader of the Nazi Party, became the Chancellor of Germany in 1933.
2) He then established a dictatorship. He governed without a parliament, banned trade unions and opposition parties, and used violence and terror against his opponents. By August 1934, he called himself the Führer — the leader.
3) Hitler had big plans for Germany on the world stage. Hitler's foreign policy had several aims:

- He wanted the Treaty of Versailles to be overturned. Hitler hated the treaty, which he saw as unfairly weakening Germany.
- He wanted rearmament. Germany had been forced to reduce its armed forces under the Treaty of Versailles. Hitler wanted Germany to be a strong military power.
- He wanted all German-speaking peoples to be united in a German Reich (empire). This would mean annexing Austria and taking territory from Poland and Czechoslovakia (which had minority German populations). This idea was known as Grossdeutschland — meaning 'Great Germany'.
- He wanted to expand Germany's territory by taking land from peoples he saw as inferior, such as the Slavs. This expansion would provide more Lebensraum (which means 'living space') for the German people.

Hitler was a charismatic speaker and was popular among the German people — his Nazi Party had been successful in German elections. This picture shows Hitler looking determined and strong, and was used by Hitler's press office.

It's important to remember that people voted the Nazis in...

Make a list of the conditions in the early 1930s that contributed to the rise of dictatorships. Write a sentence for each one, explaining the effect it had.

REVISION TASK

The Start of German Expansion, 1933-1935

From 1933, Hitler began to act upon his aim to unite all Germans in a single empire.
At the same time, the British Prime Minister was doing everything he could to avoid war.

The Dollfuss Affair was Hitler's First Step towards more Territory

1) It was no secret that Hitler wanted Austria to become part of Germany.
2) Engelbert Dollfuss was the dictator of Austria. He didn't want Austria to be joined with Germany.
3) Austrian Nazis carried out terrorist attacks, encouraged from Germany. The German government tried to persuade Dollfuss to appoint ministers who were Nazi sympathisers. Dollfuss rejected all of their demands.
4) In July 1934, a group of Austrian Nazis attempted a coup. They killed Dollfuss and took control of the government buildings. However, the coup was poorly organised and the government soon restored control after Italian troops moved to the border to warn Hitler off.
5) Hitler quickly denied any connection to the unsuccessful coup. It's still not known how far he was involved. It's likely that Hitler planned for the Austrian government to be overthrown from within — he knew he didn't have the military strength to take Austria by force. However, he may not have wanted Dollfuss to be killed — it could have led other countries to intervene, and he wasn't ready for this yet.

Comment and Analysis

The Dollfuss Affair showed Hitler to be quite vulnerable in the early years of his rule. This episode made him realise that he needed to be patient and increase his military strength.

Hitler's first Territorial Success was in the Saar

1) After the Dollfuss Affair, Hitler turned his attention to the valuable Saar — he wanted it back.
2) The Saar was an industrialised region of Germany about 30 miles wide, bordering France. Under the Treaty of Versailles, the Saar was put under the control of the League of Nations for 15 years from 1920. After this time, the plan was for the territory's status to be decided by popular vote.
3) When this plebiscite (referendum) took place in January 1935, 90% of voters chose reunion with Germany — the Saar was returned to Germany in March.

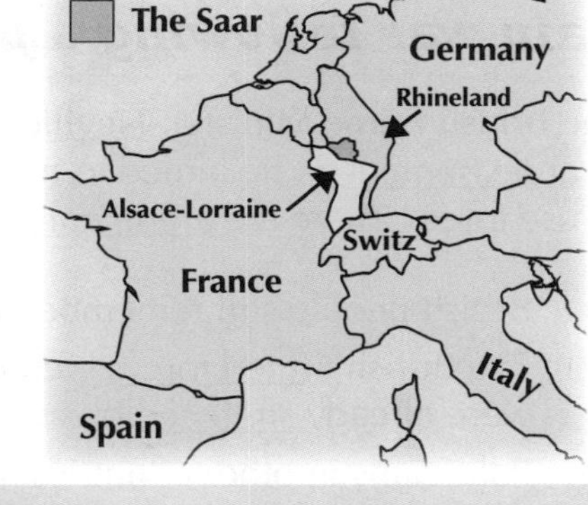

- The vote showed that people were willing to live under Hitler and the Nazis just in order to be a part of the country again.
- Lots of historians think that regaining the Saar was Hitler's first step to the Second World War. It gave him the confidence to demand more territory for Germany — see p.77.
- However, it also showed that Hitler's armed forces were still weak at this point. Some Nazis had threatened to invade the Saar, but backed down as soon as Britain threatened to send troops.

Hitler started to Rebuild Germany's Armed Forces

1) In 1933, Hitler withdrew Germany from the League of Nations' Disarmament Conference. He then withdrew Germany from the League of Nations itself.
2) In March 1935, he brought in military conscription in Germany — breaking the terms of the Treaty of Versailles. This was condemned by France, Britain and Italy at Stresa (see p.76).

Hitler was widening his territory...

Describe how the events in Austria in 1934 demonstrated some of Hitler's early weaknesses. [8]

EXAM QUESTION

The Start of German Expansion, 1933-1935

The Allies Reacted to German Rearmament at Stresa

1) Britain, France and Italy met for the Stresa Conference, in northern Italy, in April 1935.
2) Britain and France were worried about German rearmament and conscription, announced in March. Mussolini was concerned about the threat to his northern borders if Hitler united Austria with Germany.
3) In the final Stresa agreement (often called the Stresa Front) the countries condemned German rearmament. They also agreed to work together to maintain peace in Europe and to defend Austrian independence. However, they didn't decide how this would be done.
4) The agreement gave Mussolini more confidence to wage his war in Abyssinia (p.72), because it only referred to peace in Europe. He also felt that Britain and France wouldn't confront Hitler.

Stresa was Undermined by the Anglo-German Naval Agreement

1) In June 1935, Hitler reached a naval agreement with Britain. It allowed Germany to build up to 35% of British naval strength and up to 45% of their submarine strength.
2) This agreement implied that Germany had a right to rearm — even though this clearly broke the Treaty of Versailles.
3) It weakened the spirit of the Stresa Front. The three powers were supposed to form a united team against German expansion, but instead Britain was making its own pacts with Germany.
4) It also harmed Britain and France's relationship, just when they needed to unite on Abyssinia (p.72).

Comment and Analysis

Britain saw the treaty as a way to build a better relationship with Germany — and to guarantee its own naval superiority.

Britain was following a policy of Appeasement

1) The British Prime Minister, Neville Chamberlain, was following a policy of appeasement — he aimed to negotiate with Hitler, rather than threaten to use force. There are arguments both for and against this policy:

Appeasement means giving aggressive leaders (like Hitler) what they want in order to avoid a war.

For appeasement

1) British people still remembered the First World War and its devastation. They wanted peace.
2) The British armed forces weren't yet ready for another world war, and were already stretched by military commitments in the British Empire.
3) Politicians in other countries admired Hitler's success — he'd improved the economy and built impressive new infrastructure, so they didn't want to fight him.
4) The British feared communism — a strong Germany would be a barrier against communist USSR.
5) At first, Germany's army was too weak to be a significant threat, but the British weren't in a good position to go to war either — Britain wouldn't be guaranteed support from the USA and France.

Appeasement seems very unwise today — now we know it probably made war more likely.

Against appeasement

1) Hitler became more demanding as time went on. He began by asking for lands with lots of German people (e.g. the Saar — p.75), but later he threatened countries where this wasn't the case.
2) Some politicians at the time warned of the dangers of appeasement. Churchill warned that a rearmed Germany was a threat.
3) Hitler proved that he couldn't be trusted to keep his promises (p.79).

Comment and Analysis

Hitler's claims to regions like the Saar seemed fairly reasonable because they'd been part of Germany before the Treaty of Versailles.

2) Appeasement may have seemed sensible in 1933-1935 because Hitler didn't yet pose a threat to Britain.

1933-1935 — a bit of a mixed bag for Hitler...

Not all of Hitler's foreign policy moves were a success. Dollfuss would be a good example to use.

The Escalation of Tension, 1936-1938

In the second half of the 1930s, Hitler started pushing for more and more territory for Germany.

In March 1936 Hitler sent Troops into the Rhineland

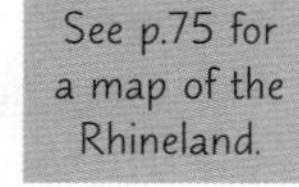
See p.75 for a map of the Rhineland.

1) The Rhineland was demilitarised by the Treaty of Versailles. While the League of Nations was busy with Italy's invasion of Abyssinia, Hitler saw his chance to overturn this.
2) The USSR and France had recently made a treaty agreeing to help each other if they were attacked (it was meant to protect them from Germany). Hitler claimed that this threatened Germany, so he should be allowed to put troops on Germany's borders, including in the Rhineland.
3) Hitler thought Britain wouldn't get involved, but he wasn't sure about France.
4) The German forces had orders to pull out immediately if the French army moved in. But France was in the middle of an election campaign — so no one was willing to start a war with Germany. The League of Nations, including Britain, was angry but took no action.

Comment and Analysis

This was a gamble. Hitler risked a war that he wasn't ready for, but appeasement and the French election worked in his favour.

Hitler started making Pacts with Mussolini

1) In 1935, Mussolini had successfully invaded Abyssinia. This made him more confident in following foreign policy that would put Italy in a more powerful position in Europe. Hitler invited Mussolini to visit Germany and showed off Germany's military strength. Mussolini decided to side with Hitler.
2) Mussolini and Hitler agreed the Rome-Berlin Axis in 1936 (which officially linked the two countries), and in 1937 Italy joined Japan and Germany in the Anti-Comintern Pact (against communism, specifically the USSR).
3) The partnership escalated the international tensions in Europe, as Germany and Italy became increasingly detached from the other European powers.

Hitler and Mussolini were still in competition with one another when it came to power in Europe. Writing about the Rome-Berlin Axis, historian A.J.P. Taylor says, 'Hitler intended to make Germany the leading power in Europe, with Italy as, at best, a junior partner. Neither was eager to promote the ambitions of the other; each planned to exploit the other's challenge to the Western Powers in order to extract concessions for himself.'

An illustration from an Italian magazine in 1937. Hitler and Mussolini are depicted as strong military leaders.

In 1938, Hitler achieved Anschluss with Austria

1) Hitler wanted 'Anschluss' (union) with Austria. This was part of his plan to unite all German people in one Reich (p.74). Anschluss would also allow Hitler to make use of Austria's armed forces and raw materials.
2) Hitler encouraged Austrian Nazis to stage demonstrations and protests in favour of Anschluss. In February 1938, he demanded that an Austrian Nazi called Seyss-Inquart be made Minister of the Interior.
3) The Austrian Chancellor Schuschnigg hoped to prevent the Nazis from taking over, but Hitler threatened to invade if he didn't resign. Schuschnigg couldn't take the risk — he and his cabinet resigned, except for Seyss-Inquart, who became Chancellor and invited the German army into Austria to 'restore order'.
4) On 12th March 1938, Hitler invaded Austria to proclaim the Greater German Reich.
5) Following its policy of appeasement (p.76), Britain didn't stop him. The whole French government had resigned two days before the German invasion, so France was in no state to intervene either.
6) In April, a referendum was held and Austrians voted overwhelmingly in favour of the Anschluss — but the vote was rigged by the Nazis.

Hitler was a difficult man to say 'no' to...

How can you tell that the illustration above supports Hitler and Mussolini? [4]

The Escalation of Tension, 1936-1938

After Hitler had taken Austria, Czechoslovakia was afraid that he'd try the same thing there.

Hitler put Pressure on Czechoslovakia in 1938

This is sometimes referred to as the Sudeten Crisis.

1) Czechoslovakia's borders had been set by the Treaty of Versailles. The Sudetenland was a part of western Czechoslovakia which had a large minority population of Germans — about 3 million.
2) Hitler said the Czechoslovakian government was discriminating against the Germans in the Sudetenland. The Nazis demanded that it should become part of Germany.
3) In May 1938, Hitler moved his armies to the border of Czechoslovakia and threatened to go to war — he wanted to take control of the Sudetenland. The Czechoslovakian leader, Benes, was ready to fight.
4) Britain, France and the USSR had agreed to support the Czechoslovakians if Hitler invaded. Hitler had promised Britain's Prime Minister Neville Chamberlain that he wouldn't invade Czechoslovakia.

Chamberlain Negotiated with Hitler

Neville Chamberlain wanted to avoid war and thought the best way to do this was to negotiate. The negotiations took place in September 1938.

15th September: Chamberlain visits Hitler to negotiate. Hitler says this will be his last territorial request in Europe. Chamberlain decides to trust him.

22nd September: Chamberlain returns to Germany and tells Hitler that the Czechoslovakians will give him the Sudetenland. Hitler then changes his demands, saying he now wants all non-Germans to leave the Sudetenland. Chamberlain calls this unreasonable and prepares the British navy for war.

29th September: Hitler invites Chamberlain, Daladier (the French PM) and Mussolini to a conference in Munich. Mussolini proposes a plan (really written by the German Foreign Office). This becomes the Munich Agreement.

The Munich Agreement

The Sudetenland would be given to Germany, but Hitler guaranteed he wouldn't invade the rest of Czechoslovakia.

1) Chamberlain gave in to Hitler's demands because he believed Hitler would honour his promise.
2) It seemed like Chamberlain had prevented war. He claimed the agreement meant 'peace for our time', and he flew back to Britain to a hero's welcome.
3) Britain's economy and armed forces were weak. Some historians say Chamberlain gave in to Hitler in order to buy time to rearm Britain.
4) Czechoslovakia and the USSR weren't invited to the Conference. So the Czechoslovakians weren't even consulted on their own future, and had now become very exposed to a possible German invasion. The USSR was worried about Hitler's hidden intentions, so it was horrified at the agreement.

This is another example of Chamberlain's appeasement policy (p.76).

An opinion poll carried out in October 1938 showed that the vast majority of the British public didn't trust Hitler.

However, another survey taken early in 1939 showed that almost half of the population did believe in Chamberlain's policy of appeasement.

You need to know all the key events and dates of the period...

REVISION TASK

Make a timeline of the events in Czechoslovakia in 1938. Your timeline needs to include all of the key dates, individuals and discussions that took place, and finish with the Munich Agreement.

The End of Appeasement

Unfortunately for Europe, Hitler broke his promise not to invade beyond the Sudetenland.

In March 1939 Hitler took over the Rest of Czechoslovakia

1) After losing the Sudetenland, Czechoslovakia began to descend into anarchy. Slovakia began to demand independence.
2) Hitler persuaded the Czechoslovakian president to allow German troops in to 'restore order'.
3) On 15th March 1939, the Nazis marched into the rest of Czechoslovakia.

Slovakia was the eastern part of Czechoslovakia.

Appeasement now Ended and countries Prepared for War

1) Britain and France did nothing — but it was clear that the appeasement policy had failed. Hitler had broken his promises. He'd also taken non-German lands, which meant many countries were at risk of German invasion.

Once the Nazis had taken the rest of Czechoslovakia, Britain abandoned appeasement and changed its foreign policy.

2) In April 1939, Britain and France made an agreement with Poland to support it if Hitler invaded.
3) Chamberlain began to prepare the armed forces for war and make arrangements for public safety.

Hitler and Mussolini continued to side with one another

- Hitler and Mussolini hadn't always been allies (p.72), but they found each other useful. For example, the lack of a reaction to Italy's invasion of Abyssinia made Hitler believe that no-one would intervene against Germany either, while Mussolini used the Munich peace conference to enhance his reputation as a statesman.
- In 1939, Germany and Italy signed the 'Pact of Steel', agreeing to support each other in war. As Germany gained more territory, Mussolini saw a chance for Italy to do the same.
- However, the Italian army was weak, and Hitler had to rescue it after a disastrous invasion of Greece in 1940. After this, Mussolini largely became a 'puppet', controlled by Hitler.

The USSR made a Pact with Hitler

1) The USSR (Soviet Union) joined the League of Nations in 1934, and signed a treaty with France in 1935 against Hitler. The Soviet leader, Stalin, was suspicious of the Nazis.
2) In 1939, Britain and France wanted the USSR to help them protect Poland. However, the USSR didn't trust France, and couldn't understand why nobody stood up to Hitler earlier. Stalin was also excluded from the Munich Agreement negotiations.

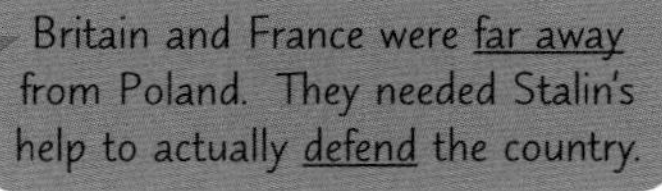

3) Stalin decided to negotiate with Germany to protect the USSR. The Nazi-Soviet Pact was signed in August 1939. Stalin and Hitler agreed not to attack each other.
4) They also secretly planned to carve up Poland. They agreed that if Germany invaded Poland, the USSR would get Latvia, Estonia, Finland and east Poland — but Hitler never really intended to let the USSR keep those areas.

Comment and Analysis

The Nazi-Soviet pact was the trigger for the German invasion of Poland, but Hitler already had plans to conquer Poland to increase Germany's Lebensraum. The Nazi-Soviet pact wasn't the underlying cause of the Second World War.

It was quite clear who wore the trousers...

EXAM TIP

If you're writing about Mussolini and Hitler's relationship, remember that Hitler had the stronger army, and so ended up being the more powerful of the two.

The Start of the Second World War

Twenty-one years after the armistice that ended the First World War, Europe was at war again.

The Second World War Started when Hitler Invaded Poland

1) On 1st September 1939, Hitler invaded Poland. Britain and France ordered him to leave, but he ignored them. Britain declared war on Germany on 3rd September 1939.
2) The invasion of Poland triggered the Second World War, but other long-term factors led to the war. You need to know why war broke out again, despite all of the efforts since 1918 to avoid it.

Long-term Factor — Treaty of Versailles, 1919

1) Germans (especially Hitler) hated the treaty. This resentment continued throughout the inter-war period (see p.61-64).
2) New countries were created by the treaty, but they were often unstable and vulnerable to German attack. Hitler knew this.
3) The treaty caused economic problems for Germany, which fuelled more resentment.

Long-term Factor — Wall Street Crash, 1929

1) This caused a global economic crisis — the Depression. It hit Germany especially hard, stirring up further resentment.
2) Countries prioritised their own economic recoveries. This made the League less effective at settling international disputes (p.70).

The League's failure also contributed to the outbreak of war. The lack of a united front against aggression made it easier for Hitler to act.

The Leaders Played Their Part in the Outbreak of war

In the short term, the outbreak of the Second World War had a lot to do with the actions of individuals.

There three key reasons why Hitler can be seen as responsible for the outbreak of war:
- He wanted to take new land for Germany from other nations, e.g. Czechoslovakia.
- He was prepared to bully and fight to get what he wanted, e.g. Austria. Hitler had an aggressive foreign policy.
- He rearmed Germany to be a military power — this suggests he had always intended to go to war with the rest of Europe.

But many historians argue that Hitler is not solely responsible for the outbreak of war, and that if other people had acted differently, war could have been avoided.

Look back at Hitler's foreign policy aims on p.74.

Chamberlain's policy of appeasement could also be seen as an important cause of World War II:
- His trust in Hitler's promises was shown to be unwise, e.g. Czechoslovakia.
- Hitler was encouraged by the fact that Chamberlain kept giving him what he wanted. This pushed him to invade Poland (the immediate cause of war).

On the other hand, you could argue that Chamberlain made the best decisions he could at the time (see the reasons for appeasement on p.76). Also, even if he only managed to delay war, he did give Britain time to get ready for it.

Stalin, the dictator of the communist USSR, also had a part to play:
- The Nazi-Soviet Pact meant that Hitler could invade Poland without worrying about Stalin defending it.

However, you could also argue that Britain and France pushed Stalin into a pact with Hitler by excluding him from their own negotiations.

The problems that led to the war were tricky to solve...

'When history asks who or what caused the Second World War, the finger must surely be pointed at Neville Chamberlain.' To what extent do you agree with this view? [16]

Revision Summary

Well, that's a whole depth study done and dusted — good going. Time to see how much you remember.

- Try these questions and tick off each one when you get it right.
- When you've done all the questions for a topic and are completely happy with it, tick off the topic.

Peacemaking (p.59-65)

1) Who suggested the Fourteen Points?
2) a) Who were the 'Big Three' who led the talks at the Paris Peace Conference?
   b) Write down three things that each of these countries wanted at the Paris Peace Conference.
3) In which year was the Treaty of Versailles signed?
4) Which area was demilitarised by the Treaty of Versailles?
5) What was Article 231 of the Treaty of Versailles?
6) Give three reasons why the German people disliked the Treaty of Versailles.
7) Name one country that was created as a result of the post-war treaties.
8) What problems were caused by creating new countries after the war?
9) Give two reasons why the Treaty of Versailles might have been the best solution at the time.

The League of Nations and International Peace (p.66-73)

10) What were the two main aims of the League of Nations?
11) a) Which country caused huge problems when they refused to join the League?
    b) Give two reasons why this was a problem for the League.
12) Choose three social issues that the League helped to improve, and explain its contribution.
13) What happened in Upper Silesia in 1921?
14) What happened in Corfu in 1923?
15) Write down two consequences of the Locarno Treaties.
16) Which event sparked the Depression and in which year did it take place?
17) Which nation invaded Manchuria in 1931?
18) Give three reasons why Mussolini invaded Abyssinia in 1935.
19) Write down two ways that the League of Nations could be judged a failure.

The Origins and Outbreak of the Second World War (p.74-80)

20) What were the four main aims of Hitler's foreign policy?
21) Write a paragraph explaining the Dollfuss Affair.
22) In which year was the Saar returned to Germany?
23) a) At which conference was German rearmament discussed?
    b) Which agreement then undermined this conference?
24) Give two reasons for and two reasons against appeasement.
25) What excuse did Hitler use for sending troops into the Rhineland?
26) Write a sentence describing the relationship between Hitler and Mussolini from 1935 to 1937.
27) Briefly describe how Hitler achieved Anschluss with Austria.
28) What is the name of the region that was given to Hitler at the Munich Conference?
29) a) On which date did Hitler invade Poland?
    b) On which date did Britain declare war on Germany?

Elizabeth's Background and Character

Elizabeth I became queen in 1558. She reigned for almost 45 years, until her death in 1603. She had a rocky start in life and faced some pretty serious problems when she first became queen.

Queen Elizabeth I was from the House of Tudor

The Tudor family had ruled England since Henry VII became king in 1485. Here's their family tree:

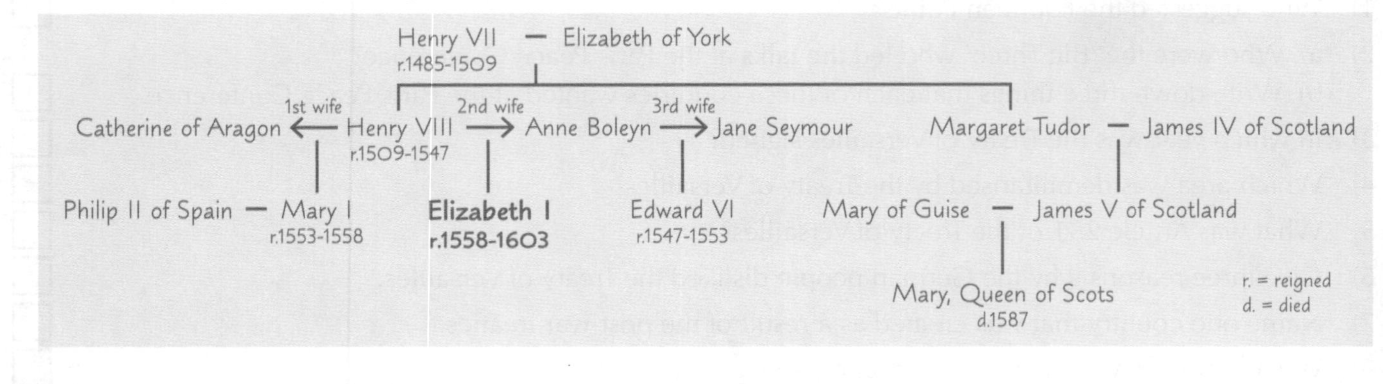

Elizabeth I was Cautious, Intelligent and Powerful

© Mary Evans / Iberfoto

1) Elizabeth was Henry VIII's second child, the daughter of his second wife, Anne Boleyn. As a child, she was third in line to the throne (behind Edward VI and Mary I), so no-one really expected her to become queen.
2) Elizabeth had a difficult upbringing and sometimes feared for her life. In 1554, she was accused of conspiring against her half-sister, Queen Mary I, and placed under house arrest for almost a year.
3) Elizabeth was very cautious and only trusted a few close advisers. She could also be indecisive — she was reluctant to make decisions without carefully considering their possible consequences.
4) She was intelligent, confident and very well educated. Despite having had little training in how to govern, she became a powerful and effective leader.

Some people Didn't want Elizabeth to be Queen

Gender

1) In the 16th century, most people believed the monarch should be a man. They thought that rule by a woman was unnatural.
2) Most people expected Elizabeth to act as a figurehead, without any real power. They thought she should let her male counsellors take control or find a husband to govern for her (see p.86).
3) However, Elizabeth was determined to rule in her own right and refused to let her counsellors take over.

Illegitimacy

1) In 1533, Henry VIII had divorced his first wife, Catherine of Aragon, and married Anne Boleyn.
2) Divorce was forbidden in the Catholic Church, so many Catholics believed Henry's marriage to Anne was not valid and their daughter, Elizabeth, was illegitimate.
3) Illegitimate children weren't usually allowed to inherit, so the issue of Elizabeth's legitimacy weakened her claim to the throne. Some people thought that Mary, Queen of Scots (see p.95) had more right to rule.

Don't let Elizabeth's character fade into the background...

It's important to understand what Elizabeth was like as a person and the early difficulties she faced — her background and character shaped many of the decisions she made during her reign.

EXAM TIP

The Elizabethan Court

Elizabeth's court was the heart of social and political life — everyone who was anyone could be found there.

The Court was the Centre of Elizabethan Social Life

1) The royal court was a large group of people who surrounded the monarch at all times. More than 1000 people attended the court, including Elizabeth's personal servants, members of the Privy Council (see p.84), members of the nobility, ambassadors and other foreign visitors, and Elizabeth's 'favourites'.

Some courtiers became Elizabeth's 'favourites'. Early in her reign, Elizabeth was very close to Robert Dudley. She made him Earl of Leicester in 1564 and may have considered marrying him (see p.86). Christopher Hatton was another of her 'favourites'. In 1587, she made him Lord Chancellor, even though he had little relevant experience. Sir Walter Raleigh came to Elizabeth's court in 1581. Elizabeth gave him many valuable gifts, including the right to colonise the New World (see p.93).

2) Courtiers were expected to flatter Elizabeth, shower her with gifts and pretend to be in love with her.
3) Courtly pastimes included plays, concerts, hunting, jousting and tennis. There were also balls and grand meals.
4) Members of the court travelled with Elizabeth when she moved between her palaces, and when great processions were held. They also went with her when she travelled around the country visiting the houses of wealthy noblemen (these trips were known as royal progresses).

Comment and Analysis

The entertainments and fashionable clothes on show at court were a way for Elizabeth to impress her subjects and foreign visitors by displaying her wealth and power.

Political Power relied on Access to the Queen

1) The Queen was the centre of government, and political power revolved around her. This meant that those closest to Elizabeth had the greatest influence and power.
2) The court was the centre of political life. Anyone who wanted to get ahead and increase their political power had to have a place at court.
3) Courtiers didn't necessarily hold government positions — they became powerful through their close relationship with the Queen.

Courtiers had to compete with one another for the Queen's attention and favour. Towards the end of Elizabeth's reign, this competition led to growing conflict at court (p.87).

Elizabeth used Patronage to ensure Loyalty and Stability

1) Patronage involved handing out titles, offices or monopolies (see p.88), which gave men a source of income. Elizabeth had a lot of these offices to give away, including high positions in the Church. Royal patronage was distributed at court.
2) Elizabeth's use of patronage helped to ensure loyalty. Those who received patronage became dependent on Elizabeth for some or all of their income and status, so they were likely to be loyal to her.
3) Elizabeth distributed patronage very widely. This helped to ensure political stability — all members of the elite felt they had a chance to be rewarded by the Queen, so they were unlikely to rebel against her.
4) Patronage was a way for Elizabeth to reward her courtiers without spending royal revenues. This was important because the English economy was weak during Elizabeth's reign and her income was limited.

Comment and Analysis

Traditionally, the elite was dominated by noble families. Their power didn't come from the monarch — it mainly came from the large amounts of land that they inherited. By promoting men who relied on her for their wealth and influence, Elizabeth limited the power of the traditional noble families and made the new elite more loyal to her.

The court was the place to be in Elizabethan England...

Jot down a quick description of Elizabeth's court, including the names of some of her favourite courtiers. Write a few sentences to explain why patronage was an important part of court life.

The Elizabethan Government

The Queen was the head of government. She was advised by her Privy Council, which included her key ministers. Parliament could be involved in granting taxes, passing laws and giving advice.

The Privy Council was Central to Elizabethan Government

1) The Privy Council had two main roles. It gave advice to the Queen and managed the administration of government.
2) The Council was made up of around twenty men, all chosen by Elizabeth. Members of the Privy Council were the Queen's closest and most trusted advisors. Some key ministers served on the Council for many years.
3) The Queen didn't have to follow the advice of the Privy Council. Councillors were expected to carry out her instructions, even when doing so went against their advice.

This involved making sure that Elizabeth's policies were enforced. The council oversaw many different areas of government, including religion, the economy, the military, foreign policy and the Queen's security.

William Cecil was Elizabeth's Closest Advisor

1) When she became queen in 1558, Elizabeth made William Cecil her Principal Secretary. He became her closest advisor, leading the Privy Council and making sure the government ran smoothly.
2) In 1571, Elizabeth gave Cecil the title Lord Burghley. The next year she made him Lord High Treasurer, giving him greater control over royal finances. Cecil continued to serve Elizabeth until his death in 1598.
3) Elizabeth's other key ministers included Nicholas Bacon, who was Lord Chancellor from 1559 to 1579, and Francis Walsingham, who became Principal Secretary in 1573.

Comment and Analysis

Cecil was a highly skilled politician and administrator. Some historians argue that Elizabeth's success as queen was as much due to Cecil's remarkable skills as it was to Elizabeth's own talents.

There were Two Chambers of Parliament

1) The House of Lords was not elected — it was made up of members of the nobility and senior churchmen.
2) The House of Commons was elected, but only men who owned property over a certain value were allowed to vote. Elections weren't free — the Crown controlled who got elected in some areas, and in others powerful local figures controlled who was chosen.

Parliament's main functions were Advice, Taxation and Legislation

Advice

Parliament was an important point of contact between central government and the leading figures in local government throughout the country. It enabled the Queen and her councillors to gauge the mood of the country and levels of support for their policies.

Taxation

When the Queen needed extra revenue, she had to ask Parliament's permission to raise taxes.

Legislation

The Queen needed Parliament's approval to pass new laws. However, she could bypass this function by issuing royal proclamations instead.

Comment and Analysis

Elizabeth took little interest in the advice of Members of Parliament (MPs), and she could bypass Parliament's role in passing new laws. For Elizabeth, Parliament's main purpose was to grant her taxes.

Elizabeth was very powerful, but she didn't rule alone...

To really ace the exam, you need to understand the key features of Elizabethan government. Make sure you know the role of the Queen, the Privy Council, key ministers and Parliament.

The Elizabethan Government

Unlike today, in the 16th century Parliament was only a secondary part of government. Its sessions were temporary and occasional, and its powers were limited.

Parliament's Powers were Limited

1) Elizabeth had the power to summon and dismiss Parliament. She disliked working with Parliament and tried to use it as little as possible — she only called 13 sessions of Parliament during her 44-year reign.
2) Parliament was not free to decide what topics it debated. It had to have permission from the Queen to discuss matters of state (e.g. religion, the succession, foreign policy). As a result, most parliamentary business focused on local matters and social or economic issues, which it could discuss without royal permission.

Elizabeth I in Parliament

Comment and Analysis

Elizabeth believed in Divine Right — that rulers were sent by God to govern their country. She believed that this gave her a royal prerogative — the right to decide about matters of state without interference from Parliament.

The Privy Council helped Elizabeth to Manage Parliament

1) The Privy Council managed relations between Elizabeth and Parliament very effectively. In particular, Cecil was highly skilled at convincing MPs to support the Queen's policies.
2) Some members of the Privy Council sat in Parliament. They acted as royal spokesmen and helped to steer debates in favour of royal policies.
3) The Speaker, who kept order in the House of Commons, was chosen by the Queen and closely monitored by members of the Privy Council. This helped the Queen's councillors to control Parliament and convince MPs to support royal policy.
4) Elizabeth was a strong public speaker. She made a number of powerful speeches in Parliament which helped to persuade MPs to obey her wishes.

There were some Disagreements, but Elizabeth stayed In Control

During Elizabeth's reign, Parliament didn't always agree with her policies:

- Throughout her reign, MPs were concerned about who would rule England after Elizabeth's death — they repeatedly tried to persuade her to marry or name an heir (see p.86).
- Some Puritan MPs challenged the religious settlement (see p.94) and tried to make England more Protestant.
- MPs were worried about the threat from Mary, Queen of Scots, and the Catholic plots surrounding her (see p.95). They tried to convince Elizabeth to take action against Mary.

Occasionally, MPs tried to force the Queen to change her mind by threatening to refuse taxation. Elizabeth never gave in to this kind of parliamentary pressure. Effective management by the Privy Council, combined with Elizabeth's powers to dismiss Parliament and select the topics it debated, meant that she remained firmly in control.

Parliament was no match for Elizabeth and her ministers...

How important was Parliament in Elizabethan England? Explain your answer. [8]

Marriage and the Succession

One of Elizabeth's biggest headaches as queen was the issue of marriage and the succession. She faced constant pressure to marry or name her successor, but was very reluctant to do so.

Elizabeth was expected to Marry and produce an Heir

1) Because people believed that women couldn't rule effectively (see p.82), there was pressure for Elizabeth to find a husband who could rule for her.
2) There were also concerns about the succession. If Elizabeth died without an heir, there would be a risk of civil war, with different groups competing for the throne. To prevent this, Elizabeth was expected to marry and produce an heir as quickly as possible.
3) The Privy Council and Parliament were deeply concerned about the succession. They repeatedly asked the Queen to marry or name her heir, but she always refused. When they asked Elizabeth to find a husband in 1563, she refused to even discuss the matter.

It was Difficult to find a Suitable Husband

1) If Elizabeth married a European prince or king, this could give a foreign country too much influence over England. In the past, Queen Mary I's marriage to King Philip II of Spain had forced England to become involved in an expensive war with France.
2) If Elizabeth chose a member of the English nobility, this would create anger and resentment among those who weren't chosen.
3) The religious settlement had made England a Protestant country (see p.94), so it was difficult for Elizabeth to marry a Catholic. Growing anti-Catholic feeling in England would have made a Catholic husband unpopular and might have undermined support for Elizabeth's rule.
4) Elizabeth was reluctant to marry anyone — women were expected to obey their husbands, so she would lose much of her power and freedom if she married.

Elizabeth Considered many Suitors, but she Rejected them All

1) Early in her reign, Elizabeth received proposals from foreign rulers, including King Philip II of Spain, Archduke Charles of Austria and King Eric of Sweden. She and her Privy Council seriously considered King Eric's proposal, but in the end all these early suitors were rejected.
2) Elizabeth seems to have been in love with her 'favourite', Robert Dudley, and seriously considered marrying him. However, members of the Privy Council and the nobility, including Cecil, were strongly opposed to this match and it did not go ahead.
3) In the 1570s, Elizabeth was courted by Duke Francis of Anjou, brother of the King of France. Although there was some support for the match, there was also strong opposition to the idea of Elizabeth marrying a French Catholic, and in the end the marriage negotiations were abandoned.

Comment and Analysis

Marriage negotiations could be a useful tool in foreign policy. Anglo-Spanish relations were breaking down in the 1570s (see p.100), and England needed a new European ally. The proposed marriage to Duke Francis played an important role in efforts to create an alliance with France.

By the late 1570s, Elizabeth was in her mid-forties and it was clear that she would never have children. The issue of the succession still needed to be resolved, but Elizabeth refused to name a successor. She was concerned that a successor might become the focus of plots to overthrow her. Towards the end of her reign, her advisors began secret negotiations to make James VI of Scotland (son of Mary, Queen of Scots) heir to the throne. When Elizabeth died in 1603, James became king of England.

Elizabeth couldn't find a suitor who suited her...

Scribble down a spider diagram showing all the reasons why it was difficult for Elizabeth to find a husband. Name two suitors Elizabeth considered and explain why she didn't marry them.

The End of Elizabeth's Reign

The last 15 years or so of Elizabeth's rule were so different to her early years that they're sometimes called her 'second reign'. One of the main differences was the growth of competing groups at court.

Elizabeth's Court split into Rival Groups in the 1590s

1) The make-up of Elizabeth's Privy Council changed towards the end of her reign. Several of her key ministers, including Christopher Hatton and Francis Walsingham, died around 1590. William Cecil died in 1598 and was succeeded by his son, Robert Cecil.
2) In 1593, Elizabeth made Robert Devereux, Earl of Essex, a member of the Privy Council. Essex's rise led to the growth of two conflicting groups at court, one around the Earl of Essex and the other around William and Robert Cecil.
3) The two groups were constantly competing for royal patronage and influence. They also disagreed over important matters, especially strategy in the war with Spain (see p.100). Elizabeth's inability to control this conflict undermined her authority.

Essex was the stepson of Elizabeth's earlier 'favourite', Robert Dudley. He came to court in 1584 and quickly became a 'favourite' himself. He was extremely ambitious for military success and could be arrogant and disrespectful, even towards the Queen.

Essex launched a Rebellion in 1601

1) In 1599, Elizabeth sent Essex to Ireland at the head of a huge army. His task was to crush Tyrone's Rebellion (also known as the Nine Years' War), which had been going on since 1594.
2) Essex made some limited attempts to fight the rebels, but when these were unsuccessful, he mad a truce with them. He then abandoned his post and returned to England without the Queen's permission.
3) As a punishment, Elizabeth put Essex under house arrest for a time, banished him from court and took away most of his public offices. In November 1600, she also took away his main source of income, a monopoly (see p.88) on the distribution of sweet wines.
4) The loss of his political power and his income drove Essex to revolt. On 8th February 1601, he launched a rebellion in London. Essex aimed to seize the Queen and force her to replace her closest advisers, especially Cecil, with himself and his followers.
5) Essex's rebellion failed within just a few hours. He received no support from ordinary Londoners, and most of his own supporters quickly abandoned him too. Essex was arrested, tried for treason and executed on 25th February 1601.

Comment and Analysis

In her later years, Elizabeth rarely appointed new men to the Privy Council, which created resentment among some courtiers. These men became frustrated at Elizabeth's refusal to promote them to government posts, and so they encouraged Essex's rebellion.

The Conflict at court Undermined Elizabeth's Authority

1) The lack of popular support for Essex's rebellion shows that it wasn't a serious threat to Elizabeth's rule. She was still a popular and respected queen, and there was no desire to overthrow her or her government.
2) However, the rebellion does suggest that Elizabeth's authority over her court became weaker towards the end of her reign. By the 1590s, she was no longer using patronage as effectively as she had in the past.
3) Instead of balancing the different groups at court, she let the Cecils become too powerful, while failing to promote many others. This led to a build-up of anger and resentment, which risked fuelling challenges to her authority — like Essex's revolt.
4) The conflict at court in the 1590s also made Elizabeth's government less effective. Constant competition and in-fighting between groups made it more difficult to make decisions and get things done.

Get to grips with the facts about the court factions...

Give an account of the reasons for Essex's rebellion in 1601. [8]

EXAM QUESTION

Poverty

The growing number of people living in poverty was a major problem in Elizabethan society.

Religious Changes meant there was Less Support for the Poor

1) Between 1536 and 1541, Henry VIII had closed down England's monasteries and sold off most of their land (this was called the 'dissolution of the monasteries').
2) The monasteries had performed important social functions, including providing support for many poor, ill and disabled people. The dissolution of the monasteries removed a valuable source of assistance for people need.

Population Growth led to Rising Prices

1) In the 16th century, England's birth rate increased and the death rate fell. This led to huge population growth — during Elizabeth's reign, the English population grew from around 3 million people to at least 4 million.
2) Food production didn't keep pace with the growth in population. As a result, food prices rose and sometimes there were food shortages.
3) Prices for food and other goods rose much more quickly than wages. Standards of living fell for many workers as they struggled to afford the necessities — many were forced into poverty.
4) Because of the rapid population growth, there was growing competition for land, and so rents increased. This trend was made worse by changes in farming practices.

Monopolies

Elizabeth often rewarded her courtiers with monopolies, which gave them the exclusive right to produce or distribute a particular item. Monopolies were unpopular with many people because they made the problem of rising prices worse. Since monopoly-holders had no competition, they could fix high prices for their goods.

Developments in Agriculture left many people Unemployed

1) Traditional farming methods involved many farmers renting strips of land in large open fields. This was subsistence-level farming — each farmer only grew enough crops to supply himself and his family.
2) This kind of farming was very inefficient, and in the 16th century landowners began changing their farming techniques to try and make more money from their land. Instead of sharing open fields among many farmers, they enclosed these fields to create a few large farms.
3) These new, enclosed farms required fewer labourers, so farmers who rented land were evicted, leaving them unemployed and homeless.
4) Exporting wool to Europe was more profitable than selling grain, so many landowners stopped growing grain and began sheep farming. This fall in grain production contributed to rising food prices. It also meant that there was a higher risk of food shortages when there was a bad harvest.

Comment and Analysis

These enclosures of farm land forced many people to leave their villages and migrate to towns or cities in search of work. The government viewed these migrant workers as 'vagabonds' and feared that they would encourage riots and rebellions.

Poverty got Worse in the 1590s

The problem of poverty reached a crisis point towards the end of Elizabeth's reign. In the late 1580s and 1590s, England suffered several failed harvests, which led to food shortages and even higher food prices. This pushed even more people into extreme poverty — in some areas people starved to death.

The enclosures closed the door to many farm labourers...

EXAM QUESTION

Why was poverty a growing problem in Elizabethan England? Explain your answer. [8]

Poverty

Elizabeth's government introduced a series of Poor Laws to try and tackle the problem of poverty.

The Government became More Involved in Poor Relief

1) Traditionally, the main source of support for the poor was charity — rich people made donations to hospitals, monasteries and other organisations that helped the poor. However, during Elizabeth's reign the problem of poverty became so bad that these charitable donations by individuals were no longer enough.
2) People began to realise that society as a whole would have to take responsibility for helping the poor, and so the government began to take action to tackle the problem of poverty.

Comment and Analysis

The government feared that the rising poverty levels were a serious threat to law and order. As poverty levels rose, crime rates increased and there were food riots in some places. The government feared that the poor might rise up in rebellion if the problem of poverty wasn't tackled.

People believed the Poor could be split into Three Categories

The Helpless Poor

Those who were unable to support themselves — including young orphans and the elderly, sick or disabled.

The Deserving Poor

People who wanted to work, but weren't able to find a job in their home town or village.

The Undeserving Poor

Beggars, criminals and people who refused to work. Also migrant workers ('vagabonds') who left their homes and travelled around looking for work.

The Poor Laws gave Help to the Helpless and Deserving Poor

1) From the 1560s onwards, the government brought in a series of Poor Laws to deal with the growing problem of poverty.
2) Because voluntary donations were no longer sufficient to fund poor relief, in the 1560s the government passed a Poor Law which introduced a tax to raise money for the poor (known as the 'poor rate').
3) Further Poor Laws were passed in 1597 and 1601 in response to the poverty crisis of the 1590s (p.88). Under these laws, the poor rate became a national system of compulsory taxation. It was collected locally by an official called the Overseer of the Poor.
4) Poor rates were used to provide hospitals and housing for the elderly, sick and disabled. Poor children were given apprenticeships, which usually lasted at least seven years, and local authorities were expected to provide financial support or work for the deserving poor. Poor people could be sent to prison if they refused to take work.

Comment and Analysis

The Privy Council researched how local government had tackled the problem of poverty. They based the national Poor Laws on the local policies that seemed to be most effective. For example, towns like London, Norwich, Ipswich and York had been using compulsory poor rates to pay for poor relief since the mid-16th century.

The Undeserving Poor were treated Harshly

Under the Poor Laws of the 1590s, the undeserving poor were to be publicly whipped and then forced to return to their home parish. Repeat offenders could be sent to prison.

Comment and Analysis

The undeserving poor were treated so harshly because they were seen as a serious threat to society. Many people believed that poor criminals and vagabonds had encouraged the Northern Rebellion in 1569 (see p.96). In response to the Rebellion, the government introduced particularly harsh punishments for the undeserving poor in 1572.

The Poor Laws helped some, but punished others...

Include plenty of specific information in your answers. For example, don't just write about the Poor Laws in general, give the dates of specific laws and explain the changes they brought in.

A 'Golden Age'

Despite the very high levels of poverty, Elizabeth's reign is often seen as a 'Golden Age'. The growing prosperity of the elite contributed to a flourishing in architecture, the arts and education.

The Gentry became Richer during Elizabeth's reign

1) Population growth and changes in farming practices (see p.88) were good for landowners, especially members of the gentry.
2) The enclosures meant that land was farmed more efficiently. At the same time, rents were increasing and prices of agricultural products like grain were rising, so landowners were earning a lot more money from their land.
3) As a result, the land-owning gentry became much wealthier during Elizabeth's reign, and members of the nobility also saw their incomes increase.
4) The growth of towns and the development of national and international trade allowed some merchants to become very rich. They often used their money to buy land and become part of the gentry.

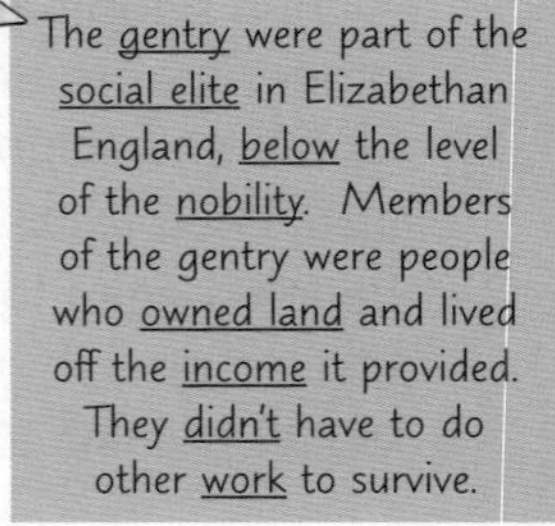
The gentry were part of the social elite in Elizabethan England, below the level of the nobility. Members of the gentry were people who owned land and lived off the income it provided. They didn't have to do other work to survive.

Some members of the Elite built New Houses

1) From the 1570s, many members of the gentry and nobility improved their homes or built new ones. This is sometimes called the 'Great Rebuilding'.
2) These building projects enabled members of the elite to show off their wealth. New houses often had many large windows — glass was very expensive, so using a lot of it was a sign of prosperity. Large landscaped gardens were also a popular way to display wealth.
3) The 'Great Rebuilding' improved living standards for the wealthy, because the new houses were much more comfortable. The large windows made them lighter, and bigger chimneys and fireplaces meant they were better heated.

Some members of the nobility built huge, elaborate houses. Burghley House in Peterborough, built for William Cecil, is a well-known example.

Art, Literature and Education were all highly Fashionable

1) The nobility and gentry had money to spend on elaborate decorations for their homes. Portraits, miniatures (very small portraits), tapestries and embroidery were all popular.
2) It was also fashionable to take an interest in literature — some people collected large libraries, and members of the elite supported the work of poets and playwrights. Elite support for playwrights and acting companies contributed to the flourishing of Elizabethan theatre (see p.91).
3) More people could afford to give their children an education. Some noble families employed a private tutor, while a growing number of children from the nobility and gentry went to grammar schools and on to university.

A miniature of Queen Elizabeth's 'favourite', Robert Dudley, painted by Nicholas Hilliard.

Comment and Analysis

Many elite fashions started at the royal court. For example Nicholas Hilliard was employed as Queen Elizabeth's miniaturist in the 1570s and painted many miniatures of Elizabeth and her courtiers. This encouraged the growing popularity of miniatures among the nobility and gentry.

Members of the elite wore elaborate clothing to show off their wealth and status. Their clothes were often made of expensive fabrics like silk, satin, velvet and lace, and were decorated with detailed embroidery. Women's dresses had very full sleeves and a large skirt, supported by a hoop-skirt, which gave it shape (see the portrait of Elizabeth on p.82). Both men and women wore wide, ruffled collars, called ruffs.

Miniatures were huge in Elizabethan England...

Write a sentence or two to explain why the gentry got richer during Elizabeth's reign. Then make a quick spider diagram showing some things that members of the elite spent their wealth on.

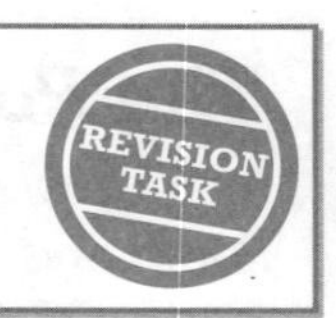

Elizabethan Theatres

The theatre became incredibly popular in the second half of Elizabeth's reign.

There were No Permanent Theatres in England until the 1570s

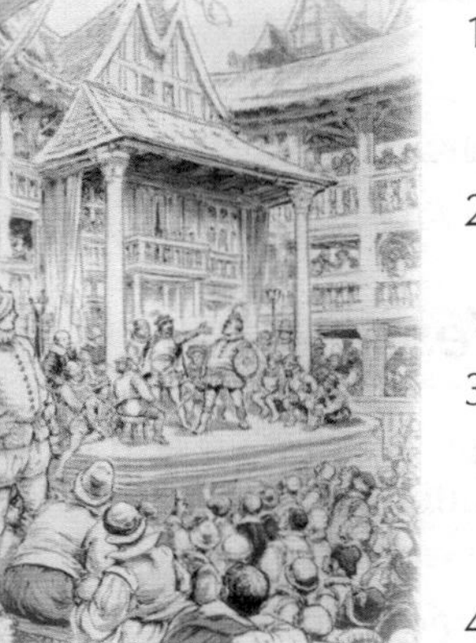

A performance at The Globe Theatre.

1) At the start of Elizabeth's reign, England didn't have any permanent theatres. Instead, companies of actors travelled around, performing in village squares or the courtyards of inns.
2) The first theatres were built in London in the 1570s. They included The Theatre and The Curtain. They were usually round, open-air buildings with a raised stage that stretched out into the audience (known as an 'apron stage').
3) The stage usually had a roof, called the 'heavens'. Actors could be lowered onto the stage from the heavens, or enter through a trapdoor in the stage floor. There were also several entrances at the back of the stage. Behind the stage was the 'tiring house' where actors got dressed and waited to enter.
4) Some theatres were very large — The Globe could hold around 3000 people. Poorer audience members, called 'groundlings', stood in the open yard around the stage, while richer people sat under cover around the theatre's walls.

Elizabeth's reign was a 'Golden Age' for Playwrights

A huge number of plays were written in the Elizabethan era, many of which are still performed today. William Shakespeare is the best-known Elizabethan playwright. He wrote 38 plays, including comedies (e.g. 'Twelfth Night'), tragedies (e.g. 'Macbeth') and histories (e.g. 'Henry V'). Other famous Elizabethan playwrights include Christopher Marlowe and Ben Johnson.

1) Plays were performed by acting companies. They often worked on a shareholder system, where members of the company contributed to its costs and received a share of its profits. Two of the most important Elizabethan companies were The Admiral's Men and The Lord Chamberlain's Men (Shakespeare's company).
2) Women weren't allowed to perform on stage, so actors were all male — boys played the female roles. One of the most famous actors was Richard Burbage. He was a member of The Lord Chamberlain's Men, and he played the lead in many of Shakespeare's plays.

Comment and Analysis

Support from the elite was essential to Elizabethan theatre — acting companies relied on members of the elite to fund or promote their performances and protect them from opponents of the theatre. Several companies were supported by members of the Privy Council.

The theatre was Very Popular, but it faced some Opposition

1) The theatre appealed to both rich and poor. Ticket prices started at just 1 penny, so it was affordable for most people. However, different social groups sat in different parts of the theatre and didn't usually mix.
2) Elizabeth enjoyed plays — she never attended a public theatre, but she often had plays performed at court. She supported her favourite performers and even set up an acting company, The Queen's Men.

The theatre wasn't popular with everyone though:

- The City of London authorities were opposed to it because they thought it was disruptive and encouraged crime. As a result, many theatres, including The Globe, were built just outside the City in Southwark.
- Some members of Elizabeth's government were worried that the theatre might be used to spread pro-Catholic or anti-government messages. As theatres grew in popularity, the government introduced censorship measures to try and control what playwrights wrote.
- Many Puritans also opposed the theatre because they thought it encouraged immorality.

All the world's a stage, especially at The Globe Theatre...

Do you find the interpretation of Elizabethan theatre in the picture above convincing? Use the picture and your knowledge of the period to explain your answer. [8]

Elizabethan Sailors

English sailors weren't that interested in voyages of discovery at first, but once they recognised the economic opportunities on offer in the Americas and Asia, there was no stopping them.

The English were Slow to take an interest in Exploration

1) The Portuguese and Spanish were the first to explore the world beyond Europe. By the time Elizabeth became queen in 1558, both countries had established many colonies in the Americas.
2) It was only from the 1560s that English sailors began to take an interest in global exploration.

Explorers were Attracted by Economic Opportunities

Spanish trade with its American colonies was very profitable — their treasure ships returned to Europe full of silver and gold. The wealth of the region attracted English privateers (men who sailed their own vessels) who hoped to get rich by trading with Spain's colonies and raiding Spanish settlements and ships.

- John Hawkins was the first English privateer to take part in the Atlantic slave trade. In the 1560s, he made three slave-trading voyages. On two of these trips, he bought slaves in west Africa, transported them across the Atlantic and sold them to Spanish colonies in the Americas.
- The Spanish didn't want English sailors to trade with these Spanish colonies, so his activities fuelled growing tensions between England and Spain (see p.100).
- Hawkins' first two voyages were very profitable, but on his last expedition he was confronted by Spanish ships in the battle of San Juan de Ulúa and most of his fleet was destroyed.

From the 1570s, English merchants also became interested in trade with Asia, and began exploring routes to the region. Some tried to find the so-called North West passage around the top of North America, while others sailed through the Mediterranean and then went overland to India. In 1591, James Lancaster sailed to India around the Cape of Good Hope (the southern tip of Africa). Following Lancaster's success, the East India Company was set up in 1600 to trade with Asia.

Francis Drake was the Second man ever to sail Around the World

1) Francis Drake was John Hawkins' cousin, and had travelled with Hawkins on two of his slave-trading expeditions. Between 1577 and 1580, Drake circumnavigated the world (sailed all the way around it).
2) Drake probably wasn't trying to sail around the world. It seems that he was sent by Elizabeth to explore the coast of South America, looking for opportunities for English colonisation and trade. He may have planned to make money from his expedition by raiding Spanish colonies and treasure ships.
3) Drake explored the South American coastline, raiding many Spanish settlements as he went. In the Pacific, he captured two very valuable Spanish treasure ships. In order to get this treasure safely home, Drake had to return by a different route — the Spanish had sent ships to intercept him off the South American coast, so he couldn't return the way he had come.
4) Instead, Drake sailed west, across the Pacific to Indonesia. He then made his way across the Indian Ocean, round the Cape of Good Hope and back to England.
5) When he returned, Drake was knighted by Elizabeth aboard his ship, the Golden Hind. This royal recognition and the vast wealth that Drake brought back from the journey encouraged more English sailors to set out on long-distance journeys.

Drake was involved in many other important naval expeditions. E.g. in 1587 he led a raid on the Spanish port of Cadiz (p.100), and in 1588 he played a key role in the defeat of the Spanish Armada. He died of disease in 1596 while trying to conquer Spanish colonies in the Americas.

Circumnavigation — taking the roundabout route...

'Francis Drake's circumnavigation of the globe made him the most successful English sailor of Elizabeth's reign'. How far do you agree with this interpretation? Explain your answer. [16]

Elizabethan Sailors

After Drake's circumnavigation, England tried to challenge Spain's dominance as an imperial power by establishing a colony in North America. But creating a permanent settlement turned out to be pretty tricky...

Drake's Circumnavigation was a Huge Achievement

Drake's expedition was only the second successful global circumnavigation, and the first by an English sailor. He and his crew had to overcome some major challenges in order to complete the expedition.

1) Navigating across vast oceans was extremely difficult. Elizabethan sailors knew how to use the Sun and stars to work out how far north or south of the equator they were (their latitude), but they couldn't measure how far east or west they had travelled (their longitude).
2) Many of the places Drake visited had never been explored by European sailors before, so there were no detailed maps or charts to help him navigate.
3) Many sailors died of disease during long journeys — one of Drake's ships had to be abandoned after crossing the Atlantic because so many of the crew had died.
4) Bad weather could blow ships off course, or even sink them. Storms destroyed one of Drake's ships as it attempted to sail around the bottom of South America, and forced another to turn back to England.

The challenges of navigation, bad weather and disease had to be faced by all Elizabethan sailors who set out on long-distance voyages.

Raleigh's attempts to Colonise Virginia were Unsuccessful

Walter Raleigh was a member of a gentry family from Devon. His family were involved with international exploration, and Raleigh first visited America in 1578. From the early 1580s, Raleigh had a powerful position at court as one of Elizabeth's 'favourites'.

1) In 1584, Elizabeth gave Raleigh permission to explore and colonise unclaimed territories. She wanted him to establish a colony on the Atlantic coast of North America.
2) In 1585, Raleigh sent 108 settlers to establish a permanent colony on Roanoke Island, Virginia (Raleigh named his colony after Elizabeth, who was known as the 'Virgin Queen'). However, the settlers (or planters) soon ran low on supplies, and when Francis Drake visited Roanoke in 1586, most of them abandoned the colony and returned to England.

Comment and Analysis

An English colony would have challenged Spain's dominance in the Americas and could be used as a base for attacking Spanish treasure ships. The colony might also provide opportunities for trade.

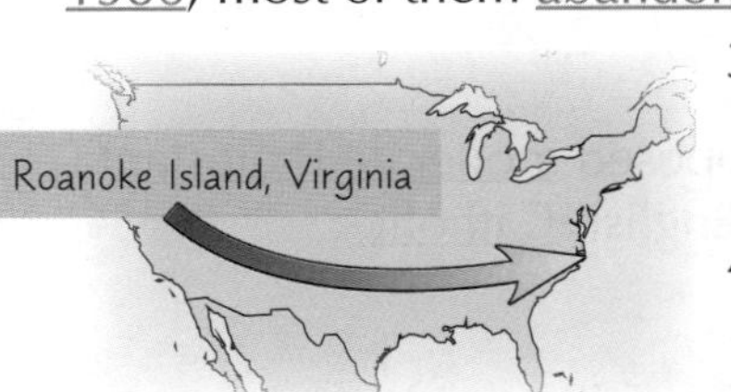

3) A second group of planters reached Roanoke in 1587. They were expecting supplies from England in 1588, but the fleet was delayed by the Spanish Armada (see p.101-102).
4) When the supply ships reached Roanoke in 1590, all the planters had disappeared. They were never found, and Roanoke became known as the 'Lost Colony'.
5) Raleigh was partly responsible for the colony's failure — his funds were too limited and the whole project was poorly planned. However, other factors like bad luck and a lack of supplies also played a part.

Raleigh's Career had Ups and Downs

1) Despite the failure of the Roanoke colony, Raleigh remained one of Elizabeth's 'favourites'.
2) However, in 1592 he was disgraced when Elizabeth found out that he had secretly married one of her ladies-in-waiting. As a punishment, Raleigh was banished from court and briefly imprisoned.
3) This wasn't the end of his career though — after his release he continued to play an important role in politics. He became a Member of Parliament and was still heavily involved with the Royal Navy.

As Raleigh learned, if you fail to plan, you plan to fail...

REVISION TASK

Make a timeline of Walter Raleigh's career. Include all the key events of his attempts to colonise Virginia and details of what happened to him after the failure of the Roanoke colony.

The Religious Settlement

By 1558, England had experienced decades of dizzying religious changes. Elizabeth's religious 'settlement', passed in 1559, aimed to put a stop to these changes and bring religious stability to England.

There had been constant Religious Changes since the 1530s

When Elizabeth became queen in 1558, England had suffered 30 years of religious turmoil, with the national religion switching repeatedly between Catholicism and Protestantism.

Henry VIII

Until the 1530s, England was a Catholic country, and most people were Catholics. However, in the early 1530s Henry VIII broke away from the Roman Catholic Church. He rejected the Pope's authority and made himself head of the Church of England.

Edward VI

Edward VI was a strong supporter of Protestantism. When he became king, he tried to reform the English Church to make it more Protestant.

Mary I

Mary I was a devout Catholic. As queen, she made England Catholic again — she restored the Pope as head of the English Church and removed Edward's protestant reforms. Protestants were harshly persecuted under Mary — more than 280 were executed, and many more fled to Protestant countries in Europe.

Elizabeth had been raised as a Protestant. She was deeply religious and committed to Protestantism. But she was also determined to end the constant religious changes of the last 30 years by creating a stable and lasting religious settlement.

Protestants questioned the authority of the Pope and rejected some Catholic beliefs — e.g. they believed that Christians were saved by faith, not by good deeds. They encouraged ordinary people to read the Bible by translating it from Latin, and thought churches should be plain and simple, unlike highly decorated Catholic churches.

The Religious Settlement was designed for Religious Stability

The Act of Supremacy gave Elizabeth Control over the Church

1) Henry VIII and Edward VI had used the title Supreme Head of the Church of England. In her Act of Supremacy (passed in 1559), Elizabeth altered this title to make herself the Supreme Governor of the English Church.
2) This gave Elizabeth control of the English Church, without actually calling her its 'Head'. This compromise satisfied those who believed a woman couldn't lead the Church.

The Act of Uniformity made Moderate Protestant Reforms

The Act of Uniformity and the Royal Injunctions, both passed in 1559, imposed moderate Protestant reforms on the English Church, but they also made some concessions to English Catholics:

Reforms

- Going to church was compulsory — there were fines for missing a church service.
- A new Book of Common Prayer was issued, which had to be used in all churches.
- All parishes had to have a copy of the Bible in English.

Concessions

- The wording of the communion service (an important Christian ceremony) was kept deliberately vague, so that it could be accepted by both Protestants and Catholics.
- Churches were allowed to keep some decorations, and priests had to wear certain Catholic vestments (robes).

Comment and Analysis

The religious settlement made England a Protestant country, but allowed some elements of Catholic belief and practice to continue. This 'middle way' was designed to satisfy the majority, who held moderate religious beliefs and were willing to make some compromises for the sake of peace and stability. But it couldn't win over the more extreme Catholics or the Puritans (see p.99).

Sometimes the 'middle way' is the only way...

Divide a piece of paper into two. Jot down the key features of the Act of Supremacy on one side and the Act of Uniformity and the Royal Injunctions on the other.

Mary, Queen of Scots

Even though Elizabeth and Mary, Queen of Scots, were cousins, Elizabeth wasn't too pleased when Mary arrived in England unexpectedly in 1568. In fact, she was so unimpressed, she put Mary in prison...

Mary, Queen of Scots, had a Strong Claim to the English Throne

1) Mary was the only child of James V of Scotland. She was related to the Tudors through her grandmother, Margaret Tudor. Margaret was Henry VIII's sister, the wife of James IV and mother of James V (see p.82).

© Mary Evans Picture Library

2) As a granddaughter of Margaret Tudor, Mary had a strong claim to the English throne. Because Mary was a Catholic, her claim was supported by many English Catholics.
3) Mary became queen of Scotland in 1542 when she was just six days old. Her mother acted as regent (she ruled on Mary's behalf), while Mary was raised in France.
4) In 1558, when Mary was 15 years old, she married the heir to the French throne. However, her husband died suddenly in 1560, and Mary returned to Scotland.

Comment and Analysis

Mary wanted to be named as heir to the English throne, but Elizabeth was unwilling to do this. She feared that making Mary her heir would encourage Catholic plots, both at home and abroad, to overthrow her and make Mary queen.

Mary Fled to England in 1568

1) In 1565 Mary married the Scottish nobleman Lord Darnley. The marriage was not a happy one. Darnley hated Mary's personal secretary, David Rizzio, and thought that the two were having an affair. In 1566 a group of Scottish nobles, accompanied by Darnley, stabbed Rizzio to death.
2) In 1567, Darnley was murdered. Many people believed that Mary and her close friend, the Earl of Bothwell, were behind the murder. Their suspicions seemed to be confirmed when Mary married Bothwell a few months later.
3) This marriage was unpopular with the Scottish nobles, who rebelled against Mary. They imprisoned her and forced her to abdicate (give up the throne) in favour of her one-year-old son, James. In 1568, Mary escaped from prison and raised an army. Her forces were defeated in battle and she fled south to England.

Some people (including Elizabeth) thought that the Scottish nobles had no right to overthrow Mary. As a result, they didn't accept her abdication, and still viewed her as the legitimate queen of Scotland.

Mary was Imprisoned, but still posed a Threat

1) Mary hoped that Elizabeth would help her regain control of Scotland. Elizabeth was not willing to do this — Mary's claim to the English throne meant that there would be a constant threat of invasion from the north if Mary regained power in Scotland.
2) Instead, Elizabeth had Mary imprisoned and set up an inquiry to investigate whether she had been involved in Darnley's murder.
3) Elizabeth didn't want the inquiry to find Mary guilty. A guilty verdict would lend support to the actions of the Scottish nobles, who had overthrown Mary, their legitimate queen.
4) However, Elizabeth didn't want a not-guilty verdict either, because this would force her to release Mary. Once free, Mary might use her claim to the English throne to try and overthrow Elizabeth.
5) In the end, the inquiry didn't reach a verdict — this enabled Elizabeth to keep Mary in captivity. Elizabeth hoped that imprisoning Mary would prevent her becoming the centre of Catholic plots, but Mary's presence caused problems for Elizabeth throughout the next 20 years (see p.97-99).

The so-called 'Casket Letters' were presented to the inquiry. They included several letters apparently written by Mary to Bothwell, which implicated the pair in Darnley's murder. Mary's supporters insisted that the letters were forgeries, but most members of the inquiry believed they were genuine.

Elizabeth really wasn't a fan of uninvited guests...

All this stuff happened before 1568, but it's still really important. Mary crops up again later, so you need to understand how she ended up in England and why she was a threat to Elizabeth.

The Northern Rebellion

Mary, Queen of Scots, had barely been in England five minutes when she began causing trouble for Elizabeth.

The Northern Nobles were unhappy for Several Reasons

1) Many northern nobles were still committed Catholics. They wanted to see the restoration of Catholicism in England under a Catholic monarch. The arrival of Mary, Queen of Scots, in 1568 (see p.95) gave them hope that Elizabeth could be replaced with Mary.
2) Elizabeth had confiscated large areas of land from the Earl of Northumberland and shared them between Northumberland's main rival in the north and a southern Protestant. Northumberland was also angry that Elizabeth had claimed all the profits from copper mines discovered on his estates.
3) Elizabeth had reduced the power of the northern nobles and increased her control in the north. In part, she did this through the Council of the North, which helped to govern the region. Under Elizabeth, the Council was controlled by southern Protestants. The northern nobles deeply resented this.
4) The northern nobles blamed Elizabeth's advisors for these policies. They believed that some privy councillors, especially William Cecil (see p.84), had become too powerful. They wanted to remove these 'evil counsellors' and replace them with men who would be more sympathetic to their interests.

The Northern Rebellion broke out in November 1569

1) In 1569 the Duke of Norfolk (the wealthiest landowner in England) hatched a plan to marry Mary, Queen of Scots, and have her recognised as Elizabeth's heir. This plan was supported by Catholic nobles, including the Earls of Northumberland and Westmorland, because it meant that Elizabeth would be succeeded by a Catholic queen.
2) When the plan was uncovered, the Earls feared they would be executed for their involvement. In a desperate attempt to escape punishment, they rebelled and tried to overthrow Elizabeth.
3) In November 1569, the Earls captured Durham, where they celebrated Catholic Mass in the cathedral. They then marched south, probably making for Tutbury in Derbyshire, where Mary was imprisoned.
4) Before the rebels reached Tutbury, a large royal army forced them to retreat. Many of their troops deserted, and the two Earls fled to Scotland. Elizabeth showed the rebels little mercy. Westmorland fled abroad, but Northumberland was executed, as were at least 400 rebel troops.

The revolt was a Serious Threat to Elizabeth's rule

1) The Northern Rebellion was the most serious rebellion of Elizabeth's reign. It posed a major threat to Elizabeth's rule and showed the danger that Mary, Queen of Scots, represented as a rallying point for English Catholics.
2) News of the rebellion created widespread fear among English Protestants about the threat posed by Catholics, and contributed to growing anti-Catholic feelings. These views were fuelled by memories of the harsh persecution of Protestants during the reign of Queen Mary I.
3) There was little support for the revolt among the rest of the Catholic nobility and ordinary people — when given a choice between Elizabeth and their religion, most Catholics chose to support the Queen. 1569-70 was the last time that English Catholics tried to remove Elizabeth by force.

Comment and Analysis

The Northern Rebellion sought to protect the long-standing independence of the northern nobles, but in the end it increased government control in the north of England. After the revolt, many rebels had their lands confiscated. The Council of the North was also strengthened under the leadership of the Puritan, Henry Hastings, Earl of Huntingdon.

Those northern earls were revolting...

As well as knowing what happened in Elizabethan England, you also need to know why things happened — so be sure to learn what caused events like the Northern Rebellion.

The Catholic Threat

The Catholic threat got even worse throughout the 1570s and early 1580s.
As a result, Elizabeth and her government became less and less tolerant of Catholicism.

The Pope Expelled Elizabeth from the Catholic Church

The excommunication was meant to strengthen the Northern Rebellion, but news of it didn't arrive until after the revolt had collapsed.

1) In 1570, Elizabeth was excommunicated (expelled from the Catholic Church) by the Pope. This meant Catholics no longer had to obey the Queen and were encouraged to overthrow her.
2) Together with the Northern Rebellion (see p.96), the excommunication changed Elizabeth's attitude towards Catholics. They were now seen as potential traitors, so Elizabeth and her government became less tolerant of recusancy (refusal to go to church) by Catholics.
3) In response to the excommunication, Parliament passed the Treasons Act in 1571. Under this Act, anyone who claimed that Elizabeth wasn't England's legitimate ruler could face the death penalty.

Missionary Priests strengthened English Catholicism

1) In 1568, William Allen founded a missionary college at Douai (now in France) to train English Catholic priests. Once trained, these missionary priests would return to England and secretly minister to English Catholics. The first missionary priests reached England in 1574.
2) In 1580, the missionaries Robert Parsons and Edmund Campion (who had both trained at a missionary college in Rome) entered the country. Campion was executed for treason in December 1581.
3) In the 1560s, Elizabeth had tolerated recusancy because she believed that English Catholicism would gradually die out as the religious settlement became more firmly established.
4) However, the arrival of the missionary priests from the 1570s changed things — with the support of these highly-committed missionaries, it was now unlikely that Catholicism in England would just fade away on its own. This strengthening of Catholicism was a major threat to the religious settlement.

In response to the threat from missionary priests, Parliament passed two anti-Catholic Acts in 1581. These Acts:
- Massively increased the fines for recusancy, making them too expensive for most ordinary Catholics.
- Introduced fines and prison sentences for people who said or attended Catholic Mass.
- Made it treason (which was punishable by death) to convert to Catholicism or persuade others to convert.
- Introduced prison sentences and the death penalty for anyone who encouraged rebellion.

Catholic Plots aimed to put Mary on the English Throne

1) Between 1571 and 1585 there were several Catholic plots to assassinate Elizabeth and replace her with Mary, Queen of Scots. They included the Ridolfi Plot (1571), the Throckmorton Plot (1583) and the Babington Plot (1586, see p.98).

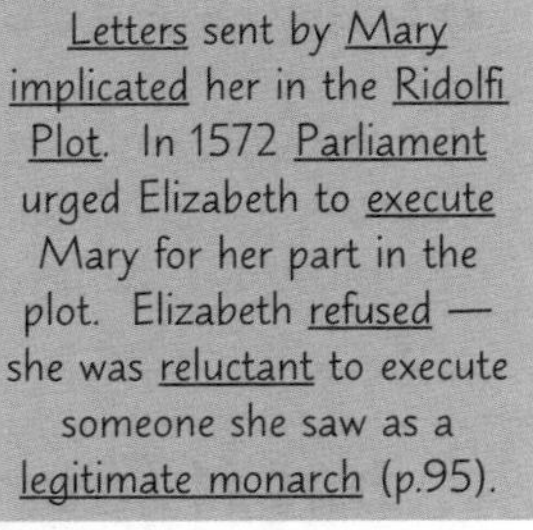
Letters sent by Mary implicated her in the Ridolfi Plot. In 1572 Parliament urged Elizabeth to execute Mary for her part in the plot. Elizabeth refused — she was reluctant to execute someone she saw as a legitimate monarch (p.95).

2) The plots involved Catholic conspirators in England and Europe. They were supported by the Pope and Catholic rulers, especially King Philip II of Spain.
3) The plots were a real threat to Elizabeth's rule and her religious settlement (p.94). Mary's strong claim to the throne (p.95) made them seem credible, and Philip II's involvement meant there was a risk they would lead to a Spanish invasion.
4) However, none of the plots succeeded. This was partly because there was little public support for a Catholic revolution (as the Northern Rebellion had shown). Also, by the 1580s Elizabeth's Principal Secretary, Francis Walsingham, had established a highly efficient spy network, which ensured that the plots were uncovered before they were carried out.

Comment and Analysis

Missionary priests supported the Catholic plots to assassinate Elizabeth. They wanted England to return to Catholicism and believed this could only be achieved if Elizabeth was removed.

Don't lose the plot, just learn this page...

REVISION TASK

Write a couple of sentences to explain why each of the following factors was a threat to Elizabeth and her religious settlement: excommunication, missionary priests, Catholic plots.

The Catholic Threat

In 1586 Walsingham used his spy network to prove that Mary had supported the Babington Plot. His evidence persuaded Elizabeth to put Mary on trial and execute her for treason.

Persecution of Catholics Increased in the 1580s

1) In 1584 the Dutch Protestant leader, William the Silent, was assassinated by a Catholic. Combined with the arrival of missionary priests and the Catholic plots against Elizabeth, this assassination made the government even more concerned about the Catholic threat in England.
2) As a result, persecution of Catholics increased. Anti-Catholic laws were enforced more strictly than they had been earlier in Elizabeth's reign, and in 1585 Parliament passed two new laws:
   - Mary, Queen of Scots, wouldn't be allowed to become queen if Elizabeth was assassinated. It was hoped that this would put a stop to the plots involving Mary.
   - Missionary priests had 40 days to leave the country. Any priests who didn't leave could be executed, as could anyone who tried to help them.

The anti-Catholic laws of 1581 and 1585 led to the execution of more than 120 Catholic priests and the deaths of many more in prison.

The Babington Plot led to the Execution of Mary, Queen of Scots

1) In 1586, Francis Walsingham used his spy network to gather evidence of Mary, Queen of Scots' involvement in the Babington Plot. He intercepted and decoded Mary's letters, including one which approved plans to assassinate the Queen and free Mary from prison.
2) Mary had been implicated in Catholic plots before, but Elizabeth had always refused to take action against her. The evidence gathered by Walsingham finally persuaded her to put Mary on trial.
3) In October 1586, Mary was found guilty of treason and sentenced to death. Despite the guilty verdict, Elizabeth was very reluctant to execute Mary. Parliament and the Privy Council believed that the execution was vital to weaken the Catholic threat and protect the religious settlement, so they put pressure on Elizabeth to sign Mary's death warrant.
4) After hesitating for several months, Elizabeth eventually agreed to the execution. Mary was executed on 8th February 1587.

Comment and Analysis

Elizabeth was reluctant to execute Mary because she was queen of Scotland. Elizabeth believed that monarchs ruled by Divine Right (see p.85), so she felt she had no right to execute a legitimate monarch. She also feared that executing Mary would undermine her own claim to rule by Divine Right and might fuel more plots against her.

Mary's execution Reduced the Threat from Catholics at Home...

The execution of Mary, Queen of Scots, removed the Catholic threat to Elizabeth at home. English Catholics now had no-one to rally around, and they lost hope of ever overthrowing Elizabeth and reversing the religious settlement. There were no more major Catholic plots during Elizabeth's reign.

...but it Increased the Threat from Abroad

1) In 1587, relations with Spain were at a low point — the two countries were now at war over the Netherlands, and King Philip II had been preparing for an attack on England since 1585 (see p.100). Mary's execution made the situation worse. Philip was now even more determined to invade.
2) There was also a danger that Mary's son, James VI of Scotland might seek revenge for his mother's death. There were fears that he would form an alliance with other Catholic powers in order to invade England.

The Babington Plot wasn't very well executed...

EXAM QUESTION

Give an account of the ways missionary priests affected England in the 1570s and 1580s. [8]

The Puritan Threat

As if the Catholic threat wasn't bad enough, the religious settlement also faced a threat from the other end of the religious spectrum. The Puritans were committed Protestants who wanted to purify the English Church.

The Puritans wanted to make the English Church More Protestant

The Puritans were committed Protestants. For them, the religious settlement of 1559 was only a first step in purifying the Church of England — they wanted further reforms that would make the Church more Protestant.

1) They were strongly anti-Catholic and wanted to remove all traces of Catholicism from the Church.
2) They believed that preaching (explaining the word of God) was very important. They thought that all priests should be well educated so that they'd be able to preach. At the time, this was unusual — many priests lacked education and didn't preach at all.
3) The Puritans also encouraged the education of ordinary people, so that they would be able to read and understand the Bible for themselves.
4) They were very strict about godly living (obeying all of God's commandments).

Comment and Analysis

For Elizabeth, the religious settlement of 1559 was final and couldn't be changed. She wanted everyone to accept the settlement, so she saw Puritan demands for further reforms as a serious threat.

Some Puritans were more radical. They wanted to get rid of the Church hierarchy of archbishops, bishops, etc. This view was a threat to Elizabeth because it called into question her authority as Supreme Governor of the Church — the head of the hierarchy.

The 'Prophesyings' taught Priests how to Preach

1) By the 1570s, the Puritans were concerned about the lack of educated priests who were able to preach. So they introduced the 'prophesyings' — a kind of training to teach priests how to preach.
2) Elizabeth thought that the 'prophesyings' would encourage more Puritan opposition to the religious settlement. In 1576, she ordered the Archbishop of Canterbury, Edmund Grindal, to put a stop to them.
3) Grindal (a moderate Puritan) thought the 'prophesyings' were good for the Church, so he refused to obey Elizabeth's order. This made Elizabeth furious. She suspended Grindal and put him under house arrest.

Archbishop Whitgift tried to Suppress Puritanism

1) In 1583 Grindal died and Elizabeth made John Whitgift Archbishop of Canterbury. With Elizabeth's support, Whitgift launched an attack on Puritan clergy — all priests had to accept the regulations of the Church of England or face suspension. Between 200 and 300 Puritan priests were suspended.
2) Whitgift's campaign made some Puritans feel that there was no hope of reforming the Church of England. Instead, they decided to break away and form a separate church.
3) These Puritan separatists were seen as a major threat to the religious settlement. The government introduced censorship laws to prevent them spreading their ideas, and in 1590 several of their leaders were arrested.
4) The threat from Puritan separatists probably wasn't as serious as Elizabeth and her government thought. There weren't many separatists and they didn't have the support of any powerful members of the elite. Most Puritans were moderates who worked within the Church of England.

Comment and Analysis

Whitgift's campaign faced some opposition from the Privy Council and Parliament. Elizabeth overcame this by threatening to dismiss any council members who opposed it, and refusing to let Parliament discuss the matter.

The Puritans wanted the Church to be pure and simple...

The different religious groups in Elizabethan England can be pretty confusing. You need to know what the Puritans believed, and how they were different from Catholics and moderate Protestants.

War with Spain

England and Spain tried to stay on good terms, but the growing tensions between them eventually led to war.

There were Political, Religious and Economic tensions with Spain

King Philip II of Spain had been married to Queen Mary I of England, and the two countries had been allies. Elizabeth and Philip tried to maintain good relations, but tensions between them gradually began to grow.

Political

Spain was a great imperial power. In Europe, Philip ruled Spain, the Netherlands, parts of Italy and (from 1581) Portugal. He also had a large empire in the Americas. By the 1570s, England was starting to have ambitions for an empire of its own (p.92-93). This led to growing rivalry and tension between the two countries.

Religious

Philip was a devout Catholic and disliked Elizabeth's religious settlement. He became involved in several Catholic plots against Elizabeth in the 1570s and 1580s (p.97-98), which damaged Elizabeth's trust in him.

Economic

Elizabeth encouraged privateers to trade illegally with Spanish colonies, raid Spanish ships and attack the treasure fleets carrying gold and silver from the Americas to Spain.

In the 1560s an English fleet, commanded by John Hawkins, traded with Spanish colonies, even though Spain had banned them from doing so (p.92). This led to the Battle of San Juan de Ulúa in 1568. Francis Drake also raided many Spanish colonies in South America during his round-the-world voyage of 1577-80 (p.92-93).

England and Spain eventually went to War over the Netherlands

1) In 1581, Protestant rebels in the Netherlands declared independence from Spain. In 1584 the rebel leader, William the Silent, was assassinated, and the revolt was in danger of being defeated.
2) Elizabeth decided to help the rebels — in 1585 she signed the Treaty of Nonsuch, which promised military assistance. Religious, economic and military factors influenced her decision:
    - Elizabeth wanted to protect Dutch Protestantism and prevent Philip forcing Catholicism on the Netherlands.
    - English exports to Europe were vital to the English economy, and many English goods reached the European market via Dutch ports, especially Antwerp. Elizabeth needed to ensure that English merchants would have access to the Dutch ports.
    - If the rebels were defeated, Philip might use the Netherlands as a base for an invasion of England.
3) Philip saw the Treaty of Nonsuch as a declaration of war on Spain. In response, he began building a huge fleet (an Armada) that he planned to use to invade England.

Drake was sent to Disrupt Spanish Preparations for the Armada

1) Elizabeth sent Drake to spy on Spanish preparations and attack their ships and supplies. In April 1587, Drake attacked the Spanish port of Cadiz. He destroyed around 30 ships and seized many tonnes of supplies.
2) This delayed the Armada by more than a year. Obtaining fresh supplies and weapons was very expensive and seriously strained Spain's finances.
3) During his raid, Drake captured planks made from seasoned wood, which were needed to make the barrels used to carry food and water.
4) As a result, the Spanish had to make their barrels from unseasoned wood, which couldn't preserve food and water very well. This caused supply problems for the Armada and affected the morale of Spanish troops and sailors. Fresh water supplies were lost and many tons of food rotted as the fleet sailed to England in 1588.

Comment and Analysis

Drake described his raid on Cadiz as 'singeing the King of Spain's beard'. He meant that he had inflicted temporary damage on King Philip's Armada, but hadn't destroyed it entirely — it would 'grow back' in time.

The Americas — a whole New World of commercial rivalry...

England's relationship with Spain was a major headache for Elizabeth throughout her reign. Make sure you understand how and why the relationship changed over time.

The Spanish Armada

The Spanish Armada was launched in 1588, but right from the start, things didn't go according to plan...

The Armada Planned to meet the Duke of Parma at Dunkirk

1) By the spring of 1588, the Spanish Armada was complete and Philip was ready to launch his 'Enterprise of England'. The Armada was a huge fleet of around 130 ships, manned by approximately 8000 sailors and carrying an estimated 18,000 soldiers.
2) Philip appointed the Duke of Medina Sidonia to lead the Armada. Philip respected the Duke's high social status and trusted him to obey instructions. However, the Duke had little military or naval experience, and he tried unsuccessfully to turn down the command.
3) The Spanish had thousands more soldiers stationed in the Netherlands under the leadership of the Duke of Parma. Philip's plan was for the Armada to meet Parma's army at Dunkirk. The combined forces would then sail across the Channel to England under the protection of the Armada's warships.

The Armada reached the English Channel in July 1588

1) The Armada set out in May 1588, but was delayed for several weeks by bad weather in the Bay of Biscay and by the attempts of an English fleet to intercept it.
2) In July the Spanish fleet was sighted off Cornwall and beacons (signal fires) were lit along the south coast to send the news to Elizabeth in London. English ships set sail from Plymouth to meet the Armada.

3) The Armada sailed up the Channel in a crescent formation. This was an effective defensive strategy, which used the large, armed galleons to protect the weaker supply and troop ships.
4) The English navy carried out a few minor raids, but was unable to inflict much damage. Only two Spanish ships were lost, and these were both destroyed by accident.

The English Attacked the Spanish at Calais and Gravelines

1) Having sailed up the Channel, Medina Sidonia anchored at Calais to wait for Parma's troops. However, Parma and his men were being blockaded by Dutch ships and weren't able to reach the coast in time.
2) In the middle of the night, the English sent eight fireships (ships loaded with flammable materials and set on fire) among the anchored Spanish ships. This caused panic among the Spanish sailors, who cut their anchor cables, broke their defensive formation and headed for the open sea.
3) The Spanish ships regrouped at Gravelines, but the weather made it impossible for them to return to their defensive position at Calais. The English moved in, and the following battle lasted for many hours. Five Spanish ships were sunk, and the rest of the fleet was forced to sail away from the French coast and into the North Sea.
4) An English fleet followed the Spanish as far north as Scotland to make sure they did not regroup and return to collect Parma's army.

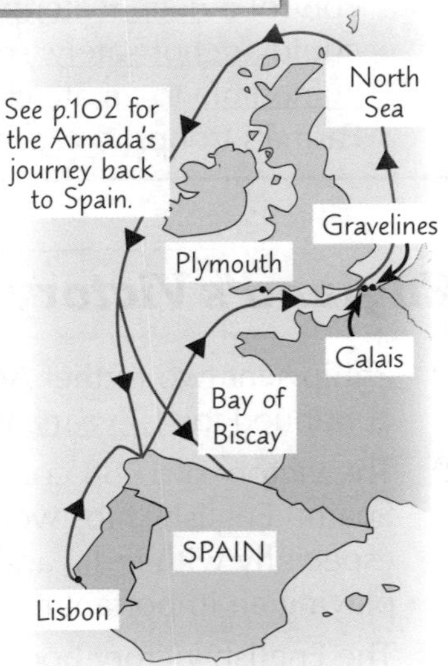

So much for King Philip's cunning plan...

Have another read of the last two pages, then cover them up and jot down a timeline of the Spanish Armada. Include all the key events from the Treaty of Nonsuch to the Battle of Gravelines.

REVISION TASK

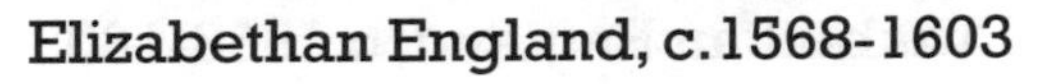

The Spanish Armada

The English navy had defeated the Armada, and the Spanish ships now faced a dangerous journey home.

The Armada's Journey back to Spain was a Disaster

1) Medina Sidonia decided to call off the attack on England and return to Spain by sailing round Scotland and Ireland. The Spanish sailors were unfamiliar with this very dangerous route, and they encountered several powerful Atlantic storms.
2) Many ships sank or were wrecked on the Scottish and Irish coasts, where the local inhabitants showed the survivors little mercy. Those ships that completed the journey ran short of supplies, and many men died of starvation and disease. In all, less than half the fleet and fewer than 10,000 men made it back to Spain.

Several Factors contributed to the Defeat of the Armada

English Strengths

- The English had improved their ship building, giving them several technological advantages. Spain relied on large ships which were heavy and difficult to handle, whereas the English built long, narrow ships which were faster and easier to handle. English cannons could also be reloaded much more quickly than Spanish ones.
- English tactics were more effective. Spanish ships aimed to come alongside their opponents, board their vessels and overcome the enemy in hand-to-hand fighting. The Spanish couldn't use this tactic against the English, who used their greater mobility to stay out of range. Instead of boarding the Spanish ships, the English fired broadsides (massive barrages of cannonballs) which could sink them.

Spanish Weaknesses

- Most of Spain's men lacked experience of naval warfare, whereas the English fleet was manned by experienced sailors.
- The Spanish plan to meet the Duke of Parma at Dunkirk was seriously flawed. Spain didn't control a deep water port where the Armada could anchor safely, so the ships were extremely vulnerable to an attack while they waited for Parma's troops to escape the Dutch blockade.

Luck

- The death of Spain's leading admiral, Santa Cruz, in February 1588, led to the appointment of the inexperienced Duke of Medina Sidonia to lead the Armada.
- The weather made it impossible for the Spanish fleet to return to the Channel after the battle of Gravelines, forcing it to travel into the dangerous waters off the Scottish and Irish coasts.

England's Victory Removed the threat of a Spanish Invasion

1) Philip sent two further Armadas in the 1590s, but they were both unsuccessful. Although war with Spain continued for 15 years, the Armada of 1588 was the last serious Spanish threat to Elizabeth's throne.
2) The victory of 1588 contributed to England's development as a strong naval power to rival Spain. English ships went on many voyages of discovery and established valuable trade routes, especially with India and the Far East (see p.92). By the end of Elizabeth's reign, the navy was also playing an important role in attempts to set up an English colony in North America (see p.93).
3) The English victory boosted Elizabeth's popularity and strengthened the Protestant cause — it was seen as a sign that God favoured Protestantism.

The defeat of the Armada — a great English victory...

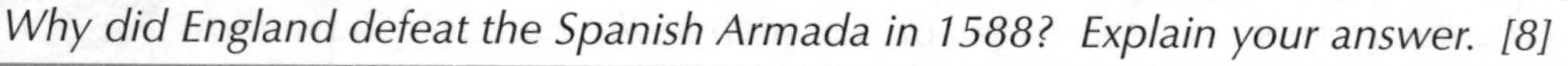

Why did England defeat the Spanish Armada in 1588? Explain your answer. [8]

EXAM QUESTION

Revision Summary

That's the Elizabethans all done and dusted — time to test your knowledge with a quick revision summary.

- Try these questions and tick off each one when you get it right.
- When you've done all the questions for a topic and are completely happy with it, tick off the topic.

Elizabeth's Court and Parliament (p.82-87)

1) Describe Queen Elizabeth I's character.
2) Explain what the term 'patronage' means.
3) What was the role of the Privy Council?
4) Name three of Elizabeth's key ministers.
5) What were Parliament's main functions?
6) Give three ways in which Elizabeth and her Privy Council managed Parliament.
7) Why was Elizabeth under pressure to find a husband?
8) How did Elizabeth's Privy Council change towards the end of her reign?
9) Who was Robert Devereux? Briefly describe his rebellion against Elizabeth.

Life in Elizabethan Times (p.88-93)

10) Why did the problem of poverty get worse in the 1590s?
11) What were the three categories of poor people in Elizabethan England?
12) Describe how the Poor Laws of 1597 and 1601 treated the deserving and undeserving poor.
13) Give four ways in which members of the Elizabethan elite spent their growing wealth.
14) Describe the layout of Elizabethan theatres.
15) Name three Elizabethan acting companies.
16) Why were some people opposed to the theatre?
17) Who was John Hawkins?
18) What did Francis Drake do between 1577 and 1580? Why was this a major achievement?
19) Who organised the attempted colonisation of Virginia in the 1580s?
20) Why is Roanoke known as the 'Lost Colony'?

Troubles at Home and Abroad (p.94-102)

21) Name the two Acts of the Elizabethan religious settlement.
22) Why did Mary, Queen of Scots, have a strong claim to the English throne?
23) Give three reasons for the 1569 Northern Rebellion.
24) How did Elizabeth's government respond to the threat posed by missionary priests?
25) Name three Catholic plots against Elizabeth.
26) Why was Elizabeth reluctant to execute Mary, Queen of Scots?
27) Explain how radical Puritans wanted to change the Church.
28) Who was John Whitgift? What was his role in dealing with the Puritan threat?
29) Why did England and Spain go to war in 1585?
30) Explain what the phrase 'the singeing of the King of Spain's beard' means.
31) Who led the Spanish Armada?
32) How did the English attack the Armada at Calais?
33) Write down four reasons why the English navy defeated the Spanish Armada.

Studying the Historic Environment

These pages are full of great advice on how to talk about your Elizabethan historic site in the exam.

The Key Features of a Site can tell you a lot about its History

The key features of a historical site are any details, characteristics or features that stand out and make the site, or part of it, special. They are the main or most important characteristics of the site. These features can show how people lived and help to paint a picture of their culture, values, and fashions.

Sites like theatres, settlements, and manor houses (and their gardens), can tell you a lot about how people lived in Elizabethan England.

Use these questions to help you to identify the key features of your site...

1) How was the site used? Did this change over time?
2) Where is the site located? What was that location like?
3) Is there anything significant about the structure of the site? e.g. the layout of a theatre was often centred around its stage.
4) What were the key design features of the site? Think about big and small features (e.g. a manor house might have impressive tall towers and glass windows, but it might also have more intricate details like family crests and initials carved in stone.)
5) Who used, designed and/or built the site? What do the site's features tell you about these people? For example, lots of manor houses were built by nobles who wanted to show off their wealth and status. Glass windows were expensive, so putting many in a manor house was a sign of great wealth.
6) Is the site connected to any key events or developments of the period?

For example, some manor houses were used as defensive strongholds as well as homes in the medieval period. In more peaceful times, they were just used as homes. As a result, the original location of a manor house might have been chosen because it was easy to defend.

You can use Key Features as Evidence of Change and Continuity

Studying the way key features changed over time at your site can help you to understand developments or key turning points in the site's history.

1) You need to know which key features of your historic environment site changed during the period that you've studied for your depth study.
2) Look for features that were different in an earlier period. Think about what this tells you about the way that society and culture changed during your time period.
3) Think about what had stayed the same. These continuities might also reflect the society and culture of your site.
4) In the exam, you'll need to use your knowledge of key features to support any arguments that you make about change and continuity. (There are some tips on how to do this on p.106.)

Make sure that you understand why these features changed — consider whether the changes are linked to any major events or developments that happened during your time period. This will help you to put the changes into context.

Historic Sites can influence Key Events and Developments

1) The nature of a historic environment can influence the events and developments which happened there.
2) Understanding the key features of a site can help you to explain how and why certain events or developments happened the way they did.

Key events like battles are often influenced by the place where they happen. The location, layout and conditions of a site can all make a difference to how an event pans out.

In 1588, the English attacked the Spanish Armada at Calais while it was waiting to pick up more Spanish soldiers, and it fled into the English Channel. After this, the Armada wanted to return to Calais, but the wind was blowing the wrong way. This meant they ended up fighting the English at Gravelines.

The leaders of the Spanish Armada were forced to fight when they weren't ready. After Gravelines, they decided to retreat. Therefore, the weather conditions of the English Channel were directly linked to the defeat of the Spanish Armada.

Biscuit barrels are a key feature of my kitchen...

Chocolatey goodness and a satisfying crunch are the key features of every good biscuit. Understanding the key features of a historic environment can be pretty useful if you're trying to put a site into context.

Writing About the Historic Environment

This handy page explains how to choose relevant key features to use as evidence in the exam.

Talk about Relevant Key Features in the Exam

In the exam, you'll be asked about the site that you've studied. You'll need to use your own knowledge of the key features of your site to answer an essay question. In your essay, you'll be asked to link the historic environment (your site) to an aspect of Elizabethan England that you've looked at in your depth study.

1) The question might focus on a key change or period of continuity, or it could ask you to examine the causes or consequences of an event or development.
2) Only talk about features of your site that are relevant to the question that you've been asked and to the points that you're making in your answer.
3) You need to select pieces of information that support your arguments.

See p.106 for some examples of how to use key features in your answer.

Different Features can tell you Different Things

When you're talking about key features, you could choose something quite broad, like the physical location of a site, or focus on very small details, like a specific type of window on a building.

1) Think about the location of your site and what was around it. There's often a reason why a certain place was chosen (e.g. it was easy to defend), and this can reveal things about the lives of those who occupied the site.
2) The way a site is used over time can be very useful — changes in function can reflect gradual change, or be a result of upheaval or a significant event.
3) Design features often reflect key attitudes or changes in the owners' lives.
4) They can also tell you a lot about the motives of the people who used or created the site. Think about the physical structure of your site and what it tells you about the way it was used and the people who designed it.
5) Pick out features that are representative of your period. Some features might be unique to your site, while others might be typical of the period and pop up in lots of sites.

For example, a family crest might be added to the wall of an Elizabethan manor house. This might suggest that the owner wanted to show off their long-standing family connections and nobility in a time when new members of the gentry were rising.

Use your Own Knowledge to put Key Features into Context

1) Use what you know about your period to put the key features of your site into context.
2) Talk about your site's development in the context of wider changes or events during your period.
3) For example, changes in design often reflect wider cultural changes — fashions change over time and key features can be used as evidence of how and when these changes affected a particular site.
4) When you identify a feature, talk about what it might suggest about the people who used the site, then link it to wider developments.

For example, new design features like fireplaces might have been added to an Elizabethan manor house by a particular owner — this could be a sign of the growing wealth of the owner. It might also show that the owner wanted to keep up with changing fashions in building design.

A key feature of the Elizabethan period was the rise of the gentry and their increasing wealth. New design features can be evidence of this wealth being used to improve living conditions. They're often evidence of owners wanting to show off their wealth by spending money in a way that was visible to everyone around them.

I was wondering why my mam chiseled that crest on our wall...

There are loads of different types of key feature that you can use in the exam. Study all of the key features of your site — it'll help you to pick out the most relevant examples for your essay.

Essay Skills

This page'll give you a few tips on how to use your knowledge of the key features to write a good essay.

You'll need to use your Knowledge of Key Features in the Exam

There'll be a question in the exam that deals with historical ideas like change and continuity, and causes and consequences (see p.2). It'll look a bit like this:

This question starts by making a statement about a key change that's linked to a particular type of site. In the exam, it'll be linked to the specific site that you've studied.

'The main change that Elizabethan theatres demonstrated was the increasing popularity of plays as a form of entertainment.'

How far does a study of the Globe Theatre support this statement?

Explain your answer.

Refer to the Globe and your contextual knowledge. [16 marks]

It'll name a specific site (in the exam, it'll be the one that you've studied).

You'll need to use evidence from your site to answer the question. Always support your points by drawing on your knowledge of your site's key features.

Use the Key Features of your site to Support your Answer

Select key features that are relevant to the question and use them to support your points. Make sure you clearly link the features to the argument that you're making. Explain how the key features of your site support (or go against) the statement in the question.

The Globe was designed to be permanent. This suggests that the theatre was becoming more popular as a form of regular entertainment. The Globe was a wooden structure that was used as a permanent theatre venue in Elizabethan London. This meant that plays could be performed more regularly and in a fixed place. As a result, its owner and designer, Richard Burbage, could make a steady and reliable income out of the theatre. He couldn't do this when plays were performed across the country in inns and village squares in the earlier part of Elizabeth's reign.

The design of the Globe shows that theatre was becoming popular among both the rich and the poor. Richer people sat underneath a thatched cover that stretched around the edge of the theatre. Poorer people, known as groundlings, stood around the apron stage. This was an open air stage that pushed into the crowd. This meant that everyone in society could enjoy plays, without having to mix with each other and weaken the gap in social status that existed between the rich and the poor.

Use your knowledge of the period to support your arguments and link your site to wider developments. Don't just write down everything you know about the period — you need to answer the question. You can use your knowledge to argue against the statement in the question too.

You can also use the actions or motives of people who were linked to your site to support your arguments. Try to link the attitudes of people who are linked to your site to the values held by wider society.

Burbage used classical features like pillars when he built the Globe to try and make theatre seem more respectable and improve its status. These design features were popular and well-respected in Elizabethan England, so he hoped they would improve the reputation of the Globe. The Globe also had to be built outside the City of London, because the London authorities and the Puritans disapproved of the theatre. They thought that it encouraged poor behaviour. This shows that, although the popularity of the theatre was growing, not everyone in Elizabethan London approved of it.

Who knew key features could be so revealing...

This question might seem a bit daunting, but if you learn the key features of your site inside-out and know how to use them to support your argument, then you'll be off to a great start in the exam.

Exam Skills for the Thematic Study

These two pages are all about how to answer the thematic study section of your exam.

The Thematic Study covers a Long Period of time

1) The thematic study covers around 1000 years of history and goes right up the present day.
2) The study focuses on what changed over time and why — this means it's really important to know the main features of different ages within the period you're looking at (e.g. the Middle Ages, the Renaissance).
3) You'll be expected to understand social, political and economic changes during your period. You'll need to think about the importance of different factors from your period, e.g. the role of the government, war, religion or important individuals.
4) You'll also need to know how these factors impacted developments in your thematic study. For example, how improvements in science helped the prevention of disease.
5) You need to practise analysing visual and written sources from the period you're studying. You should be able to apply your knowledge of context to work out what the source is saying and why.

There are Four basic types of exam question

1) The first question involves a visual or written source. You'll be asked how useful the source is in studying something from your topic.

   How useful is Source A to a historian studying cholera? [8 marks]

2) The next question will ask you to 'explain' the significance of something — you'll have to assess its impact on the period that you've studied.

   Explain the significance of the Germ Theory in the development of medicine. [8 marks]

3) The third question will be a comparison. You'll have to write about the similarities and/or differences between two aspects of the period you've studied.

   Compare surgery in the Middle Ages with surgery in the 19th century. In what ways were they similar? [8 marks]

4) In the fourth question, you'll need to make an argument about the role one factor (e.g. religion) played in your topic. You'll need to give your own opinion.

   Has the role of the government been the main factor in the development of medicine in Britain since Medieval times? [20 marks]

The first three questions could all ask about an important event or development, or the role of an individual or group.

There are 4 marks for spelling, punctuation and grammar in this question (see p.137).

You'll need these Skills to answer the questions

1) When you're analysing the usefulness of a source, always look at what it's saying and where it's from. Use the source and your own knowledge to decide if the source is reliable and if the content is relevant.
2) Always support your points with relevant evidence and explain how it backs up the point. Specific information will get you more marks than making generalisations, so having a good knowledge of the facts is important.
3) For the final question, have a clear argument in your head before you start writing. Consider the importance of other factors, as well as the one you've been asked to discuss, and think about how their significance has changed over time.
4) For more general advice on how to answer exam questions, see p.136.

Make sure you get your dates right in the exam — remember that the seventeenth century refers to the 1600s, the eighteenth century refers to the 1700s, and so on.

Exam Skills for the Thematic Study

Here are some sample answers for questions in the thematic study section of your exam.

Have a look at this Sample Answer

This sample answer will help you to assess the usefulness of a source.

Source A

An English cartoon by John Leech, published in 1858. Its caption says, 'Father Thames Introducing his Offspring to the Fair City of London'. It shows figures representing diphtheria, scrofula and cholera rising from the river.

How useful is Source A to a historian studying cholera? [8 marks]

Source A was published in 1858 and is useful because it shows the fear surrounding cholera in Britain at the time. The corpse-like figures rising out of the water suggest that cholera symbolised death, and that Londoners were under attack from the disease. Indeed, an epidemic in 1848 killed 53,000 people. The source therefore gives historians an idea of people's views of cholera, but doesn't reveal much about other aspects of the disease, e.g. its impact on London.

Source A is also useful because it gives historians an insight into people's beliefs in 1858 about how cholera was spread. The figure of cholera is rising from the river, which is clearly polluted — dead animals have been washed ashore. The link the cartoonist makes between pollution and cholera suggests people's continued belief in the 'miasma theory' — the idea that inhaling bad smells caused disease.

The first sentence directly addresses the question.

Details from the source are used to back up points.

The answer talks about why it might not be useful.

Using your own knowledge shows a good level of understanding.

This refers back to the source for evidence.

This is a shortened example — in the exam, you'd need to finish this paragraph and make more points.

Here's another Sample Answer to help you

This sample answer will give you an idea of how to respond to the final question.
Look at the points that have been made and how they have been supported with evidence.

Has the role of the government been the main factor in the development of medicine in Britain since medieval times? Explain your answer with reference to the government and other factors. [20 marks]

The government has played an increasingly important role in medicine since medieval times, and is one of the leading factors in its development today. The establishment of the National Health Service (NHS) in 1948 was a crucial turning point for the government's role in medicine, as it took on the responsibility of providing free healthcare for all. The NHS has resulted in a dramatic improvement in health in Britain. Life expectancy rose by over ten years between 1951 and 2011.

However, before the 19th century the government's role in medical development was limited. In medieval times (1000-1500), the supernatural dominated beliefs about disease, and many people believed illness was a punishment from God. This meant that the Catholic Church played an important role in medicine.

This gives a basic answer to the question straight away.

The answer considers how the government's role changed over time.

Specific details show understanding.

You'll need to think about the role of other factors, too.

This is a shortened example — in the exam, you'd need to finish this paragraph and make more points.

My opinion of this sauce? — It's delicious...

Thematic studies are a long old haul, but don't worry — you might already know some of it because they go right up to the present day. That's sixteen-ish years in the bag. Just 984 years to go, then...

Disease and the Supernatural

In medieval England (and for the purposes of this section we're talking roughly 1000 to 1500), treatment of disease was a bit... medieval. The key problem was a lack of understanding of the causes of disease.

Disease was thought to have Supernatural Causes

1) Many people believed that disease was a punishment from God for people's sins. They thought that disease existed to show them the error of their ways and to make them become better people. Therefore, they thought that the way to cure disease was through prayer and repentance.
2) Disease was also thought to be caused by evil supernatural beings, like demons or witches. Witches were believed to be behind outbreaks of disease — many people were tried as witches and executed.
3) People believed that some diseases could be caused by evil spirits living inside someone. Members of the Church performed exorcisms, using chants to remove the spirit from the person's body.

The Church had a big Influence on medieval medicine

1) The Roman Catholic Church was an extremely powerful organisation in medieval Europe. It dominated the way people studied and thought about a range of topics, including medicine.
2) The Church encouraged people to believe that disease was a punishment from God, rather than having a natural cause. This prevented people from trying to find cures for disease — if disease was a punishment from God, all you could do was pray and repent.
3) The Church made sure that scholars of medicine learned the works of Galen (see p.110) as his ideas fit the Christian belief that God created human bodies and made them to be perfect. It also stopped anyone from disagreeing with Galen.
4) The Church outlawed dissection. This meant that medieval doctors couldn't discover ideas about human anatomy for themselves — they instead had to learn Galen's incorrect ideas.

Comment and Analysis

The Church's influence over medieval medicine meant that there was very little change in ideas about the cause of disease until the Renaissance — the Church and its messages were so influential that people were unable to question them.

Astrology was used to Diagnose disease

1) Astrology is the idea that the movements of the planets and stars have an effect on the Earth and on people. Astrologers in medieval England believed that these movements could cause disease.
2) Astrology was a new way of diagnosing disease. It was developed in Arabic medicine and brought to Europe between 1100 and 1300.
3) Medieval doctors owned a type of calendar (called an almanac) which included information about where particular planets and stars were at any given time. The doctor then used this information to predict how patients' health could be affected.
4) Different star signs were thought to affect different parts of the body.

A woodcut from 1490 showing two astrologers looking at the positions of the Sun and Moon.

The medieval period — a dark age for medicine...

Look at the woodcut of the astrologers above. Scribble down a few sentences explaining how useful you think it would be to a historian studying medieval beliefs about the causes of disease.

Natural Explanations

Some treatments in medieval Britain were based less on religious faith and more on natural theories and observation of the physical world. But a reason-based theory can still be wrong.

Medicine was dominated by the Four Humours Theory

After the fall of the Roman Empire, much Ancient Greek and Roman medical knowledge was lost in the West. The Theory of the Four Humours was eventually brought back to western Europe via the Islamic world (see p.111). Many medieval doctors based their diagnosis and treatment on this theory.

1) The Theory of the Four Humours was created by the Ancient Greek doctor Hippocrates (c.460-c.377 BC). Hippocrates believed that the body was made up of four fluids (or humours) — blood, phlegm, yellow bile and black bile. These were linked to the four seasons and the four elements. They needed to be in balance for good health.

E.g. in winter we get colds. So Hippocrates thought that in winter the body created an excess of phlegm. Sadly, Hippocrates failed to see that a bunged up nose, fevers, etc. are symptoms of the disease — he thought they were the cause.

2) The Theory of the Four Humours was developed further by another Greek doctor, Galen, who was born in AD 129 and worked for much of his career in Rome.
3) Galen believed that diseases could be treated using opposites. He thought that different foods, drinks, herbs and spices had a humour, which could balance the excessive humour that was causing the disease.

E.g. someone with a cold (too much cold, wet phlegm) could be given chicken, pepper or wine (all considered hot and dry) to correct the imbalance.

The Miasma Theory blamed Bad Air for causing disease

1) The miasma theory is the idea that bad air (or miasma) causes disease when someone breathes it in. This bad air may come from human waste or dead bodies — anything that creates a bad smell.
2) The miasma theory originated in Ancient Greece and Rome, and was incorporated by Galen into the Theory of the Four Humours. The idea became extremely popular in medieval Britain.
3) The miasma theory was so influential that it lasted until the 1860s, when it was replaced by the Germ Theory (see p.122). Miasma often prompted people to do hygienic things, like cleaning the streets, which sometimes helped to stop the spread of disease (but for the wrong reasons).

Comment and Analysis

The Four Humours and miasma were both incorrect theories. But they assumed disease had a natural cause, rather than a supernatural one. This was important, as it suggested that people weren't powerless against disease — they could investigate and take action against it.

Hippocrates and Galen were very Influential

The work of Hippocrates and Galen was extremely influential in medical diagnosis and treatment.

1) Hippocrates and Galen wrote down their beliefs about medicine. These were translated into Latin books, which were considered important texts by the Roman Catholic Church. Like the Bible, Hippocrates' and Galen's ideas were considered the absolute truth.
2) Many of their ideas were taught for centuries after their deaths, including the incorrect ones. For example, Galen only ever dissected animals — animal and human bodies are very different, so some of his ideas about anatomy were wrong. Medieval doctors were not allowed to perform their own dissections, so they continued to learn Galen's incorrect ideas.
3) Some of Hippocrates' and Galen's ideas were so influential that they continue to be used today. The Hippocratic Oath is the promise made by doctors to obey rules of behaviour in their professional lives — a version of it is still in use today. Hippocrates and Galen also believed that doctors should observe their patients as they treat them.

The four humours — it's totally hilarious...

In the exam it's important to take a couple of minutes before the start of each question to plan your answer. This will make sure that you answer the question and don't veer off topic.

Islamic Medicine

In the medieval period, Islamic medicine was miles ahead of European medicine. Arabic ideas eventually made their way to Europe — including knowledge of the all-important Galen and Hippocrates.

Arab doctors kept Classical Knowledge alive

1) While a lot of medical knowledge was lost in the West after the fall of the Roman Empire, medical ideas like the Four Humours and treatment by opposites (see p.110) were kept alive by Islamic scholars.
2) In the 9th century, Hunain ibn Ishaq (also known by his Latin name Johannitius) travelled from Baghdad to Byzantium to collect Greek medical texts. He translated these into Arabic.
3) This classical knowledge was eventually brought to Europe by Avicenna (or Ibn Sina), a Persian who lived from around AD 980-1037. Avicenna wrote the 'Canon of Medicine', which brought together the ideas of Galen and Hippocrates, and was the most important way that classical ideas got back into Western Europe.
4) This work and other Islamic texts were translated into Latin in Spain (which was partly Christian and partly Islamic) or Italy. The Crusades also made Europeans aware of the scientific knowledge of Islamic doctors.

Comment and Analysis

Islamic medicine was generally more rational and evidence-based than European medicine, partly due to their knowledge of classical (Ancient Greek and Roman) medical texts.

The Crusades were a series of wars fought by Christian Europeans against Muslims. They were an ultimately unsuccessful attempt to retake Jerusalem and the surrounding areas associated with the early history of Christianity.

Islamic doctors made several New Discoveries

1) Albucasis (or Abu al-Qasim, born c.AD 936) wrote a well thought-out book describing amputations, the removal of bladder stones and dental surgery — as well as methods for handling fractures, dislocations and the stitching of wounds.
2) In the 12th century, Avenzoar (or Ibn Zuhr) described the parasite that causes scabies and began to question the reliability of Galen.
3) Ibn al-Nafis, who lived in the 13th century, also questioned Galen's ideas. He suggested (correctly) that blood flows from one side of the heart to the other via the lungs — and doesn't cross the septum (the dividing wall between the left and right sides of the heart). Ibn al-Nafis' work wasn't recognised in the West until the 20th century.

Comment and Analysis

In the Islamic world, as in Western Europe, religion strongly influenced the development of medicine. For example, Islam, like Christianity, prohibited dissection.

The autobiography of Usama ibn Munqidh, a 12th century Muslim doctor, suggests the difference between Islamic and European medicine. Usama describes how he treated a knight with a sore on his leg by using a poultice, and a woman who was 'feeble-minded' by advising a new diet. Then a French doctor arrived and claimed Usama knew nothing. He cut off the knight's leg with an axe, and cut the woman's head with a razor and rubbed the skull with salt. Both patients died.

Alchemy helped to develop New Drugs

1) Alchemy was the attempt to turn base (ordinary) metals into gold and to discover the elixir of eternal life.
2) Alchemy traces its origins back to the Egyptians and it was preserved in the Islamic world.
3) Unlike modern chemistry, much superstition was included — an unsuccessful experiment was as likely to be blamed on the position of the stars or the spiritual purity of the alchemist as anything else.
4) Even so, Arabic alchemists invented useful techniques such as distillation and sublimation, and prepared drugs such as laudanum, benzoin and camphor.

Who needs gold when you've got health?

Imagine that you've been tasked with 'selling' Islamic medicine to Europe. Write an advert for Islamic medicine, including a list of the ways it was more advanced than European medicine.

Treating Disease

As the Middle Ages went on, medical treatments continued to be based on ideas we'd nowadays consider very unscientific. Treatments were ambitious though, and theories quite sophisticated in their own ways.

Prayer and Repentance were major treatments

1) Disease was believed to be a punishment from God, so sick people were encouraged to pray. The sick often prayed to saints, in the hope they would intervene and stop the illness. Medieval people also believed that pilgrimages to holy shrines (e.g. sites containing the remains of saints) could cure illnesses.
2) Others took their repentance one step further. Flagellants were people who whipped themselves in public in order to show God that they were sorry for their past actions. They were particularly common during epidemics, such as the Black Death (see p.115).
3) Many doctors had superstitious beliefs — e.g. some used astrology to diagnose and treat illness (see p.109), or believed that saying certain words while giving a treatment could make that treatment more effective.

Bloodletting and Purging aimed to make the Humours balanced

1) Bloodletting and purging were popular treatments because they fitted in with the Four Humours Theory.
2) If someone apparently had too much blood inside them, the doctor would take blood out of their body through bloodletting — they might make a small cut to remove the blood or use blood-sucking leeches.
3) Some people were accidentally killed because too much blood was taken.
4) Purging is the act of getting rid of other fluids from the body by excreting — doctors gave their patients laxatives to help the purging process.

Comment and Analysis

Bloodletting caused more deaths than it prevented, but it remained a popular treatment. This shows the strength of medieval people's beliefs in the face of observational evidence.

Purifying the Air was thought to Prevent Disease

1) The miasma theory (see p.110) led people to believe in the power of purifying or cleaning the air to prevent sickness and improve health.
2) Physicians carried posies or oranges around with them when visiting patients to protect themselves from catching a disease.
3) During the Black Death (see p.115), juniper, myrrh and incense were burned so the smoke or scent would fill the room and stop bad air from bringing disease inside.

Purifying the air was also seen as important for helping with other health conditions. In the case of fainting, people burned feathers and made the patient breathe in their smoke.

Remedies were Early Natural Medicines

1) Remedies bought from an apothecary, local wise woman or made at home were all popular in medieval Britain and contained herbs, spices, animal parts and minerals.
2) These remedies were either passed down or written in books explaining how to mix them together. Some of these books were called 'Herbals'.
3) Other remedies were based on superstition, like lucky charms containing 'powdered unicorn's horn'.

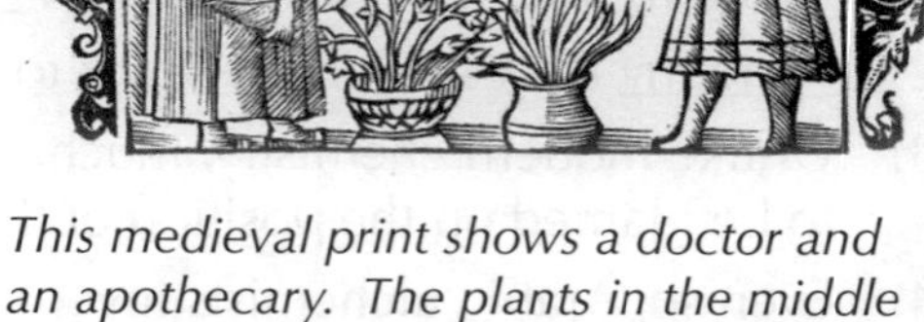

This medieval print shows a doctor and an apothecary. The plants in the middle show the importance of herbal remedies.

Medieval medical treatment was varied and diverse...

Look at the print of the doctor and apothecary above.
How useful would this source be to a historian investigating medieval medicine? [8]

Treating Disease

If you were ill in the Middle Ages, you couldn't just go to your local GP. But as there were various kinds of medical healers, there could still be an element of 'patient choice'...

People used lots of Different Healers

1) Physicians were male doctors who had trained at university for at least seven years. They read ancient texts as well as writings from the Islamic world (see p.111) but their training involved little practical experience. They used handbooks (vademecums) and clinical observation to check patients' conditions. But there were fewer than 100 physicians in England in 1300, and they were very expensive.
2) Most people saw an apothecary, who prepared and sold remedies (see p.112), and gave advice on how best to use them. Apothecaries were the most common form of treatment in Britain as they were the most accessible for those who could not afford a physician.
3) Apothecaries were trained through apprenticeships. Most apothecaries were men, but there were also many so-called 'wise women', who sold herbal remedies.

There were Few Public Hospitals

1) Most public hospitals were set up and run by the Church. There were relatively few such hospitals, but they were very popular and highly regarded.
2) The main purpose of hospitals was not to treat disease, but to care for the sick and elderly. The hospital provided its patients with food, water and a warm place to stay. Most hospitals were also more hygienic than elsewhere, because they had developed water and sewerage systems.
3) Some monasteries also cared for the sick, the elderly or the poor (see p.114).
4) Most sick people were treated at home by members of their family.

Famous hospitals like St. Bartholomew's and St. Thomas' in London started life as church establishments. The monastery at Canterbury Cathedral already had a complex water and sanitation system by 1250.

Surgery — work for Barbers, not doctors

1) Medieval surgery was very dangerous — there was no way to prevent blood loss, infection or pain. It was therefore only attempted rarely and for very minor procedures, e.g. treating hernias or cataracts.
2) There were a few university-trained, highly paid surgeons, but surgery as a whole was not a respected profession in medieval times — most operations were carried out by barber-surgeons (who also cut hair).

Some Progress was made in Surgery

1) Hugh of Lucca and his son Theodoric worked as surgeons in Italy in the early 13th century. They recognised the importance of practical experience and observation, and questioned some of Galen's ideas — their thoughts appear in Theodoric's textbooks.
2) They began dressing wounds with bandages soaked in wine, because they noticed that the wine helped to keep wounds clean and prevent infection. They made this discovery by chance.
3) They also realised that pus was not a healthy sign, unlike other doctors at the time who might try to cause wounds to pus because they believed it would release toxins from the body.
4) Some surgeons tried to find ways to reduce pain during operations. For example, John of Arderne created a recipe for an anaesthetic in 1376 which included hemlock, opium and henbane (a relative of deadly nightshade). In carefully controlled doses this may have worked — but was very likely to kill.

Comment and Analysis

Hugh and Theodoric's approach was unusual in the Middles Ages. It wasn't until the Renaissance that people started to question widely-held beliefs about the causes of disease, and to carry out experiments to find more effective methods of treatment and prevention.

Get the terminology right — no funny spellings...

Some of the marks in the exam are for using specialist terminology — so make sure you know it.

EXAM TIP

Health in Towns and Monasteries

In the medieval period, how healthy people were had a lot do with the area where they lived.

Living Conditions in Towns were pretty Poor

1) Most towns were small, especially after the Black Death when a lot of people died (p.115). Houses were usually made of wood and were crammed together — overcrowding and fires were common problems.
2) A lot of towns didn't have clean water supplies or sewerage systems — waste was chucked into the street or into rivers to be washed away. Sewage from latrines (pits with wooden seats) leaked into the ground and got into wells.
3) Businesses and homes weren't separated — butchers, tanners and dyers threw toxic waste into rivers and residential streets. People had to get their drinking water from rivers and wells that were contaminated.
4) In the 13th century, a water channel called the Great Conduit was built to bring clean water into London, as the Thames was getting too toxic.
5) In 1388, the government ordered town authorities to keep the streets free of waste. Towns introduced public health measures to tackle waste, sewage and pollution and to create a clean water supply.

'When passing along the water of Thames, we have beheld dung and lay stools and other filth accumulated in diverse places within the city, and have also perceived the fumes and other abominable stenches arising therefrom...' King Edward III commenting on the state of the Thames in London in 1357.

York and London both banned people from dumping waste in the street. These cities also built latrines over rivers so that sewage could be carried away.

London eventually banned any waste from being thrown into the Thames — carters were hired to collect waste and take it out of the city.

Many towns, like York, ordered toxic businesses like butchers, tanners, fishmongers and dyers to move outside the city walls.

Comment and Analysis

People broke these rules and officials struggled to enforce them. People knew that dirty water and bad health were linked, but they didn't really understand the risks. Town authorities didn't have enough money or knowledge to properly fix these public health issues.

Monasteries were Healthier than Towns

Monasteries had cleaner water than towns and had good systems for getting rid of waste and sewage. Monks also had access to books on healing and they knew how to grow herbs and make herbal remedies.

© Historic England / Mary Evans

It was easier to create healthy living conditions in monasteries than it was in towns.

1) Monasteries were wealthy, so they could afford to build infrastructure like latrine buildings and waterways to keep their water clean. Towns had to rely on wealthy individuals to fund these kinds of projects.
2) Monastery populations were small and had one leader (the Abbot) — he had the power to enforce rules about cleanliness and waste disposal. Getting hundreds of townspeople to adopt cleaner habits was trickier — towns didn't have one person in charge who could easily enforce public health measures.

City livin' ain't all it's cracked up to be...

Draw two boxes — one with the heading 'Towns' and the other with the heading 'Monasteries'. Fill in the boxes with bullet points about health and living conditions in each location.

The Black Death in Britain

The Black Death first struck in the 14th century. People tried to limit its spread, but couldn't stop the disease.

The Black Death was a devastating Epidemic

1) The Black Death was a series of plagues that swept Europe in the 14th century. It was really two illnesses:
   - Bubonic plague, spread by the bites of fleas from rats carried on ships. This caused headaches and a high temperature, followed by pus-filled swellings on the skin.
   - Pneumonic plague was airborne — it was spread by coughs and sneezes. It attacked the lungs, making it painful to breathe and causing victims to cough up blood.
2) The disease first arrived in Britain in 1348. Some historians think at least a third of the British population died as a result of the Black Death in 1348-50. There were further outbreaks of the Black Death throughout the Middle Ages.

People Didn't Know what Caused the Black Death

No-one at the time knew what had caused the plague.

1) Some people believed that the Black Death was a judgement from God. They thought the cause of the disease was sin, so they tried to prevent the spread of the disease through prayer and fasting.
2) Some blamed humour imbalances, so tried to get rid of the Black Death through bloodletting and purging. Those who thought that the disease was caused by miasma (see p.110) carried strong smelling herbs or lit fires to purify the air.
3) Some people also carried charms or used 'magic' potions containing arsenic.

Comment and Analysis

One of the main reasons why the Black Death killed so many was because people didn't know what caused the disease. Their ideas about the cause of disease were wrong, so their attempts at prevention and treatment were mostly ineffective.

Local Governments tried to Prevent the spread of the disease

1) Some people in Winchester thought that you could catch the plague from being close to the bodies of dead victims. When the town's cemetery became too full to take any more plague victims, the townspeople refused to let the bishop extend the cemetery in the town centre. Instead, they insisted that new cemeteries be built outside of the town, away from the houses.
2) The town of Gloucester tried to shut itself off from the outside world after hearing the Black Death had reached Bristol. This suggests that they thought the plague was spread by human contact. Their attempt at prevention was unsuccessful — many people in the town died of the Black Death.
3) In November 1348, the disease reached London. In January 1349, King Edward III closed Parliament.

The Black Death caused Social Change

1) After the Black Death, there were far fewer workers around. This meant that they could demand higher wages from their employers, and move around to find better work. The cost of land also decreased, allowing some peasants to buy land for the first time.
2) These changes threatened the power of the elites. The government created laws, such as the 1349 Ordinance of Labourers, to try and stop peasants moving around the country.
3) Some people think the Black Death helped cause the Peasants' Revolt in 1381, and, eventually, the collapse of the feudal system in Britain.

Don't plague aims — this Black Death is serious stuff...

It really helps to add some important facts — a useful date, for example. But make sure it's relevant to what you're trying to say — the details should be used to support your argument.

The Renaissance

The Renaissance was a time of new ideas and fresh thinking. People began to challenge old beliefs, and put forward new theories — such as Vesalius' ideas about practical observation.

The Renaissance was a time of Continuity and Change

1) In the Renaissance there was a rediscovery of knowledge from classical Greek and Roman times. Western doctors gained access to the original writings of Hippocrates, Galen and Avicenna (a Persian physician who lived between 980 and 1037 AD). These hadn't been available in the medieval period. They led to greater interest in the Four Humours Theory and treatment by opposites (see p.110).
2) But the Renaissance also saw the emergence of science as we know it from the magic and mysticism of medieval medicine. People thought about how the human body worked based on direct observation and experimentation.
3) This was partly because many of the new books that had been found said that anatomy and dissections were very important. This encouraged people to examine the body themselves, and to come to their own conclusions about the causes of disease.
4) People began to question Galen's thinking and that of other ancient doctors. However, his writings continued to be studied.

Protestant Christianity spread to Britain in the 16th century, during the Reformation. This reduced the influence of the Catholic Church in many areas of people's lives, including medicine. Although religion was still important, the Church no longer had so much control over medical teaching.

This woodcut shows physicians debating over a medicine book.

Vesalius wrote Anatomy books with Accurate Diagrams

1) Vesalius was born in 1514 and was a medical professor at Padua University, Italy. He believed that successful surgery would only be possible if doctors had a proper understanding of the anatomy.
2) Vesalius was able to perform dissections on criminals who had been executed. This let him study the human anatomy more closely.
3) He wrote books based on his observations using accurate diagrams to illustrate his work. The most important were 'Six Anatomical Pictures' (1538) and 'The Fabric of the Human Body' (1543).
4) His works were printed and distributed around Europe, including to Britain. This allowed British doctors to read about Vesalius' findings and learn from his discoveries.
5) Vesalius' work helped point out some of Galen's mistakes. For example, in the second edition of 'The Fabric', he showed that there were no holes in the septum of the heart.
6) His findings encouraged others to question Galen. Doctors also realised there was more to discover about the body because of Vesalius' questioning attitude.
7) Vesalius showed that dissecting bodies was important, to find out exactly how the human body was structured. Dissection was used more and more in medical training for this reason (see p.119).

Printing was invented in the 1440s, and the first British printing press was set up in the 1470s. The invention of printing meant books could be copied more easily. This allowed new ideas to be shared and old ideas (e.g. Galen's theories) to be discussed and questioned.

Comment and Analysis

The work of Vesalius didn't have an immediate impact on the diagnosis or treatment of disease. However, by producing a realistic description of the human anatomy and encouraging dissection, Vesalius provided an essential first step to improving them.

Without you, Vesalius, I've got a hole in my heart...

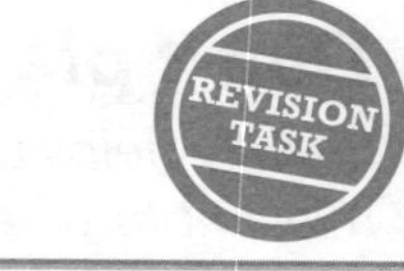

Vesalius was a pretty important Renaissance dude. Note down three ways he had an impact on the development of medicine. Was his impact short-term or long-term?

The Renaissance

William Harvey and Ambroise Paré were key individuals in the history of Renaissance medicine. Harvey discovered how blood circulates around the body, and Paré made surgery safer and more effective.

Harvey discovered the Circulation of the Blood

1) William Harvey was a British doctor, born in 1578. He studied medicine at Padua University, Italy, then worked in London at the Royal College of Physicians (see p.119), before becoming Royal Physician to James I and Charles I.
2) Harvey studied both animals and humans for his work. He realised that he could observe living animal hearts in action, and that his findings would also apply to humans.

Harvey was one of many British doctors who studied medicine at a university in Italy or France. During the Renaissance, major new discoveries were being made at these European universities — the discoveries of Vesalius (see p.116) were made at Padua University. British doctors who studied in Europe learnt the latest ideas in medicine and brought them back to Britain.

3) Before Harvey, people thought that there were two kinds of blood, and that they flowed through two completely separate systems of blood vessels. This idea came from Galen.

© Mary Evans / Everett Collection

A diagram from Harvey's book 'On the Motions of the Heart and Blood' (1628), showing blood circulation in the arm.

4) Harvey realised Galen's theory was wrong. From experiments, he knew that too much blood was being pumped out of the heart for it to be continually formed and consumed. Instead he thought that blood must circulate — it went round and round the body.
5) Harvey's ideas, shown in his books, gave doctors a map of how the body worked, changing their understanding of anatomy.
6) However, not everyone believed his theories, and it took a long time before doctors used them in their treatments. For example, people continued to perform bloodletting (see p.112), even though Harvey had shown the reasoning behind it to be wrong.

Paré improved Surgical Techniques

1) Ambroise Paré was a French barber-surgeon born in 1510. Surgery was still a low status profession. Paré worked for a public hospital, then became an army surgeon.
2) As an army surgeon, Paré treated many serious injuries caused by war. His experience treating these wounds led him to develop some improved surgical techniques.

Paré also designed quite sophisticated artificial limbs.

- At this time, gunshot wounds often became infected. Doctors didn't understand why this happened or how to treat it. The usual treatment was to burn the wound with a red hot iron, or to pour boiling oil onto it. This may have worked in some cases, but it often did more harm than good.
- During one battle, Paré ran out of oil and resorted, by chance, to a simple cool salve instead. To his surprise the patients treated in this way did better than the ones scalded with oil.
- Paré also improved the treatment of amputations. Before Paré, the severed blood vessels left by amputation were sealed by burning their ends with a red hot iron (cauterisation). Paré invented a method of tying off the vessels with threads (ligatures). This was less painful than cauterisation, so it reduced the chances of the patient dying of shock. However, it did increase the risk of infection.

A cool salve is a type of ointment.

3) Paré published his ideas to enable other doctors to read about them — British surgeons used the methods of Paré and took inspiration from his work. Over time, his ideas helped improve surgical techniques.

Paré's ideas were resisted by doctors who felt that a lowly surgeon shouldn't be listened to. He eventually became surgeon to the King of France, and it was only with the King's support that his ideas started to be accepted.

The circulation of the blood goes round and round...

Look at Harvey's diagram of the blood circulation in the arm above. How useful would this source be to a historian investigating Renaissance medicine? [8]

EXAM QUESTION

Medical Treatment: Continuity and Change

Medical treatment improved in the Renaissance. But traditional treatments continued to be popular among ordinary people. Both these trends were seen in the way people responded to the Great Plague.

People used both Old and New Treatments

1) Many doctors were reluctant to accept that Galen was wrong. This meant that they continued to use similar treatments to the Middle Ages, like bloodletting and purging (see p.112). Doctors tended to focus more on reading books than on treating patients.
2) Doctors were also still very expensive. As a result, most people used other healers, such as apothecaries or barber-surgeons (see p.113), or were treated in the home. Herbs were still the main ingredient in many drugs.
3) Superstition and religion were still important. People thought the King's touch could cure scrofula (a skin disease known as the 'King's Evil'). Thousands of people with scrofula are thought to have visited King Charles I (1600-1649) in the hope of being cured.
4) Some people sold medicines that didn't work, and often did more harm than good — this was known as quackery. Quacks sold their wares at fairs and markets and often had no medical knowledge. From 1600 the College of Physicians (see p.119) started to license doctors to stop quackery.
5) In the 1700s, electricity started to be used in some medical treatments, although it was rarely effective.

Comment and Analysis

The invention of printing in the 1440s was a huge development. But because most people couldn't read or write (or couldn't afford the books in the first place) new ideas could only be shared within a small part of society. Most people in the Renaissance were using the same cures and treatments as medieval people.

Responses to the Great Plague showed Continuity and Change

1) The Great Plague struck London in 1665 — it was a rare but deadly recurrence of the medieval Black Death (see p.115).
2) Responses to the Great Plague were both similar and different to how people reacted to the Black Death.

Similarities

- Many treatments for the Great Plague were based on magic, religion and supersition, including wearing lucky charms or amulets, saying prayers and fasting.
- Bloodletting was still used, even though this probably made the plague worse — it created wounds which could become infected.
- Some people also thought that miasma caused the disease (see p.110), so they carried posies of herbs or flowers to improve the air.

Differences

Town and Parish Councils tried to prevent the disease's spread.

- Plague victims were quarantined (isolated) to stop them passing on the disease. The victim's house was locked and a red cross was painted on their door.
- Areas where people crowded together, such as theatres, were closed.
- The dead bodies of plague victims were buried in mass graves away from houses.

3) The responses to the plague came from local councils — they did more to try to combat the Great Plague than they had done for the Black Death 300 years previously. But there were no national government attempts at prevention.
4) The plague gradually began to disappear. Many people think the Great Fire of London in 1666 helped wipe it out, by effectively sterilising large parts of London — it burned down the old, crowded houses, killing the plague bacteria.

Change and continuity — just a fancy 'spot the difference'...

How were the responses to the Great Plague and the medieval Black Death similar? Explain your answer and refer to both epidemics. [8]

Doctors and Surgery

Over time, doctors started to have more training, and surgeons became more important. John Hunter was a surgeon who established a better approach to surgery, based on learning and experimentation.

Doctors' Training and Knowledge began to Improve

1) Many doctors in Britain trained at the College of Physicians, which was set up in 1518. Here they read books by Galen, but also studied recent medical developments. Doctors who trained at the college gained a licence, which separated them from the large numbers of quack doctors (see p.118).
2) However, a licence didn't guarantee that a doctor would give the most effective treatment — sometimes an experienced, unlicensed doctor could be just as good.
3) New weapons like cannons and guns were used in war. This meant surgeons had to treat injuries they hadn't seen before, forcing them to quickly find new treatments.
4) Explorations abroad brought new ingredients for drugs back to Britain, including guaiacum — believed to cure syphilis — and quinine, a drug for malaria from the bark of the Cinchona tree. Other exotic drugs that were sold might have just been advertising gimmicks.
5) Dissections, which enable doctors to see how the body actually works, became a key part of medical training in the 1700s.

The College of Physicians was later called the Royal College of Physicians.

Surgeons became more Important

1) In the Middle Ages, there were two types of surgeons. There was a small group of professional surgeons, who trained at university and were highly paid by their rich patients. Then there were unqualified barber-surgeons (see p.113). In general, surgeons weren't respected compared to doctors.
2) In the 1700s and 1800s, surgeons began to gain the same status as doctors. In 1800, the London College of Surgeons (later the Royal College of Surgeons) was created, which set training standards for surgeons for the first time.

John Hunter developed Better Approaches to Surgery

John Hunter (1728-93) was a well-known surgeon and scientist.

1) Hunter joined his brother William, a successful doctor, at his anatomy school in London. Dissecting human corpses was a large part of the school's teaching. Over 12 years, Hunter was present at more than 2000 dissections, developing an unrivalled knowledge of the human body.
2) Hunter became an army surgeon in France and Portugal and a popular surgeon and teacher in England. During his work, he made several important medical discoveries. He learned more about venereal disease (sexually transmitted infection), a major cause of illness at the time, and introduced a new approach to the treatment of gunshot wounds.
3) In an operation in 1785, he introduced a new way to treat an aneurysm (a bulge in a blood vessel) in a man's thigh. Hunter tied off the blood vessel to encourage the blood to flow through the other vessels in the leg, preventing it from having to be amputated.
4) Hunter is especially remembered for encouraging better approaches to surgery. This included good scientific habits like learning as much about the body as possible to understand illness, experimenting to find better ways to treat disease, and testing treatments (e.g. on animals) before using them on people.

Comment and Analysis

Hunter's pupils included doctors like Edward Jenner (see p.121). This meant that his methods and ideas were passed on, improving the way people conducted scientific research as a whole.

Dissect this joke to find pure comedy gold...

Make some notes comparing surgery between 1500 and 1800 with surgery in medieval times. Keep adding to your notes as you read on — things got pretty fancy in the 20th century.

Hospitals

From the 18th century, hospitals focused more on treating patients — rather than just caring for them — as well as teaching. Nursing standards also improved — largely thanks to Florence Nightingale.

Hospitals focused more on Treatment and Learning

In the 1530s, Henry VIII closed down most of Britain's monasteries (this was called the 'dissolution of the monasteries'). Since most hospitals had been set up and run by monasteries (see p.114), this also led to the closure of a large number of hospitals. As a result, Britain had relatively few hospitals until the 18th century.

1) From the early 18th century, several charity hospitals opened, including the Middlesex Infirmary, The London Hospital and Guy's Hospital. They were funded by the rich, and offered largely free treatment to the poor. Some specialised in treating certain illnesses, or provided somewhere for mothers to give birth.
2) Only those who were likely to recover quickly were admitted — this was partly because of a lack of space and because of the risk of contagious illnesses spreading. The 'deserving' poor (those who led hardworking, respectable lives) had a greater chance of being admitted.
3) Dispensaries provided free non-residential care to poor people. Medicines and non-surgical services from people like dentists and midwives were given without charge.
4) Most poor people were treated in workhouses — large buildings that people went to if they could no longer look after themselves (e.g. because of unemployment, illness or old age). Conditions were poor — from the 1850s a partially successful movement began to improve conditions in workhouse infirmaries.
5) In the 19th century, some hospitals were founded alongside universities or medical schools, including Charing Cross Hospital, University College Hospital and King's College Hospital. These hospitals were used as training schools for doctors, and for conducting scientific research.
6) Cottage hospitals, run by GPs, opened from the 1860s. They provided care for people in rural areas.

Comment and Analysis

Before the 18th century, many hospitals focused only on caring for people. In the 18th and 19th centuries, treating diseases became more important.

Florence Nightingale Improved Nursing Standards

1) Florence Nightingale (1820-1910) studied to become a nurse in 1849, despite opposition from her family. During her career, she helped nursing became more professional and disciplined.
2) When the Crimean War broke out in 1853-54, horror stories emerged about the Barrack Hospital in Scutari, where the British wounded were treated. Sidney Herbert (the Secretary of War and a friend of her family) asked for Nightingale to go to Scutari to sort out the nursing care in the hospital.
3) The army opposed women nurses, as they were considered inferior and a distraction. Nightingale went anyway, taking 38 hand-picked nurses with her.
4) Using methods she had learned from her training in Europe, Nightingale ensured all the wards were clean and hygienic, that water supplies were adequate and that patients were fed properly.
5) Many of Nightingale's nursing practices were used in hospitals in Britain.

Nightingale improved the hospital a lot. Before she arrived, the death rate in the hospital stood at 42%. Two years later it had fallen to just 2%.

- In 1859, Nightingale published a book, 'Notes on Nursing'. This explained her methods — it emphasised the need for hygiene and a professional attitude. It was the standard textbook for generations of nurses.
- The public raised £44,000 to help her train nurses, and she set up the Nightingale School of Nursing in St. Thomas' Hospital, London. Nurses were given three years of training before they could qualify. Discipline and attention to detail were important.

Like it or lamp it, you've got to learn it...

Individuals like Nightingale can have an impact on the rate of change. But so can factors like war, government, communication, science and technology and just chance. Don't forget any of these.

Jenner and Vaccination

Until the 1700s, people had few effective ways to prevent the spread of disease. Edward Jenner's discovery of the smallpox vaccine was a landmark in the development of preventive medicine.

Before Jenner the only way to prevent Smallpox was Inoculation

1) In the 1700s, smallpox was one of the most deadly diseases — in 1751, over 3500 people died of smallpox in London alone.
2) At the time, the only way to prevent smallpox was inoculation. This was promoted in Britain by Lady Mary Wortley Montagu, who learned about it in Turkey.
3) Inoculation involved making a cut in a patient's arm and soaking it in pus taken from the swelling of somebody who already had a mild form of smallpox.

Inoculation was successful in preventing the disease, but it meant patients had to experience smallpox before they could become immune — some died as a result.

Jenner discovered a link between Smallpox and Cowpox

1) Edward Jenner (born in 1749) was a country doctor in Gloucestershire. He heard that milkmaids didn't get smallpox, but they did catch the much milder cowpox.
2) Using careful scientific methods Jenner investigated and discovered that it was true that people who had had cowpox didn't get smallpox.
3) In 1796 Jenner tested his theory. He injected a small boy, James Phipps, with pus from the sores of Sarah Nelmes, a milkmaid with cowpox. Jenner then infected him with smallpox. James didn't catch the disease.
4) Jenner published his findings in 1798. He coined the term vaccination using the Latin word for cow, vacca.

Comment and Analysis

Jenner was important because he used an experiment to test his theory. Although experiments had been used during the Renaissance, it was still unusual for doctors to test their theories.

Jenner's vaccination was Successful despite Opposition

1) Jenner faced some opposition to his vaccine...
   - Many people were worried about giving themselves a disease from cows.
   - Some doctors who gave the older type of inoculation saw it as a threat to their livelihood.
   - One doctor, William Woodville, claimed Jenner's vaccination worked little better than inoculation, after several smallpox deaths occurred at his hospital.
   - When vaccination became compulsory in 1853, several groups were formed to campaign against it — they didn't like the idea of the government telling them what to do.

A cartoon from 1802 by James Gillray, with cows bursting out of vaccinated patients' sores.

2) ...but his discovery got the approval of Parliament.
   - In 1802, Parliament gave Jenner £10,000 to open a vaccination clinic. It gave Jenner a further £20,000 a few years later.
   - In 1840, vaccination against smallpox was made free for infants. In 1853, it was made compulsory.
   - The vaccine was a success — it contributed to a big fall in the number of smallpox cases in Britain.

Comment and Analysis

Jenner didn't know why his vaccine worked. This lack of understanding meant Jenner couldn't develop any other vaccines. This was only possible after the Germ Theory was published in 1861, when Pasteur and others worked to discover vaccines against other diseases, like chicken cholera, anthrax and rabies (see p.122-123).

Jenner's vaccine got things mooving on disease prevention...

Draw (or print out) a picture of a cow. Fill it with facts about Jenner's discovery and about the opposition to his vaccination. Stick it on the fridge — your mum'll be chuffed.

Germ Theory

Although people's understanding of anatomy had improved greatly during the Renaissance, there was still plenty to learn. The causes of disease was an area that still needed proper explanation.

People knew about Germs but hadn't linked them to Disease

Germs and other micro-organisms were discovered as early as the 17th century. Scientists thought that these microbes were created by decaying matter, like rotting food or human waste — this theory was known as spontaneous generation. It led people to believe that disease caused germs.

Pasteur was the first to suggest that Germs cause disease

1) The French chemist Louis Pasteur was employed in 1857 to find the explanation for the souring of sugar beet used in fermenting industrial alcohol. His answer was to blame germs.
2) Pasteur proved there were germs in the air — he showed that sterilised water in a closed flask stayed sterile, while sterilised water in an open flask bred germs.
3) In 1861, Pasteur published his Germ Theory. In it he argued that microbes in the air caused decay, not the other way round. He also suggested that some germs caused disease.
4) In 1867, Pasteur published evidence proving there was a link between germs and disease, demonstrating that germs caused a disease in silkworms.

Pasteur's discovery was partly due to Antonie van Leeuwenhoek's invention of the microscope in the 17th century. More advanced microscopes were developed during the 1800s. They allowed scientists to see much clearer images with a lot less light distortion.

The Germ Theory had a major Impact on medicine

The Germ Theory was first met with scepticism — people couldn't believe tiny microbes caused disease. It didn't help that the germ responsible for each disease had to be identified individually, as this meant it was several years before the theory became useful. Eventually, however, it gained popularity in Britain.

- The theory helped inspire Joseph Lister to develop antiseptics (see p.125).
- The theory confirmed John Snow's findings about cholera (see p.126).
- The theory linked disease to poor living conditions (like contaminated water). This put pressure on the government to pass the 1875 Public Health Act (see p.127).

Robert Koch used dyes to identify microbes

1) The German scientist Robert Koch built on Pasteur's work by linking specific diseases to the particular microbe that caused them. This technique was called 'microbe hunting'.
2) Koch identified anthrax bacteria (1876) and the bacteria that cause septicaemia (1878), tuberculosis (1882) and cholera (1883).
3) Koch used revolutionary scientific methods:
   - He used agar jelly to create solid cultures, allowing him to breed lots of bacteria.
   - He used dyes to stain the bacteria so they were more visible under the microscope.
   - He employed the newly-invented photography to record his findings.
4) Koch's techniques were important as they allowed other microbe hunters to find the specific bacteria which cause other diseases (see p.123).

Pasteur's theory — more than the germ of an idea...

Split your page into three sections, with the headings: individuals, technology and changing attitudes. Under each heading, list the ways in which that factor contributed to the Germ Theory.

REVISION TASK

The Fight against Germs

Pasteur and Koch weren't friends — in 1871 Germany beat France in the Franco-Prussian War, so there was a great national and personal rivalry between the two scientists. This competition fuelled their next discoveries.

Pasteur developed Vaccines for Anthrax and Rabies

1) In 1877, hearing of Koch's discovery of the anthrax bacteria (see p.122), Pasteur started to compete in the race to find and combat new microbes.
2) Pasteur's assistant, Charles Chamberland, injected some chickens with a cholera culture that had been weakened by being accidentally left out on the desk while he was on holiday. The chickens survived. The team tried again with some newly cultured cholera, but the chickens still survived.
3) They worked out that the weakened (attenuated) cholera had made the chickens immune. Chamberland's error had produced a chance discovery.
4) The team produced an attenuated version of the anthrax bacteria to make sheep immune. They showed this in a public experiment in 1881. They used a similar method to find a vaccine for rabies.

Koch's Methods helped other Microbe Hunters

Other scientists used Koch's methods (see p.122) to find and combat the bacteria that caused other diseases.

1) The diphtheria germ was discovered by Edwin Klebs in 1883.
2) Friedrich Loeffler cultured the diphtheria germ and thought that its effect on people was due to a toxin (poison) it produced. Emile Roux proved Loeffler right.
3) In 1891, Emil von Behring produced an antitoxin (a substance that cancels out the toxins produced by germs) from the blood of animals that had just recovered from diphtheria. This could be used to reduce the effect of the disease.
4) Ronald Ross received the Nobel Prize in 1902 for his discovery of how malaria is transmitted. Ross' Nobel Prize was disputed by Giovanni Battista Grassi, who also discovered how malaria is transmitted. However, Koch supported Ross' claim and so he retained the prize.

Paul Ehrlich discovered the first Magic Bullet — Salvarsan 606

Antibodies were identified as a natural defence mechanism of the body against germs. It was known that antibodies only attacked specific microbes — so they were nicknamed magic bullets. In 1889, Paul Ehrlich set out to find chemicals that could act as synthetic antibodies.

1) First, Ehrlich discovered dyes that could kill the malaria and sleeping sickness germs.
2) In 1905, the bacteria that causes the sexually transmitted disease syphilis was identified.
3) Ehrlich and his team decided to search for an arsenic compound that was a magic bullet for syphilis. They hoped it would target the bacteria without poisoning the rest of the body. Over 600 compounds were tried, but none seemed to work.
4) In 1909, Sahachiro Hata joined the team. He rechecked the results and saw that compound number 606 actually appeared to work. It was first used on a human in 1911 under the trade name Salvarsan 606.

Comment and Analysis

The Germ Theory led to the introduction of new vaccines, antiseptics (see p.125) and government intervention in public health (see p.127). But it didn't really affect treatments in Britain that much — Salvarsan 606 was only a treatment for one specific disease, and the second magic bullet (prontosil) wasn't discovered until 1935. It wasn't until the pharmaceutical industry took off in the 1940s (see p.130) that ordinary people began to feel a benefit from the Germ Theory.

When it comes to magic bullets, Ehrlich hit the mark...

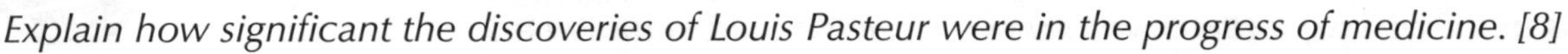

Explain how significant the discoveries of Louis Pasteur were in the progress of medicine. [8]

EXAM QUESTION

Anaesthetics

Improving hospitals helped to prevent many unnecessary deaths. But the three problems of pain, infection (see p.125) and blood loss (see p.128) were yet to be solved. The solution to pain was anaesthetics.

Anaesthetics solved the problem of Pain

Pain was a problem for surgeons, especially since patients could die from the trauma of extreme pain. Natural drugs like alcohol, opium and mandrake had been used for a long time, but effective anaesthetics that didn't make the patient very ill were more difficult to produce.

- Nitrous oxide (laughing gas) was identified as a possible anaesthetic by British chemist Humphry Davy in 1799 — but he was ignored by surgeons at the time.
- The gas had been dismissed as a fairground novelty before American dentist Horace Wells suggested its use in his area of work. He did a public demonstration in 1845, but had the bad luck to pick a patient unaffected by nitrous oxide — it was again ignored.

- In 1842, American doctor Crawford Long discovered the anaesthetic qualities of ether, but didn't publish his work. The first public demonstration of ether as an anaesthetic was carried out in 1846 by American dental surgeon William Morton.
- Ether is an irritant and is also fairly explosive, so using it in this way was risky.

- James Simpson was a Professor of Midwifery at Edinburgh University who tried to find a safe alternative to ether that women could take during childbirth. He began to experiment with other chemicals by testing them on himself.
- In 1847 Simpson discovered the effects of chloroform. He found it was easier to use than ether — it took effect more quickly and less was needed to achieve the same result.
- After Queen Victoria gave birth to her eighth child while using chloroform in 1853, it became widely used in operating theatres and to reduce pain during childbirth.

General anaesthesia (complete unconsciousness) is risky, so local anaesthesia (numbing of the part being treated) is better for many operations. In 1884, William Halsted investigated the use of cocaine as a local anaesthetic. His self-experimentation led to a severe cocaine addiction.

Early Anaesthetics actually led to a Rise in death rates

1) Anaesthetics led to longer and more complex operations. This was because surgeons found that unconscious patients were easier to operate on, meaning they could take longer over their work.
2) Longer operating times led to higher death rates from infection, because surgeons didn't know that poor hygiene spread disease. Surgeons used very unhygienic methods:

- Surgeons didn't know that having clean clothes could save lives. Often they wore the same coats for years, which were covered in dried blood and pus from previous operations.
- Operations were often carried out in unhygienic conditions, including at the patient's house.
- Operating instruments also caused infections because they were usually unwashed and dirty.

Comment and Analysis

Anaesthetics helped solve the problem of pain, but patients were still dying from infection. This meant the attempts at more complicated surgery actually led to increased death rates amongst patients. The period between 1846 and 1870 is sometimes known as the 'Black Period' of surgery for this reason.

Anaesthetics revision — don't let it put you to sleep...

Remember to check the number of marks each question is worth. If a question's worth double the marks of the other questions, you'll need to give it double the time.

Antiseptics

Anaesthetics had solved the problem of pain, but surgeons were still faced with a high death rate from operations due to the amount of infection. Antiseptics and later asepsis helped prevent this by killing germs.

Antisepsis and Asepsis reduce infection

There are two main approaches to reducing infection during an operation:

- Antiseptic methods are used to kill germs that get near surgical wounds.
- Aseptic surgical methods aim to stop any germs getting near the wound.

Joseph Lister pioneered the use of Antiseptics

1) Ignaz Semmelweis showed that doctors could reduce the spread of infection by washing their hands with chloride of lime solution between patients. However, it was very unpleasant, so wasn't widely used.
2) Joseph Lister had seen carbolic acid sprays used in sewage works to keep down the smell. He tried this in the operating theatre in the early 1860s and saw reduced infection rates.
3) Lister heard about the Germ Theory in 1865 — he realised that germs could be in the air, on surgical instruments and on people's hands. He started using carbolic acid on instruments and bandages.
4) The use of antiseptics immediately reduced death rates from as high as 50% in 1864-66 to around 15% in 1867-70.
5) Despite these early successes, Lister faced opposition from many doctors. They didn't like to use the carbolic spray, which they found unpleasant on their skin or to breathe in.
6) In 1877, Lister used a well-publicised operation at King's College Hospital to promote the use of his carbolic spray.
7) Antiseptics allowed surgeons to operate with less fear of patients dying from infection. The number of operations was ten times higher in 1912 than 1867 as a result.

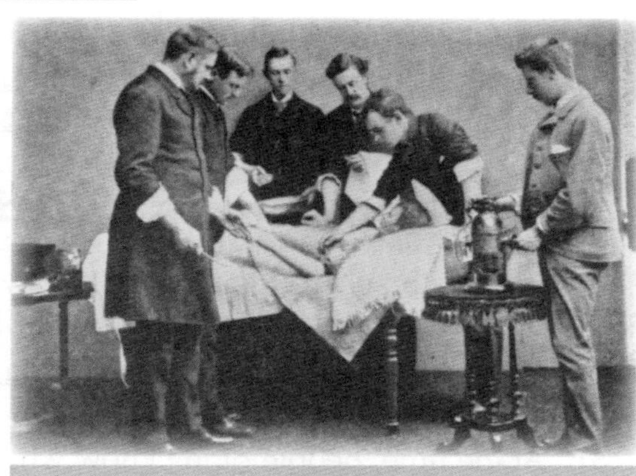

A photo of an operation from the late 1800s. You can see Lister's carbolic spray on the table on the right. The operating theatre isn't aseptic though — the surgeons aren't wearing sterile gowns or surgical gloves.

Comment and Analysis

Antiseptics (and later asepsis) solved the problem of infection. This, combined with the use of anaesthetics (see p.124) to stop pain, improved British surgery and prevented many deaths.

Asepsis reduced the need for Nasty Chemicals

Since the late 1800s, surgeons have changed their approach from killing germs to making a germ-free (aseptic) environment. Aseptic surgery reduced the need for a carbolic spray.

1) Instruments are carefully sterilised before use, usually with high temperature steam (120°C).
2) Theatre staff sterilise their hands before entering — and wear sterile gowns, masks, gloves and hats. Surgical gloves were invented by William Halsted in 1889.
3) The theatres themselves are kept extremely clean and fed with sterile air. Special tents can be placed around the operating table to maintain an area of even stricter hygiene in high risk cases.

Make a Lister them facts — then germ up on them...

Write a paragraph summarising whether you think anaesthetics or antiseptics were a greater breakthrough for 19th century surgery.

Public Health

The industrial revolution began in the 18th century. Lots of people moved into cities like London to work in the factories. The places they lived were cramped, dirty and great for spreading diseases like cholera.

Overcrowding in Towns led to Poor Living Conditions

1) During the 18th and 19th centuries, lots of people moved from the countryside to towns to work in factories. The towns grew so quickly that good housing couldn't be built fast enough — instead, houses were built as close together as possible, with little outside space and poor ventilation.
2) Overcrowding was a big problem. Workers had little money, so tried to live in the smallest possible space — families with four or more children often lived in a single room. The poorest lived in cellars.
3) People didn't understand the need for clean water or good sewerage systems. Most houses had no bathroom — they instead shared an outside toilet, called a privy.
4) Each privy was built above a cesspit. Cesspit and household waste was collected by nightmen, who threw the waste into rivers or piled it up for the rain to wash away.
5) Water companies set up water pumps in the streets, which were shared between many houses. The pump's water supply was often contaminated by waste from the cesspits or rivers.

Cholera epidemics Killed Thousands of people

1) Cholera reached Britain in 1831. By 1832 it was an epidemic — over 21,000 people in Britain died of cholera that year.
2) Cholera spreads when infected sewage gets into drinking water. It causes extreme diarrhoea — sufferers often die from loss of water and minerals. Both rich and poor people caught the disease.
3) At the time, people didn't know what caused cholera — the best theory was miasma (see p.110). The government started regulating the burial of the dead, but this did little to halt the spread of cholera. The 1832 epidemic declined and interest was lost.
4) Cholera epidemics recurred in 1848, 1853-54 and 1865-66.

Chadwick's Report led to the 1848 Public Health Act

1) In 1842, the social reformer Edwin Chadwick published a report on poverty and health. The report showed that living conditions in towns were worse for people's health than conditions in the countryside.
2) Chadwick's report suggested that the government should pass laws for proper drainage and sewerage systems, funded by local taxes.
3) Chadwick's report and another cholera epidemic in 1848 (which killed 53,000 people) put pressure on Parliament to pass a Public Health Act.
4) The 1848 Act set up a central Board of Health (which included Chadwick as a member) and allowed any town to set up its own local board of health as long as the town's taxpayers agreed.

Comment and Analysis

The impact of the 1848 Act was limited — towns could set up health boards but very few chose to, and those that did often refused to spend any money to improve conditions. Chadwick annoyed a lot of people, and was forced to retire in 1854. The central Board of Health was dismantled in 1858.

Snow linked Cholera to Contaminated Water

John Snow showed that there was a connection between contaminated water and cholera in 1853-54. He studied a cholera outbreak in the Broad Street area of London and noticed that the victims all used the same water pump. So he removed the handle from the pump and ended the outbreak.

Snow's work received little attention at first. Most people still believed diseases were spread by miasma ('bad air').

I hope you're not Bored of Health, as there's more to come...

Explain the differences between public health in the Middle Ages and public health during the industrial revolution. [8]

Public Health

Despite the work of Chadwick and Snow, public health didn't improve — cholera returned to Britain in 1865. But then, thanks to several factors, things began to change and the government took action.

The 'Great Stink' struck London in 1858

1) As in other towns, a lot of waste in London drained into water sources, including the River Thames.
2) In the summer of 1858, the hot weather caused the river's water level to drop and bacteria to grow in the waste. This produced a smell that was so bad it affected large parts of London and stopped Parliament from meeting.
3) To reduce the stink, engineer Joseph Bazalgette was appointed in 1859 to build a new London sewer system. The sewers transported waste that was normally dumped into the Thames away from heavily populated areas to the Thames Estuary. About 1300 miles of sewers were built.
4) The sewer system was officially opened in 1865. Bazalgette's design became the blueprint for most cities in Western Europe.

Comment and Analysis

When Bazalgette started work on his sewers, people still didn't understand how diseases spread. They were trying to get rid of the bad smells coming from the Thames. The fact they stopped cholera by cleaning the drinking water was unintended.

Public Opinion began to Change

For most of the 19th century, people believed in a laissez-faire style of government — they thought the government shouldn't intervene in public health. But then things began to change.

1) Evidence from Chadwick and Snow (see p.126), and Pasteur's Germ Theory (see p.122), showed that cleaning towns could stop the spread of disease.
2) In 1867, the Second Reform Act was passed giving nearly 1 million more men the vote, most of whom were industrial workers.
3) Several reformers helped change attitudes towards health. William Farr was a statistician who recorded causes of death. He used his statistics to press for reforms in areas where death rates were high.

Now they had the vote, workers could put pressure on the government to listen to concerns about health. For the first time, politicians had to address workers' concerns in order to stay in power.

The 1875 Act improved Public Health

In the 1870s the government finally took action to improve public health.

1) In 1871-72, the government followed the Royal Sanitary Commission's proposal to form the Local Government Board and divide Britain into 'sanitary areas' administered by officers for public health.
2) In 1875, Benjamin Disraeli's government passed another Public Health Act. It forced councils to appoint health inspectors and sanitary inspectors to make sure that laws on things like water supplies and hygiene were followed. It also made councils maintain sewerage systems and keep their towns' streets clean.
3) The 1875 Public Health Act was more effective than the one passed in 1848 because it was compulsory.
4) Disraeli also brought in the Artisans' Dwellings Act in 1875. This let local councils buy slums with poor living conditions and rebuild them in a way that fit new government-backed housing standards.

Few councillors used the Artisans' Dwellings Act. An exception was Joseph Chamberlain, who became Mayor of Birmingham in 1873. Chamberlain persuaded the city authorities to buy the local gas and water companies to make sure people had good supplies of both. In 1875, he cleared an area of the city's slums and built a new street in their place. He also improved some of the slum housing.

Comment and Analysis

There were several changes to public health during the industrial revolution, and the 1875 Public Health Act was the biggest. The work of the government and individuals like Chadwick, Snow and Farr were key to these changes. Technology (like Bazalgette's sewers), the 1867 Reform Act and the cholera epidemics were other factors that prompted improvement.

Turns out laissez-faire had made things less fair...

Write a list of the factors which led to the 1875 Public Health Act. For each factor, write a sentence explaining how that factor helped cause the Act.

REVISION TASK

The Impact of the First World War

The First World War (1914-1918) caused devastation in Europe. But the soldiers' injuries gave surgeons opportunities to find new techniques for diagnosis and for carrying out more complex operations.

The First World War made X-rays more Reliable and Mobile

Wilhelm Röntgen discovered X-rays in 1895. X-rays pass easily through soft flesh, but less well through bone. X-ray images could therefore be produced by directing X-rays at a body part in front of a photographic plate.

A photograph from 1915, showing a First World War hospital car equipped with mobile X-ray equipment.

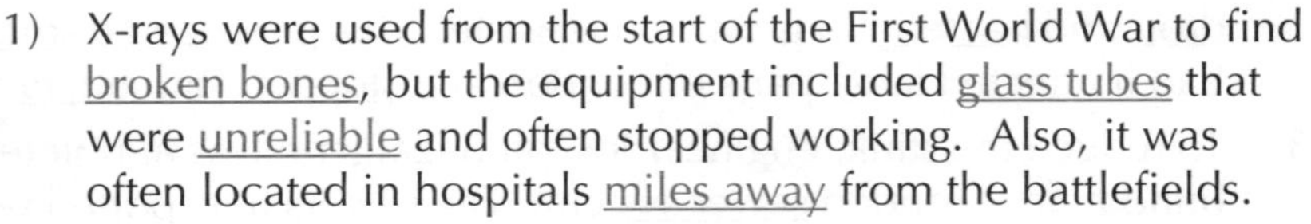

1) X-rays were used from the start of the First World War to find broken bones, but the equipment included glass tubes that were unreliable and often stopped working. Also, it was often located in hospitals miles away from the battlefields.
2) The American scientist William Coolidge had invented a more reliable X-ray tube in 1913. The 'Coolidge tube' became widely used by the end of the war, and is still used today.
3) In 1914, the Polish scientist Marie Curie developed mobile X-ray units (ambulances equipped with X-ray machines) which allowed doctors to transport X-ray equipment.

The war also increased the number of radiologists — people who know how to operate X-ray equipment. Curie and French scientist Antoine Béclère set up training schools to teach doctors how to use X-ray equipment.

The problem of Blood Loss was overcome as a result of the war

The idea of blood transfusions was known from the 17th century, but they were rarely successful because the blood of the recipient often clotted. Blood also clotted if it was stored outside the body.

1) In 1900, Karl Landsteiner discovered blood groups. Certain blood groups couldn't be mixed together as the blood would clot, blocking the blood vessels. Landsteiner's discovery meant doctors could perform more successful blood transfusions, as long as the donor's blood group was the same as the patient's.
2) During World War I the seriousness of wounds from gunshots and explosive shells meant that many soldiers died of blood loss. This made being able to store blood very important.
3) In 1914, doctors found that sodium citrate stopped blood clotting so it could be stored. In 1917, this discovery allowed the first ever blood depot to be set up at the Battle of Cambrai.
4) In 1946, the British National Blood Transfusion Service was established.

Patients always suffer some blood loss during surgery. If a lot of blood is lost, this can be fatal. Blood transfusions helped to prevent this cause of death by enabling surgeons to replace any blood lost during surgery.

War sped up the development of Plastic Surgery

1) Doctors in France and Germany had been working on skin graft techniques since before the First World War. Their work helped pave the way for Harold Gillies, who set up a plastic surgery unit for the British Army during the war.
2) Gillies was interested in reconstructing facial injuries so that patients could have a normal appearance. He developed the use of pedicle tubes, and kept detailed records of his achievements.
3) Gillies' work was continued during the Second World War by his assistant, Archibald McIndoe. A lot of McIndoe's patients were pilots who had been trapped inside burning aircraft.

A pedicle tube is a skin graft technique where skin is partially cut from a healthy part of a patient's body, grown and then attached to the damaged area of the patient to cover any scarring.

Doctors search for broken bones — X-ray marks the spot...

In the exam, you need to think about the factors that caused change. One of the most important of these was war, which improved both modern surgery and modern public health (see p.133).

Penicillin

In the 1800s, Pasteur discovered that bacteria cause disease. But it wasn't until the 1900s that doctors were able to treat bacterial diseases. This was partly due to the discovery of penicillin, the first antibiotic.

Fleming discovered Penicillin — the first Antibiotic

1) Alexander Fleming saw many soldiers die of septic wounds caused by staphylococcal bacteria when he was working in an army hospital during the First World War.
2) Searching for a cure he identified the antiseptic substance in tears, lysozyme, in 1922 — but this only worked on some germs.
3) One day in 1928 he came to clean up some old culture dishes on which he had been growing staphylococci for his experiments. By chance, a fungal spore had landed and grown on one of the dishes.
4) What caught Fleming's eye was that the colonies of staphylococci around the mould had stopped growing. The fungus was identified as Penicillium notatum. It produced a substance that killed bacteria. This substance was given the name penicillin.
5) Fleming published his findings in articles between 1929 and 1931. However, nobody was willing to fund further research, so he was unable to take his work further. The industrial production of penicillin still needed to be developed.

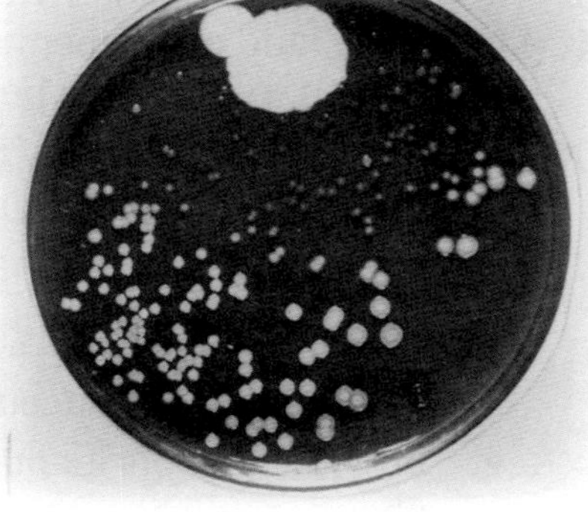

The original plate on which Fleming first observed the growth of Penicillium notatum.

Florey and Chain found a way to Purify Penicillin

1) Since it is a natural product, penicillin needs to be purified. A breakthrough was made by Howard Florey's team in Oxford between 1938 and 1940. Ernst Chain, a member of the team, devised the freeze-drying technique which was an important part of the purification process.
2) At first Florey and Chain didn't have the resources to produce penicillin in large amounts. They made penicillin for their first clinical trial by growing Penicillium notatum in every container they could find in their lab. Their patient began to recover, only to die when the penicillin ran out.

Florey took penicillin to America for Mass Production

Florey knew that penicillin could be vital in treating the wounds of soldiers fighting in World War II. British chemical firms were too busy making explosives to start mass production — so he went to America.

1) American firms were also not keen to help — until America joined the war in 1941. In December 1941, the US government began to give out grants to businesses that manufactured penicillin.
2) By 1943, British businesses had also started mass-producing penicillin. Mass production was sufficient for the needs of the military medics by 1944.
3) After the war, the cost of penicillin fell, making it more accessible for general use.
4) Fleming, Florey and Chain were awarded the Nobel Prize in 1945.

Today, penicillin is used to treat a range of bacterial infections, including chest infections and skin infections. Other antibiotics were discovered after 1945, including treatments for lung infections, acne and bacterial meningitis.

Comment and Analysis

While individuals (like Florey, Chain and Fleming) were important in making the discovery of penicillin, it was large institutions like governments that funded its mass production.

Penicillin isn't just mould news — it's still used today...

How significant has Alexander Fleming's discovery of penicillin been in the development of medicine since c.1900? Explain your answer. [8]

Modern Treatments

Penicillin became one of the first mass-produced drugs, helping to build a new pharmaceutical industry. Pharmaceutical companies research and develop new medicines for doctors and patients to use.

The Pharmaceutical Industry has really taken off

1) In the late 1800s, the chemical industries in places like Britain, Germany, Switzerland and the United States were booming. The late-19th and 20th centuries also saw the discovery of new drugs including aspirin (1899), insulin (1921), sulphonamides (1932) and penicillin (see p.129).
2) The chemical companies were best placed to manufacture these new drugs and medicines on a large scale, and make them available for lots of people. The success of their mass-produced drugs in the 1940s (particularly penicillin) helped the modern pharmaceutical industry take off.
3) Pharmaceutical companies have played an important role in researching and developing new medicines. They also mass produce these drugs to sell worldwide.
4) These companies have been important in curing new diseases and researching new forms of treatment:

- Chemotherapy is the treatment of cancer using drugs. It began to be developed during World War II, and pharmaceutical companies have been producing cancer drugs since the 1960s.
- In 1981, doctors identified a new illness, AIDS, which is caused by the HIV virus. In 1987, pharmaceutical companies began mass producing a drug called AZT, the first approved drug to treat HIV. They have since been involved in developing more effective treatments for HIV.
- In 2002, there was an outbreak of a new virus called SARS in China. The virus quickly spread to many different countries. SARS can cause severe breathing difficulties that are sometimes fatal. To date there is no cure for SARS, but companies produce treatments that reduce the symptoms.

The pharmaceutical industry has faced several Problems

1) Drugs have to go through a series of clinical tests before they are given to patients. This is to make sure that they work properly and don't cause any damaging side-effects.

- In the 1950s, the drug thalidomide was released without thorough testing. It was originally used as a sleeping pill, but it soon became popular among pregnant women as a treatment for morning sickness. Tragically, thalidomide affected the women's unborn babies, causing thousands of children to be born with under-developed limbs and other issues.
- The thalidomide tragedy forced pharmaceutical companies to test drugs more thoroughly. The government responded to the tragedy in 1963 by setting up a Committee on Safety of Drugs to make sure all new drugs were safe before being given to patients.

2) Pharmaceutical companies have high costs for research and development of new medicines. Rare diseases sometimes go unresearched because companies tend to focus on treatments for common diseases that will make a lot of money.
3) Antibiotic resistance is when a type of bacteria adapts so it isn't affected by antibiotics anymore. This resistance develops when doctors and patients overuse antibiotics — the more antibiotics are used, the more likely it is that bacteria will become resistant to them.

- Antibiotic resistance stops antibiotics from working properly, making it more difficult to treat some diseases. This has increased the levels of disease and the time taken for patients to recover.
- Around 25,000 people in the European Union die every year as a result of infections caused by antibiotic-resistant bacteria.

The only disease Farmer Ceutical cares about is cowpox...

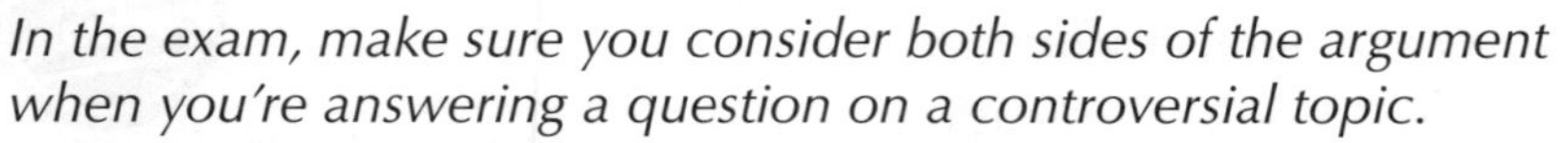

In the exam, make sure you consider both sides of the argument when you're answering a question on a controversial topic.

EXAM TIP

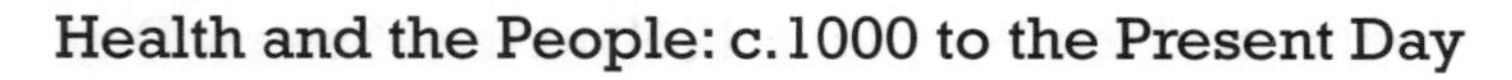

Modern Treatments

Advances in science and technology during the 20th century led to improvements in how doctors treat many medical conditions. However, some people don't trust modern techniques and prefer alternative medicine.

Transplants have been made more Successful

1) In 1905, the first successful transplant of the cornea of the eye was performed.
2) The first complete organ to be successfully transplanted was the kidney. Livers, lungs, pancreases and bone marrow can now also be transplanted.
3) The first successful heart transplant was carried out by the South African surgeon Christiaan Barnard in 1967. The patient only survived for 18 days — he died of pneumonia.

The problem for transplants is rejection. The immune system attacks the implant as if it was a disease.

- The success of early transplant operations was limited because doctors lacked effective immunosuppressants — drugs that stop the immune system attacking.
- Since the 1970s, researchers have developed increasingly effective immunosuppressants, making transplants safer and more likely to be successful.

Technology has improved modern surgery

1) Advances in science and technology have led to improvements in the treatment of diseases like cancer. The discovery of radiation in 1896-1898 by Antoine Henri Becquerel, Marie Curie and Pierre Curie led to the creation of radiation therapy. Radiation therapy is the use of radiation to kill cancer cells.
2) The development of lasers since the 1950s led to their widespread use in medicine in the 1980s. Laser surgery is used to correct vision problems, and lasers are also used in cancer treatment and dentistry.
3) Advances in video technology led to the development of keyhole surgery in the 1980s.

- A type of camera called an endoscope is put through a small cut, letting the surgeon see inside the body. Other surgical instruments are then introduced through even smaller cuts in the skin.
- Keyhole surgery is useful for investigating the causes of pain or infertility. It's also used for vasectomies, removing cysts or the appendix, mending hernias and other minor operations.
- Keyhole surgery leaves patients with smaller scars and allows them to recover more quickly, with less risk of infection.

Some people use Alternative Treatments

1) Mistrust of modern medicine and technology means some people use alternative therapies instead.
   - Acupuncture is the method of putting needles in specific points of the patient's skin to relieve pain.
   - Homeopathy is treatment using extremely weak solutions of natural substances.
2) Unlike mainstream treatments, alternative therapies aren't based on evidence gathered from scientific research. As a result, there is little scientific evidence that alternative treatments work effectively, and some doctors believe that they might do more harm than good.
3) However, some doctors are now working with alternative therapists to see if using a mix of alternative and mainstream medicine might result in benefits to the patient.

All you need to do is transplant these facts into your brain...

To what extent has technology been the main factor in the development of medicine in Britain? Refer to technology and other factors in your answer. [16]

The Liberal Social Reforms

In the 19th century, people believed government should have little involvement in public health. This all began to change after 1900, when the Liberal social reforms were introduced to deal with poverty.

Booth and Rowntree showed the effects of Poverty

1) Slums and other poor, overcrowded housing were all still common in industrial towns in 1900. The poor worked long hours for low wages. Many people couldn't afford doctors or medicine — they could barely provide their children with three decent meals a day.

There was no unemployment benefit, or pensions for the elderly. Workhouses were the only help — they provided basic food and lodging in exchange for working long hours in brutal conditions.

2) Two reports showed how widespread poverty was:

Booth's Report

Charles Booth's 1889 'Life and Labour of the People in London' showed that 30% of Londoners were living in severe poverty, and that it was sometimes impossible for people to find work, however hard they tried. He showed that some wages were so low they weren't enough to support a family.

Rowntree's Report

Seebohm Rowntree had a factory in York. He didn't believe the problem was as bad there as in London — so he did a survey of living conditions. His report, 'Poverty, a Study of Town Life' (published 1901), showed that 28% of people in York couldn't afford basic food and housing.

3) The lack of access to good healthcare meant that most people's health was pretty poor. When the Boer War broke out in 1899, army officers found that 40% of volunteers were physically unfit for military service — mostly due to poverty-related illnesses linked to poor diet and living conditions.
4) The Government realised that it needed to improve basic healthcare in order to have an efficient army.

The Liberal Reforms improved health by tackling Poverty

Booth, Rowntree and the Boer War showed that there was a link between poverty and ill health. The newly-elected Liberal government and its Chancellor, David Lloyd George, realised it had to take action.

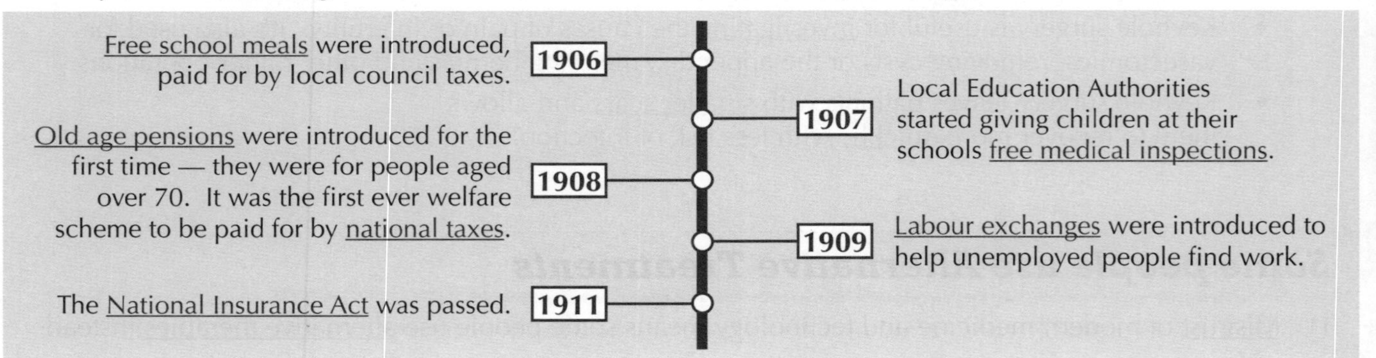

The National Insurance Act introduced health insurance for workers — the worker, their employer and the government all contributed to a central fund that the workers could use for sick pay or to pay for a doctor.

Comment and Analysis

The Liberal reforms were the first real effort by the national government to improve people's living conditions as a way of improving their health. The reforms were a result of changing attitudes towards the role of government, and changed people's attitudes further.

'Doc, I feel poorly.' 'Try taking two shillings once a week...'

Create flashcards about the Liberal reforms — some with the dates and some with the names of the reforms. Match them up, then write a paragraph explaining why the reforms were important.

Public Health and the World Wars

After World War II, housing standards began to improve. The Beveridge Report argued that the state should provide support to people, resulting in the creation of the welfare state and the NHS.

The World Wars created Pressure for Social Change

The First World War (1914-1918) and the Second World War (1939-1945) broke down social distinctions and brought people together whose lives had been very separate.

1) Raising mass armies made government and military officials more aware of the health problems of the poor, because so many recruits were in poor health. Powerful people were more concerned with solving these health problems when at war, because of the need for a strong army to defend the country.
2) The evacuation of children during the Second World War increased awareness in richer rural communities of how disadvantaged many people were in other parts of the country.
3) After the Second World War, people looked for improvements in society. Such feelings led to the 1945 victory for the Labour Party, which promised healthcare for everyone and full employment.

Housing and Health Improved after the Second World War

1) Towards the end of the First World War, Prime Minister David Lloyd George promised to tackle poor-quality housing by building 'homes fit for heroes' to tackle bad housing. Some new council houses were built in the 1920s and 1930s, but many of them were too expensive for the poorest families, who still lived in slums.
2) During the Second World War, destruction from bombing and a lack of construction led to severe housing shortages, making the situation worse.
3) After the war, the Labour government built 800,000 homes between 1945-51. In 1946, it passed the New Towns Act — this created completely new towns near major cities. Governments in the 1950s and 1960s demolished over 900,000 old, cramped slums — around 2 million inhabitants were rehoused.
4) In 1961, a report called 'Homes for Today and Tomorrow' gave specific standards for new housing, including adequate heating, a flushing toilet and enough space inside and outside. This was the final step in tackling the issues of overcrowding, poor nutrition and poor waste disposal that had caused major public health problems.

The Beveridge Report led to the Welfare State

1) In 1942, during the Second World War, economist and social reformer William Beveridge published his famous report. The Beveridge Report became a bestseller — it was widely read and hugely popular.

In his report, Beveridge called for the state provision of social security 'from the cradle to the grave.' Beveridge argued that all people should have the right to be free from want, disease, ignorance, squalor and idleness. He called these the five 'giants.'

2) Beveridge said that the government had a duty to care for all its citizens, not just the poor or unemployed. To achieve this, Beveridge suggested the creation of a welfare state — a system of grants and services available to all British citizens.
3) The 1945 Labour government was elected with the promise to implement Beveridge's proposals. One of their first acts was to pass a new National Insurance Act in 1946 to support anyone who couldn't work, whether as a result of sickness, pregnancy, unemployment or old age.

Comment and Analysis

The Labour Party's National Insurance Act went further than the one introduced by the Liberal government (see p.132) — anyone could apply for Labour's National Insurance without having to take a test to see if they were eligible.

Beveridge Report — nothing to do with your favourite drink...

EXAM QUESTION

Explain how significant the two world wars were for the improvement of housing and public health in Britain. [8]

National Health Service

One of the most important changes in modern British medicine was the creation of the NHS.

The National Health Service was established in 1948

1) In 1948, the Labour government implemented Beveridge's last proposal — a National Health Service.
2) Aneurin Bevan was the Labour Minister for Health who, after a lot of negotiation, introduced the National Health Service (NHS). The government nationalised hospitals and put them under local authority control. Treatment was made free for all patients. There were arguments for and against the NHS:

For the NHS

- During World War Two the government took control of all hospitals, creating the Emergency Medical Service. Its success led many to support the creation of the NHS.
- The NHS would make medical care free so it was accessible to everyone.
- The NHS guaranteed that hospitals would receive government money, rather than having to rely on charities for money.

Against the NHS

- Many Conservatives opposed the NHS as they believed the cost would be huge.
- Doctors saw themselves as independent professionals — they didn't want to be controlled by the government. They also worried that they would lose a lot of income.
- Many doctors threatened to go on strike in protest against the NHS.

The government finally convinced doctors by offering them a payment for each patient and letting them continue treating fee-paying patients.

The NHS was Very Popular

1) Although many Conservatives were opposed to the creation of the NHS, they couldn't abolish it when they came back into power in 1951 — it was too popular.
2) The NHS increased the number of people with access to healthcare — the number of doctors doubled between 1948 and 1973 to keep up with demand.
3) Today, the NHS provides a range of health services, most of which are free and accessible to everyone. They include accident and emergency care, maternity care and major surgery, as well as pharmacies, dentists, mental health services, sexual health services and general practitioners (GPs).

In the long term, the NHS has contributed to a dramatic improvement in people's health and a rise in life expectancy. In 1951, men could expect to live to 66 and women to 72 — by 2011 this had risen to 79 for men and 83 for women.

Today the NHS faces several Challenges

1) The increase in life expectancy means there are many more older people in Britain today than there were in 1948, who are more likely to suffer from long-term conditions like diabetes and heart disease. They need regular medical attention and require a lot of NHS time and resources.
2) Many people's lifestyle choices are putting strain on the NHS. Smoking, obesity and alcohol consumption can all harm people's health and may require expensive treatment — for example, smoking can cause lung cancer and drinking too much alcohol can cause serious liver disease.
3) Many modern treatments, equipment and medicines are very expensive, and the NHS has had to face rising expectations of what it can and should offer.
4) As a result of all these factors, the cost of the NHS is rising rapidly — in 2015/16 the NHS budget was £116 billion overall. In order to stay within its budget, the NHS sometimes has to make difficult choices about which treatments it can and can't provide.

A 2015 poll suggested that around 60% of British people are satisfied with the NHS, showing that it is still relatively popular.

Sadly the NHS doesn't offer an exam revision service...

Split your page in two. On one side, write down the successes of the NHS.
On the other side, write down the problems and challenges it faces.

Revision Summary

Well, that was a healthy amount of information to revise. Now treat yourself to these revision questions.
- Try these questions and tick off each one when you get it right.
- When you've done all the questions for a topic and are completely happy with it, tick off the topic.

Medicine Stands Still (p.109-115)

1) Give two supernatural causes of disease believed by people in medieval Britain.
2) Briefly describe two natural explanations for disease believed by people in medieval Britain.
3) Describe two medical discoveries made by Islamic doctors.
4) Name six treatments for disease used by people in medieval Britain.
5) List three types of people you might visit if you felt ill in medieval Britain.
6) List two approaches to health in towns and two approaches to health in monasteries.
7) Give three ways people tried to prevent the Black Death.

The Beginnings of Change (p.116-121)

8) How did Vesalius help to advance medical knowledge?
9) What did Harvey discover and why did he have a limited impact on diagnosis and treatment?
10) Describe how Paré found a better way to treat wounds.
11) List four medieval treatments that were still used during the Renaissance.
12) List four treatments and four prevention methods people used against the Great Plague in 1665.
13) Give two factors that improved doctors' training during the Renaissance.
14) Who was Florence Nightingale and how did she improve hospital care?
15) Describe how Edward Jenner proved the link between smallpox and cowpox.

A Revolution in Medicine (p.122-127)

16) In what year did Louis Pasteur publish the Germ Theory?
17) Who was Robert Koch? Name three new methods he used and three discoveries he made.
18) Name the first magic bullet and describe how it was discovered.
19) Give the year that chloroform was discovered and explain why it initially led to higher death rates.
20) What is the difference between antisepsis and asepsis?
21) Describe the contribution to public health made by these individuals:
Edwin Chadwick, John Snow, William Farr, Joseph Bazalgette.
22) Give three things that the 1875 Public Health Act forced local councils to do.

Modern Medicine (p.128-134)

23) List three advances in medicine and surgery that were made during World War I.
24) Explain how the following individuals or institutions contributed to the production of penicillin:
Fleming, Florey and Chain, the United States government.
25) Describe three challenges that the pharmaceutical industry has faced.
26) Explain how technology has improved modern surgery.
27) List five of the Liberal social reforms and describe what they involved.
28) State three ways in which housing and public health were improved as a result of World War II.
29) Describe the different reactions to the National Health Service (NHS) when it was founded in 1948.
30) Give three challenges the NHS faces today.

Exam Hints and Tips

These pages will show you how to use your knowledge to get those all-important marks.
Make sure that you read all of this very very carefully.

You will take 2 Papers altogether

1) Paper 1 is 1 hour 45 minutes long. It's worth 84 marks — 50% of your GCSE. It's all about 'Understanding the Modern World'. This paper will be divided into 2 sections:
   - Section A: Period Study (see pages 3-4 for more information).
   - Section B: Wider World Depth Study (see pages 57-58 for more information).
2) Paper 2 is 1 hour 45 minutes long. It's worth 84 marks — 50% of your GCSE. It's all about 'Shaping the Nation'. This paper will be divided into 2 sections:
   - Section A: Thematic Study (see pages 107-108 for more information).
   - Section B: British Depth Study (see pages 57-58 for more information). This also includes questions on the Historic Environment (see pages 104-106 for more information).

The Period Studies covered in this book are America, 1840-1895: Expansion and Consolidation (on pages 5-30) and Germany, 1890–1945: Democracy and Dictatorship (on pages 31-56).

The Wider World Depth Study covered in this book is Conflict and Tension, 1918-1939 (on pages 59-81).

The Thematic Study covered in this book is Health and the People: c.1000 to the Present Day (on pages 109-135).

The British Depth Study covered in this book is Elizabethan England, c.1568–1603 (on pages 82-103).

Make sure you know which Thematic Study, Period Study and Depth Studies you're studying. They might not be the ones we've covered in this book. And remember... some of your exam papers will contain questions on topics you haven't studied — IGNORE THOSE. Only answer questions on the topics you've studied.

Remember these Four Tips for Answering Questions

1. Don't spend Too Long on Short Questions

1) Learn the rule — the more marks a question is worth, the longer your answer should be.
2) Don't get carried away writing loads for a question that's only worth 4 marks — you need to leave time for the higher mark questions.

2. Plan your Essay Answers, but not the others

1) You don't need to plan answers to the shorter questions in the exam. That will waste time.
2) For longer essay questions, it's very important to make a quick plan before you start writing.
3) Think about what the key words are in the question. Scribble a quick plan of your main points — cross through this neatly at the end, so it's obvious it shouldn't be marked.

3. Stay Focused on the Question

1) Make sure that you directly answer the question. Back up your points with relevant facts. Don't just chuck in everything you know about the period.
2) You've got to be relevant and accurate — e.g. if you're writing about the rise of the Nazi Party, don't include stories about a London camel called George who moved rubble during the Blitz.
3) It might help to try to write the first sentence of every paragraph in a way that addresses the question, e.g. 'Another way in which Chamberlain was an important cause of World War Two is...'

4. Use a Clear Writing Style

1) Essay answers should start with a brief introduction and end with a conclusion.
2) Remember to start a new paragraph for each new point you want to discuss.
3) Try to use clear handwriting — and pay attention to spelling, grammar and punctuation (see next page).

Exam Hints and Tips

In both papers, the examiner will be marking you partly on your spelling, punctuation and grammar (SPaG). SPaG is worth nearly 5% of your overall mark, so don't forget to write nicely (as my mum would say).

Remember to Check your Spellings

1) You should leave about five minutes at the end of the exam to check your work.
2) Check as many questions as you can, but make sure you read over the questions which award SPaG marks especially carefully. (Marks are shown very clearly at the end of each question.)
3) 5 minutes isn't long, so there won't be time to check everything thoroughly. Look for the most obvious spelling mistakes...

If you're not confident with any of these things, learn them now.

- where / wear / were
- your / you're
- silent letters, e.g. know, science, could
- names of historical figures or places, e.g. Mussolini, Khrushchev, Scutari
- there / their / they're
- to / too / two
- of / off
- effect / affect
- double letters, e.g. aggression, success
- don't confuse 'past' with 'passed'
- though / thought / through / thorough

You need to Punctuate Properly...

1) Always use a capital letter at the start of a sentence. Use capital letters for names of particular people, places and things. For example:

In 1933 Hitler was made Chancellor of Germany.

All sentences start with capital letters. The name of a person. A title.

2) Full stops go at the end of sentences, e.g. 'General Custer was killed in June 1876.' Question marks go at the end of questions, e.g. 'How successful was the Nazi propaganda?'
3) Use commas when you use more than one adjective to describe something, or to separate items in a list:

Elizabeth I was intelligent, confident and powerful.

4) Commas can also join two points into one sentence with a joining word (such as 'and', 'or', 'so' or 'but'):

The work of Galen was central to medieval medical teachings, so doctors found it difficult to disagree with him.

5) Commas can also be used to separate extra information in a sentence:

The Civil Rights Act, which was enacted in 1870, was opposed by President Andrew Johnson.

...and use Grammar Correctly

1) Don't change tenses in your writing by mistake:

The mountain men explored the West first — they hunted animals for their skins.

Both verbs are in the past tense — which is correct. Writing 'hunt' instead of 'hunted' would be wrong.

2) Write your longer answers in paragraphs.
   - A paragraph is a group of sentences which talk about the same thing or follow on from each other.
   - You need to start a new paragraph when you start making a new point.

You show a new paragraph by starting a new line and leaving a gap (an indent) before you start writing:

From 1933, Hitler started a programme of public works, such as the building of huge new motorways. This gave jobs to thousands of people.

Even though there was increased employment, the Nazis altered the statistics so that things looked better than they were. Wages were also poor.

That's that, then — all that's left to do now is to sit the exams...

Good SPaG is a great way to get marks in the exam. So make sure you've learnt all the stuff on this page, and also everything about anything that's ever happened in all of history, and you should be okay.

Index

Index

Index